"Disillusioned by an academy that too often seemed to be divorced from the social realities of the outside world, James Downs and Jennifer Manion sought to locate a tradition of historian-activists from which students and scholars might take inspiration. The result is a challenging and engaging collection of essays that is essential reading for aspiring and seasoned academics alike. *Taking Back the Academy* brings together a dynamic cast of scholars and activists representing a broad range of generational, institutional, and disciplinary backgrounds. They invite us to consider the multiple ways in which colleges and universities can stimulate social change.

"While celebrating the achievements of past scholar-activists, this book also offers a searching look at the present state of the field and a provocative call for future action. In an age of increasingly demanding hiring and tenure committees, *Taking Back the Academy* challenges scholars to recognize that their duties nonetheless extend far beyond the profession. In considering the broad social and political responsibilities of intellectuals in society, this book calls for a revitalized definition of what it means to be a scholar-citizen in the twenty-first century. For scholars in the humanities, that call could not be more timely. Alternatively maligned as politically irrelevant or dangerously subversive, historians and other stewards of society's subjective truths increasingly must be prepared to articulate—and defend—their function in today's marketplace of ideas and corporatized universities. *Taking Back the Academy* reflects honestly on the perils of uncritically linking scholarship and politics, but it ultimately insists that both as a matter of civic duty and professional survival historians must unapologetically embrace opportunities to put the past in open dialogue with the pressing needs of the present."

Jacquelyn Hall, past president Organization of American Historians and Spruill Professor of History, University of North Carolina at Chapel Hill

TAKING BACK THE ACADEMY!

History of Activism, History as Activism

EDITED BY
**JIM DOWNS &
JENNIFER MANION**

ROUTLEDGE New York • London

Published in 2004 by
Routledge
270 Madison Avenue
New York, NY 10016
www.routledge-ny.com

Published in Great Britain by
Routledge
2 Park Square
Milton Park, Abingdon
Oxon, OX14 4RN, U.K.
www.routledge.co.uk

Routledge is an imprint of the Taylor & Francis Group.

Printed in the United States of America on acid-free paper.

10 9 8 7 6 5 4 3 2 1

Library of Congress Cataloging in Publication Data

Taking back the academy! : history of activism, history as activism /
    James T. Downs, Jr., and Jennifer Manion, editors.
      p. cm.
    Papers derived from a conference held at Columbia University in New York, N.Y. in 2002.
    ISBN 0-415-94810-X (hardback : alk. paper) — ISBN 0-415-94811-8 (pbk. : alk. paper)
    1. Historians—United States—Political activity—Congresses. 2. Learning and scholarship—Political aspects—United States—Congresses. 3. Student movements—United States—Congresses. 4. Social movements—United States—Congresses. 5. Political activists—United States—Congresses. 6. Historians—Political activity—Congresses. 7. Learning and scholarship—Political aspects—Congresses. 8. Student movements—Congresses. 9. Social movements—Congresses. 10. Political activists—Congresses. I. Downs, James T., 1973– II. Manion, Jennifer, 1974–
    E175.45.T35 2004
    378.1'981'0973—dc22

                    2004014171

Dedicated to our parents,

Concetta Sepielli Downs and James T. Downs
and
Dorothy Chiccine Manion and Edward Michael Manion

Contents

Acknowledgments

JIM DOWNS
JENNIFER MANION

We would like to acknowledge the truly energetic and dynamic participation of all those who attended and made the conference a success. For making the conference possible, we are grateful to the Columbia University faculty and administration for their financial and administrative support, particularly Alan Brinkley, Elizabeth Blackmar, the Graduate Student Advisory Council, La Maison Francaise, and the Dean's Office. Most of all, we would like to thank the graduate students who designed Web pages, hung posters, found A.V. equipment, reviewed proposals, poured coffee, and assisted with the registration table, most especially Aparna Balachandran, Shannan Clark, Jennifer Fronc, Laura Hornbake, Nancy Kwak, Ted McCormick, Lisa Ramos, Jennifer Tammi, Jennifer Tappan, James Tejani, Janice Traflet, Toru Umezaki, and Theresa Ventura.

Catherine Clinton first saw the value of pulling together essays from the conference to be published in book form, and without her, this volume would not exist. Before even seeing our dissertation proposals, Eric Foner and Nancy Hewitt, our respective advisors, each offered important feedback about the book proposal and publishing process. They, along with Barbara Balliet, David Rosner, Todd Anten, Jodi Bromberg, and George Davilas, have provided us with extremely useful advice and encouragement. We are also very grateful to Jaclyn Bergeron and Karen Wolny who provided editorial assistance and support.

As undergraduates, we learned that teaching and writing were powerful vehicles for social change through the examples of Drew Gilpin Faust, Farah J. Griffin, Lynn Hollen Lees, Kathy Brown, Nancy Bentley, Ellie DiLapi, Gloria Gay, Carroll Smith-Rosenberg, and Herman Beavers. Lynda Hart, to whom the conference was dedicated, has profoundly shaped our intellectual, political, and even personal endeavors, in life and in death.

Finally, our deepest gratitude to the contributors whose energy, idealism, and passionate commitment to bridging the gap between activism and the academy made this book possible and continues to inspire us.

Foreword

ERIC FONER

The chapters in this excellent volume derive from a path-breaking conference held at Columbia University in 2002 to explore the links between historical scholarship and political activism. Columbia was a most appropriate site for this event. Perhaps because of its location in New York City, the university has a long tradition of scholarly involvement in public affairs. In 1912, Columbia professors like Charles Beard and E. R. A. Seligman, helped to develop the program for Theodore Roosevelt's Progressive Party, which helped to establish the political and social agenda for twentieth-century liberalism. During the New Deal, A. A. Berle, Rexford Tugwell, and other Columbians became part of Franklin D. Roosevelt's group of advisers known as the Brains Trust. In the 1950s, Richard Hofstadter and C. Wright Mills, among other Columbia scholars, commented frequently and incisively on national affairs. In recent years, Columbia professors like the late Edward Said, Manning Marable, and Jeffrey Sachs have been actively involved in national and international public affairs.

Student activism also has a long history at Columbia. In the late 1950s and early 1960s, students took a prominent role in the local civil rights movement and the campaign for a ban on nuclear testing. The well-known Columbia upheaval of 1968, perhaps the pivotal moment in the university's modern history, was followed by many other examples of student activism, often forgotten today, including demonstrations against the invasion of Cambodia in 1970, the campaign in the 1980s that resulted in Columbia becoming the first Ivy League university to "divest" from South Africa, and the student hunger strike in the 1990s that led to the formation of an ethnic studies program.

As the chapters that follow demonstrate, scholarship and activism are not mutually exclusive pursuits, but, at their best, are symbiotically related.

Activism without detached analysis can become mere rebelliousness; scholarship divorced from consideration of the problems of the real world can become sterile. The issues confronted by scholar-activists today, at the dawn of the twenty-first century, are in some ways very old—economic justice, the rights of citizens, civil liberties, racial equality—and in other ways quite new. We need scholars to produce new analyses of the process of globalization, of the decline of public engagement in politics, of the prospects of democracy at a time when decisions affecting individuals' day to day lives are increasingly made by supranational institutions—the World Bank, multinational corporations, and the like—over which there is no semblance of democratic control.

Scholarship should be "relevant." But this does not mean simply drawing the issues one investigates from the day's headlines. Relevance is impossible to predict. In the 1960s, the black and feminist movements went back to academic writing by W. E. B. Du Bois, Mary Beard and others, seemingly "irrelevant" when they were produced but made relevant by subsequent social movements. Studies of the long history of American empire, which attracted little attention during the 1990s, have suddenly become relevant because of the imperial ambitions of George W. Bush.

Scholarship can itself be a form of activism. The rewriting of American history begun by scholars of the Old Left in the 1930s, in which African Americans and laborers more generally became active agents of historical change rather than passive recipients of the actions of others, was largely ignored in the mainstream academy for many years. But it helped to provide a "usable past" for subsequent struggles for racial justice and economic democracy. By the same token, social movements can inspire entirely new branches of scholarly knowledge—as the gay movement has helped to produce a flourishing subfield in gay and lesbian history.

More generally, humanism, an intellectual commitment premised on the idea that the historical world having been created by men and women can be understood through the exercise of human reason, is itself a highly liberating outlook. Today, humanism is, to say the least, beleaguered. The humanities have lost their prominence in U.S. universities. Higher education is increasingly corporatized. At Columbia and other institutions, the arts and sciences seem to live in perpetually straitened circumstances, while more technically and professionally based branches flourish. In society at large, market values pervade all relationships. At such a time, it is hardly surprising that anti-humanism abounds. We are often told that we live in a post-Enlightenment world in which the idea of "truth" is itself passé, or worse, oppressive. Certainly, as recent scholarship has insisted, claims to historical truth have often been deeply complicit in the exercise of power. The assumed universality of man, it is now clear, was predicated on the exclusion of women, colonial populations, and others.

Yet uncovering the truth about the past can also be liberating—as South Africa's Truth and Reconciliation Commission and similar investigations of the crimes committed by American-backed governments in El Salvador and Guatemala have shown. Today, the airwaves and op-ed pages reverberate with talk of a "clash of civilizations," in which something called "Islamic civilization" is depicted as inherently intolerant, backward, and violent, and "western" or "American civilization" as the unproblematic home of rationality, tolerance, and freedom. It is a form of political activism, as well as of valuable scholarship, to remind readers that essentializing ourselves and others in this way is a form of myth-making, not history. At its best, activist scholarship is a mode of questioning, a challenge to what is taken for granted, a worldwide exchange of ideas rather than the now dominant complacent dialogue with ourselves.

During the 1880s, the American labor journalist John Swinton visited Karl Marx in London. He asked the author of *Capital* and *The Communist Manifesto* what he foresaw for the future. Marx answered: "struggle." The answer would be the same were Marx alive today. In the struggle, scholars and activists both have critical roles to play.

Bench Talk

JIM DOWNS
JENNIFER MANION

The voice of a student activist announcing the time for the annual "Take Back the Night" rally resonates across the college green. It is one of those days when the campus seems alive and bursting with energy. Wherever you look, people are enjoying one of the first days of spring. Underneath the large oak tree, in front of the library—within view of Frisbee tossing, students sunning, and activists strategizing—we like to sit on our favorite bench and discuss ideas from our lectures and seminars. Today, we are discussing the ideology of pro-slavery thought in the United States antebellum South. Inspired by a lecture given by one of our favorite professors, we are on the lookout for her to pass by and settle our pressing question of the day, "Was James Henry Hammond a racist?"

It was on the bench, with each other, in front of the imaginary cameras that recorded our daily talk show, *Benchtalk*, that we held our own class. We spouted out positions we were too shy to take in class. We took on the ideas of our professors and our classmates and argued them into the ground. It was on the bench, not inside a classroom, that we began to realize that we would not join our classmates in corporate America, but instead would pursue academic and activist work. Jen already devoted a significant amount of time to lesbian and feminist groups on campus and in the city, while Jim worked as a research assistant and became heavily involved in some of our mentoring professors' fights for tenure.

Unlike many of our classmates, our introduction to the world of ideas and intellectual debate excited us. We wanted to know more, debate more,

1

probe issues more deeply. Our professors inspired, challenged, and energized us. They were not stereotypical academics who dusted dandruff off their corduroy blazers as they presented ideas in an unwieldy, incomprehensible, and monotone manner, but were smart, sassy, and sometimes too sexy to be historians and literary scholars. They were activists, social critics, and academic geniuses. And to us, they were rock stars, and we were the groupies.

We wrote letters to the editor of the local newspaper, started our own campus publications, and imagined one day we'd become part of the world that our professors and cool graduate school friends inhabited. After college, however, we took separate paths. Jim devoted himself to challenging both historical and educational problems as a teacher at the junior high and secondary level. Jen pursued similar goals, but in a slightly less conventional way as a basketball coach and sailing instructor.

In the fall of 2000, we both began graduate school at different institutions. But the experience was depressing and frustrating. In graduate school, it seemed that disciplinary jargon and rigors overrode intellectual curiosity and political passion. Fewer voices inspired us, less hope burned within us, and the light at the end of the tunnel seemed turned off. After our first semester Jim came up with the idea of having a history graduate student conference. We met briefly for a cup of coffee in Philadelphia and talked about his idea that the conference would be a chance for us to bring together everyone who inspired us.

Jen didn't make much of it; she wasn't really interested in volunteering to spend *more* time with other academics. For me, the conference needed to happen; I desperately needed a way to break free from the stifling intellectual structures and approaches to history that some of my professors attempted to impose on me.

Sometime in the fall, Jim was moving full speed ahead with the planning. Despite my apprehension, he encouraged me to get involved and asked me to think about writing the call for papers. It was fun to conceptualize the conference—to be broad, but specific, appeal to many people, but not just any people. Our aim was to bring together a few dozen graduate students from history departments of universities located on the northeast coast of the United States. But we called and people answered—several hundred faculty, activists, and graduate students from all over the United States, even Australia, Europe, and South America. We called for historians, but social workers, lawyers, doctors, anthropologists, writers, and filmmakers answered.

Despite her initial apprehension, by the winter break, we sat in a seminar room carpeted with proposals, and with the prospect of my orals exam just a few short weeks away, Jen took over full force. As I read for orals, she designed the panels, contacted the presenters, and invited additional faculty.

The topics of our daily conversations shifted from school, family, and relationships to the conference, the conference, and the conference.

With the conference quickly approaching, I began to worry that we didn't have enough nonacademics presenting. I envisioned a revolt of the activists accusing us of being elitist, relying on empty academic jargon, and not really speaking to their needs. We talked about the conference in my feminist theory class one day. Drucilla Cornell, Professor of Law, Women's Studies and Political Science at Rutgers University, alluded to this dynamic of standing accused by activists who claim they do the "real work." How often, she explained, these people reinforce the systems and structures they want to overthrow. Activists reacting to specific situations often fail to consider the bigger picture, to develop a coherent strategy for the desired end. If they do not know their own theory, she argued, they are enacting someone else's.

Finally, April 5, 2002 arrived. The conference was packed and alive in a way I didn't imagine possible. After the opening comments in the standing room only crowd, there was a buzz of excitement that remained the entire weekend. People were enthused. They were engaged with ideas, feelings, and each other. The activists did not revolt. They were hungry for the time and space to connect, think, and learn in an intellectual environment. They cherished the space which sometimes stifles and isolates me, which many academics take for granted.

We want to continue those discussions, and broaden our audience. We want to inspire those out there who are trying to create change, but face seemingly impenetrable resistance. We want to ensure that university campuses remain hotbeds for intellectual inquiry and political dissent. We want to ensure that there is a bench, a place, a space, for students to find activism and hope—even when all around them appears bucolic and ideal. We want to take back the academy!

History has long been used by governments and elite classes to promote the existing power structure, maintain the status quo, and justify contemporary political agendas. The most violent erasure of the truth and silencing of the past occurred under the guise of an objective academic discipline. In the 1960s and 1970s, the production of historical knowledge was transformed when activists from a variety of social justice movements entered the field. Just as history had been used to maintain power, they believed it could be used to usurp it. Studies of working people, communities, and everyday life proliferated, redefining the boundaries of legitimate historical inquiry to incorporate the lives, struggles, and passions of all kinds of people. Social history, the subcategory under which much of this work is grouped, is now as institutionalized as political history was a generation ago.

What does this mean for the future of activist scholarship, now that it is more commonly self-referential than sparked by or accountable to activist movements? How can an academically-based activist bridge the gaps between intellectual inquiry, disciplinary expectations, political ideologies, and movement demands? Has the professionalization of history created a generational divide between the academic activists who created the space within the field for social histories of oppressed and marginalized groups and younger social historians who are not consciously vested in the political significance and consequences of their teaching and scholarship?

Taking Back the Academy attempts to answer these questions. Written against the political rantings by right wing authors such as Ann Coulter and Lynne Cheney, who view liberal academics as "treasonous" and "unpatriotic," these authors defend political dissent and powerfully document the importance of activism and public debate on college campuses.[1] From the controversies surrounding the war in Iraq to continuing problems of identity politics on campus, *Taking Back the Academy* covers a number of issues raging on today's university campuses. The authors represent a range of perspectives—from graduate students to senior scholars, from Ivy League to state run universities, from history to women's studies departments.

The chapters that form the bulk of this volume address how academics in the last thirty years have worked to take back the academy. The book is broken down into four distinct sections: "Student Movements—Beyond the University," "Students in Unions—Rethinking the University," "Historians for Social Justice," and "Bridging the Gap Between Academia and Activism." The first section challenges our understanding of student movements as a purely United States phenomenon of the late 1960s and early 1970s. By exploring the history of student protest movements in the United States, Mexico, and Europe, the authors offer a comparative framework for understanding the politics of social activism and the possibility of social change.

In the opening chapter, Eileen Eagan's "Teaching Student Activism" forms the conceptual framework for the first section. From her work as a teacher in dismantling the idea that student activism is purely a phenomenon in the United States to her advocating that student activism be included in all history courses, Eagan powerfully expands contemporary understandings of student protest and offers interesting pedagogical suggestions. Moreover, Eagan stresses the need to examine the ways in which student activism moves beyond campus and how students around the world are involved in issues relating to globalism, racism and the environment.

Eagan's gesture to move beyond the traditional geographic boundaries of the United States provides the ideal segway to both Martin Klimke's chapter on student movements in a transatlantic context and to Vania Markarian's article on the thirty-year public debate on the Mexican Student Movement. Klimke calls for an analytical approach that allows for the historian to compare the connections and exchanges among student movements in Berkeley and Berlin and in San Francisco and Frankfurt. His essay also serves as a historiographical intervention by exposing new sites of archival excavation and by demonstrating how scholarship can be used as a vehicle for change. Markarian takes a closer look at October 2, 1968 when several men, women, and children participating in a student rally in Tlatelolco Square in Mexico City were killed. Markarian analyzes the debates surrounding this still-unanswered controversy. Markarian's chapter reveals how student movements can be used as metonymy to examine larger social and political questions in Mexico today. Yet the most powerful trope connecting the three chapters is the authors' unwavering attempt to view student activism as not only a phenomenon of the United States in the 1960s, but as a global movement that persists to the present to serve as an important political backdrop to contemporary social issues.

Defying the overbearing stigma of "generation x" as the "sleeper generation," Anita Seth, Kim Phillips-Fein, and John McMillian show how the legacy of the 1960s continues in the next section, "Students in Union—Rethinking the University." As Union organizers and activists, these authors uphold the legacy of the 1960s college activists by powerfully demonstrating their commitment to social justice on college campuses. Each of their chapters reveals how contemporary students continue to question hegemony, to organize on campus, and to imagine a university in which social justice is not just a concept taught in a philosophy course but one that is fundamental to a university's vitality and purpose.

Kim Phillips-Fein and Anita Seth both extensively document one of the most important student movements in the country in the last twenty years: graduate student unionization. Both Phillips-Fein and Seth are active union organizers and are at the forefront of union agitation: Philips-Fein was one of the original organizers at Columbia University, and Seth has been involved with the Yale Unionizing effort, long before it received national attention. Both chapters provide perspectives on the work of the union and the goals each has accomplished.

Seth meticulously details how the union effort began at Yale and shows how the graduate student union movement is intricately connected with other unions on campus. Additionally, she describes how the union is not only a mouthpiece for better wages and rights for student labor, but also how it bears on concerns regarding the treatment of medical personnel, university patents, and other pertinent issues related to the New Haven community. By documenting the various activities and concerns of the graduate student union at Yale that are beyond the traditional purview of graduate student life, Seth unwittingly endorses Eagan's position that students involved in student protest movements are inherently drawn to other movements that seek social justice.

Phillips-Fein offers a personal perspective on the union struggle. She explains how being a union activist has caused her to see the university from a different, more cynical perspective. Ultimately, Phillips-Fein's piece imagines a university in which social justice is extended to all—even graduate students. John McMillian's chapter is based on his own experience as not only a historian of the New Left, but as a scholar committed to social change. His personal narrative reveals his frustration with his own generation's turning away from their activist legacy, and forgetting the underlying motivations for studying history.

In section three, "Historians for Social Justice," Nancy A. Hewitt, David Rosner, and Glenda Gilmore each present a compelling narrative in which they wrestle with the position of historians outside of the archives. Navigated by their own personal journeys and experiences, their chapters, richly insightful and persuasive, speak to the larger political implications and ethical considerations of history in political debates and public discourse.

As a feminist in the academy for the past twenty years, Hewitt looks back on the beginning of her career and the challenges that many young female historians faced as history departments became eager to hire women. Hewitt vividly describes the pressures of young feminist historians as they juggled professional obligations with teaching responsibilities—while building women's studies departments and publishing anthologies on the history of women. Hewitt's experience, as both a historian and an activist in the academy, illuminates the often untold stories of women historians in the 1970s and 1980s as they continued the work and followed the mission set forth by activists of the 1960s.

Building on the role of the historian as an activist, by campaigning for civil legislation and influencing public opinion, David Rosner exposes the dangerous ways in which historians of public health and medicine use their positions of power and their roles as experts unscrupulously. In his chapter, "Toxic Torts: Historians in the Courtroom," Rosner looks at the recent recruitment of historians into the world of toxic tort law and examines the various ways the craft of history is abused in the legal system. He identifies the important ways that historians' skills can be used on behalf of people victimized by a variety of industries as well as the ways that these same skills can be abused in order to defend the activities of huge corporations.

Using her role as a historian of twentieth century politics, Glenda Gilmore protested against the United States government going to war against Iraq in 2003. Her courageous participation landed her in the middle of national controversy. Attacked by conservatives, her experience exposes the ramifications for socially-minded historians who take public political positions.

Adding to the chorus on the subject of academics and the war in Iraq, Drucilla Cornell and Kitty Krupat engage in a provocative dialogue in the final section of the book, "Bridging the Gap Between Academia and Activism." In this unique dialogue, Cornell, a former labor activist and current feminist theorist, explores the intersections between feminism and racism, ideology and identity, and labor and peace with Kitty Krupat, a labor activist and graduate student. Elaborating on these connections, Jennifer Manion in her piece, "Calling All Liberals," explains the ways in which feminist theory offers an analytical strategy to rethink not only how we conceptualize United States history, but also to serve as a bridge between social justice activism and academic practice. Also, illuminating the connections between history and activism, Kathy Brown and Tracey M. Weiss engage in an intriguing dialogue about the ways in which teaching can be used as a bridge, linking scholarly interests with political and intellectual concerns. Brown and Weiss discuss how the differences of educational setting, i.e., public vs. private institutions, shape the ways in which they make these connections.

Bringing together both Manion's vision of history as a form of social change and Brown and Weiss' ideas about the classroom as a viable setting for such collaboration, Jim Downs in his chapter, "Teaching Across the Color Line" warns against the problem of basing a curriculum committed to social change on the merits of identity politics, and not historical truth. Finally, Jesse Lemisch returns to the broader question in his chapter, "2.5 Cheers for Bridging the Gap Between Activism and the Academy. " Lemisch describes the recent efforts of union activists as an opportunity for scholars to rethink the function and purpose of the university. By taking a look at union activists on college campuses, Lemisch gratefully welcomes the return of protest and agitation on campus. Yet surprisingly he reserves half a cheer and offers some good reasons not to build a coalition between activism and the academy. Told from the perspective of someone involved in labor strikes and campus activism for well over thirty years, Lemisch offers some important advice for the next generation of activists as they prepare for the challenges that lie ahead.

It is our hope that this volume will awaken some to the political and social responsibilities of the historian, facilitate connections between academics and activists, as well as across generations, and remind us that even in these oppressive times of restricted civil liberties and threatened intellectual freedom, we are not alone in our desires to end the violences of war, classism, racism, sexism, homophobia, environmental destruction, and religious intolerance. When the conference took place in Spring 2002, the blind nationalism sweeping across the country threatened to delegitimate movements which call attention to the social injustices deep-seeded in American soil. It is as crucial now as it was then, that we—as activists, academics, workers, students, and administrators—get up and stand up for justice.

Note

1. See Ann Coulter, *Treason: Liberal Treachery from the Cold War to the War on Terror* (Crown Forum, 2003); Lynne Cheney, *Telling the Truth* (Touchstone Books, 1996).

Student Movements—
Beyond the University

CHAPTER 1

Teaching Student Activism

EILEEN EAGAN

Handcuffed, they sit together in a police bus, and head toward the Cumberland County jail. Ages range from eighty-three to eighteen; some are longtime peace activists; some are college students; some are faculty at the local university. All have been arrested for "obstructing a public way" in downtown Portland, Maine, for sitting down in the street to protest impending war. The two eighteen-year-old students refused bail and got to stay in jail over night. The war came the next day but the protests continue, in Maine, across the United States, around the world.

In Burma/Myanmar, students have taken the lead in uprisings against oppressive governments, first the British, then, after World War II, against a series of military regimes. In 1974 students joined workers in demonstrations that lead to the shutting down of the universities. Again in 1976 and in 1988 demonstrations, often lead by students, shook the control of the authorities. Confronting a disasterous economy and martial law, professors called a return to civilian, parliamentary government, democracy, and human rights. The authorities responded with massive force and murder. When the Myanmar government refused to abide by the election victory of the National League for Democracy in 1990, some students joined an armed resistance force and others continued in nonviolent protest.[1]

In Iran in the summer of 2003, students protested against conditions on campuses and in commemoration of the violent attacks on students in their dormitories the previous year.[2]

In the twentieth century, struggles for democracy—national and academic—and freedom—personal and political—have brought students out of the classroom and into the streets. Often very immediate issues like campus food or rising tuition trigger organization that develops a broader critique of the university and of the society. In the United States, where student activism has ebbed and flowed, the widest movements have developed around civil rights and war and peace. Campus activists have also had ties to the labor movement and workers issues. Students went to Harlan County, Kentucky in the 1930s to support striking coal miners and to investigate their living conditions. In recent years some students have supported campus employees' efforts to organize, notably at Yale University.

Student political protest has many roots. Some activism is spontaneous, coming from immediate provocation and economic issues; some, in Latin America for example, comes from a traditional role of students as elites in their societies. Part is a generational clash and rejection of authority. "Two, Four, Six, Eight/Smash the Family, Church, and State" and "No Class Today/ No Ruling Class Tomorrow" are chants with a basic appeal to young people still being controlled by their elders. Campus issues like free speech, bad food, or boring classes can set off a movement that becomes more political. In some countries the lack of jobs for college graduates sets up a willingness to challenge the university and the government.

National and international organizations help coordinate campus activism. Student activism can be on the left or on the right, religious or secular. Occasionally, students fight other students, as in Iran where religious fundamentalists attacked the reformist and prodemocracy students, and in other areas like Israel and Palestine where, despite some efforts to work together, students are caught up in the dominant conflict.

There is a history of international student organization going back to 1900 and including Marxists and religious student groups. Today, organization and technology, including the Internet, facilitate ties among students around the world.[3] These connections take the form of individual as well as group commitment of students to global as well as local issues. While student activism usually arises from immediate and local issues, as it develops commitment it can take an international trajectory.

Concern with international issues can be strong on campuses with large numbers of international programs or international students, with substantial study abroad or exchange programs, or with a committed cadre of organizers. Global and local issues can be tied together, especially with an analysis of the role of corporations at home and abroad. At Occidental College in California students protested Atlantic Richfield's (ARCO) corporate role in Burma and its support for its oppressive government.[4] Geographic knowledge may not be Americans' strong point; many students on that campus might have never previously heard of Myanmar (or Burma.) However through the protests they learned about the connection between profit and human rights violations, and about a part of the world they didn't know. Other American students' interest carried them further. Five students from American University, Washington, D.C. and Yale University law school went to Burma/Myanmar in 1998 and were arrested, and expelled from the country for passing out leaflets about repression and government violence ten years earlier.[5]

Individual students and graduates find that travel abroad broadens their perspective and deepens their commitment. Sometimes they pay a great price. Ben Linder, a graduate of the University of Washington (Seattle), was murdered in 1988 by the Nicaraguan Contras who were funded by the U.S. government. He was there as an engineer trying to improve living conditions. Rachel Corrie, a student at Evergreen State College in Olympia, Washington, was killed by an Israeli bulldozer tearing down houses in the Gaza Strip in the spring of 2003 as she worked with the International Solidarity movement in a Palestinian camp. Lori Berenson went from MIT in Cambridge, Massachusetts, to Latin America and is now in a Peruvian prison, sentenced to life for alleged involvement with a radical, armed group.[6]

Student protest, and the lifelong commitment that it may involve—efforts at reform or revolution—is not without consequence. Teaching student activism may also have effects that might give us pause.

Students around the world continue to challenge political and academic authority. In Myanamar/Burma, Iran, Taiwan, Bangladesh, Nigeria, Mexico, Chile, Bosnia, France, Canada, the United States, and elsewhere on campus and off, students are important components of activism and challenges to governments and social, economic and political powers. Sometimes this is peaceful and responded to peacefully. Often, however, rather than being places for friendly debate—Ivory Towers—campuses are battlefields, sometimes scenes of carnage, as opposition provokes repression and outside conflict comes onto campus. Suppression of student dissent and shut downs of universities are marks of authoritarian governments of all sorts. In part, this is because student protest is not confined to the campus. Students combine with other protestors in their communities. "Globalization," racism, and environmental issues draw students into the streets. Broad social issues combine with educational concerns such as increasing access to education and to obtaining good jobs after graduation. For public or state funded universities in particular, academic issues are inseparable from political ones.

Student protest is hardly new. It is as old as education. Mass media have made it increasingly visible. In nineteenth-century Russia and early twentieth century China students played important roles in revolutionary movements. In colonial countries, including those in the Americas, student elites have been rebellious. In postcolonial societies, student protests continue or increase. Irish students played important roles in the late 1960s and early

1970s Civil Rights movement in Northern Ireland. Historical scholarship (including that of political scientists, sociologists and others) has documented the role of students, on the left and right, in social movements.

For many historians who were student activists themselves, teaching about activism as part of history is natural, if a little unnerving. To other historians (and perhaps the students) the subject may seem less obvious, and less important. The two key questions are why to teach about student activism and how to teach it in historical perspective. For historians who are committed activists themselves a third set of questions asks how academics/ activists use their own experience to teach and not preach, how to reach students who don't necessarily share their views, and how to work within often undemocratic colleges and universities. Student political activity can (and should) be considered in all kinds of history courses—national, regional, world or comparative—but has a particularly important place in United States history courses, where students on campuses can learn about their own (perhaps untraditional) traditions.[7]

Like other groups (women, farmers, workers, indigenous peoples) young people in high schools, colleges and universities can draw on common bonds and traditions of resistance to create a force capable of promoting (or sometimes resisting) change. In some countries, including many in Latin America, students and the public are fully conscious of their role in society. Faculty, administrators and the government also know the potential for student activism on and off campus. In other countries, including the United States, that student role is less assumed, the tradition of activism is uneven.

There are many reasons for this. Other segments of the population, especially workers, farmers, racial and ethnic minorities, and women, have been major engines of social change in the United States. Class, race, and gender in general have divided students and young people; those differences have often been more important than common ties of age or educational status. Part of the story, or its absence, however, is the neglect by scholars, in particular of United States history, of the important role that education and students (and faculty and staff) have played in social conflict and change. Despite interest, if not obsession, with student activism in the 1960s, the longer tradition of student activism is relatively neglected.[8] Some attention has been paid to students in the Progressive era, the 1920s and the 1930s. An early study of African American students is *The New Negro on Campus: Black College Rebellion of the 1920s* by Raymond Wolters.[9] Another major body of work has addressed discrimination in higher education.

However, the overwhelming percent of research on student activism (at least that which has been published) has focused on the 1960s (and its beginning with the civil rights movement in the 1950s). Even there, despite important work, the American students usually have been seen in relative isolation rather than as part of an international movement of students and national and international movements. Uprisings in the sixties also tend to be portrayed as a momentary aberration rather than part of a history of student activism in the United States. Finally, despite some studies of protest movements at state universities, most attention and memory of student activism focuses on certain campuses—Columbia, Berkeley, Wisconsin.

Many of the accounts of this activism have been in the form of memoirs, or memoirs disguised as history, and much of this deals with only segments of "the movement"—focusing on Students for a Democratic Society (SDS) or on the Student Nonviolent Coordinating Committee (SNCC) or on Vietnam. While this makes sense—some campuses were more involved than others, and SNCC and SDS were key organizations—that concentration obscures the depth of student activism on all kinds of campuses and around a variety of issues. In addition, it tends to minimize the importance then and in other periods of activism at traditionally black colleges, women's colleges, and religious and teacher's colleges. Recent attention to conservative student groups begins to fill another gap. Conservativism in the Bush administrations, in Congress, and in think tanks in Washington has its roots in the "new right" of the 1960s that included youthful supporters of 1964 Republican presidential candidate Barry Goldwater as well as members of the Young Americans for Freedom, a conservative group in the 1960s.[10]

A cursory examination of United States history survey textbooks shows that few mention student activism at all except in the late 1950s and 1960s. In fact, except for discussion of the origins of public education before the Civil War in the North, and during the Reconstruction in the South, and some discussion of the role of schools in "Americanization" of immigrants in the early twentieth-century, the history of education is generally missing from textbooks. Schoolbooks do not examine the history of schooling. Higher education pops up for discussion of the Morrill Land Grant Act (1862) which gave federal land to states to fund public ("land-grant") colleges and universities, then generally disappears for a hundred years. Many textbooks discuss, at least briefly, young people and their culture in the 1920s. However, the image of the young woman as "flapper" is generally presented with no ties to campus life or consideration of the changing place of women in higher education. Some texts do mention the role of students in the radicalism of the 1930s. More texts mention the role of the GI Bill of Rights on college enrollment, but few relate it to the political activity of students themselves (or the effect on women's enrollment). Many prominent monographs about the 1930s omit any mention of students and campuses from the discussion of the turmoil of the period.[11]

In some countries student protest has been deliberately written out of history texts to avoid embarrassing the government (and perhaps to avoid rekindling similar protests). Only recently, since 2000, with a change of political parties in power in Mexico, have that nation's textbooks begun acknowledging the massacre of hundreds of students and others in Mexico City in 1968. In the United States the issue seems to be less a matter of direct censorship than historians' own downplaying of the significance of student political activity and of the political role of education. Perhaps it is also the avoidance of difficult issues. The role of students in the civil rights movement can be rightly, and without much controversy, portrayed as heroic; their role in more radical groups, some of which advocated more radical goals, or more violent methods are harder to fit into a conventional narrative. The divisions in student groups like the SNCC and SDS reveal issues of racial and gender conflict that are not easily dealt with by iconic photographs or eloquent speeches. The use of violence by the SDS spin off the Weather Underground has been hard to fit into a progressive historical narrative without resort to good radicals/bad radicals rhetoric.[12] Especially since the violence of September 11, 2001, historians may be cautious about acknowledging violence that has been part of student activism.

Of course much historical memory is carried on outside of textbooks and outside of the classroom. Memories of social movements are transmitted in other ways -through word of mouth and oral tradition and in local or mass popular culture. Mass media now plays a key role. As a result, in the United States the word "Tienanamin" conveys an image of repression of students in China. "Kent State" carries some of the same force. Famous photographs of each violent incident, and in the case of Kent State, a song by Crosby, Stills, Nash and Young, have kept these images alive, while the shootings of students at Jackson State, Mississippi, at about the same time, are less visible. Films portray the uprisings in Europe in 1968. However, the word "Tlatelolco," despite more attention in United States media since the election in 2000 of Vicente Fox as president of Mexico and the opening of official records, is less familiar to most Americans. That massacre of hundreds of students and others in Mexico City in 1968 was overshadowed in the U.S. media by the Olympics a month later (and by the dramatic photo of the black power salute by four U.S. athletes).

"The Port Huron Statement, " written in 1960 by members of the SDS became a major document of the New Left. Its critique of U.S. society and call for participatory democracy helped introduce a new ideology on the left, a new approach to social change, and to the role of students. While books about the sixties discuss The Port Huron Statement at length, it rarely makes the cut in textbooks. The phrase may ring a bell for some people, but is not exactly the answer to a question on television quiz shows.[13] The Vietnam military veteran is a prominent figure in popular culture, but the antiwar "veteran" is likely to be a figure of ridicule (as in the film "Forrest Gump") or ignored. While in Mexico and Europe student radicals have been the subject of serious films, in the United States, even in films about the civil rights movement, student activists are at best, "ghosts."[14]

Still, memories persist, are perpetuated, and redefined. Student activists who have gone into government, journalism, teaching, union organizing, filmmaking, public history, and the arts carry their memories into the U.S. culture and help shape collective memory. Sometimes memory is deliberately revived. In the aftermath of the murder of students by the National Guard at Kent State on May 4, 1970, the university administration, like the state government tried to pave over the past, and in doing so created new student resistance. The administrators also rejected a memorial, which portrayed biblical figures Abraham and Isaac (signifying the willingness of patriarchs to sacrifice their children); the sculpture went off to Princeton University (which presumably wouldn't let the National Guard on its campus). Forty years later, Kent State University has a memorial and a Web page that discusses the war on campus.[15]

On some campuses, small ones like Oberlin in Oberlin, Ohio or large ones like the University of California at Berkeley, students (and staff, and faculty, and presumably, administrators) do have a sense of their campus traditions. Indeed, some students choose their college based on that image of the school and its students.

At many schools, there is less history of activism or perhaps less memory. Students come to college with no knowledge of past activism and no idea of their own potential role as activists. Campus culture may appear as predominantly vocational; students may see it as a site of sports or parties not debates or barricades.[16] On campuses with existing student political organizations, this can change as students are moved to deal with specific issues and look for a way to act on their concerns. On other campuses, though, there may be no carry over.

Teaching the history of student activism should be an integral part of teaching about social movements and political history. However it may also offer students a way to approach their own concerns as well as to understand the dynamics of historical change. It can teach them to examine the institutions of which they are a part, and to think of social structures as shaping their own lives, not just abstractions somewhere out there to be examined abstractly.

Like the textbooks that skip over the history of education, many history (and other) courses ignore the history of students and their role in society. There is something a little bizarre about a dynamic in which students and faculty seriously examine every institution except their own. It is also ironic when faculty who are engaged in struggle over campus governance issues leave that behind when they enter their classrooms. Should democracy on campus be discussed in class? Will it interrupt the day's lecture? There is of course the obvious problem of teaching about students questioning authority. What happens to your authority? Alert students may suggest that academic democracy begins in the classroom.

Whatever its risks, teaching about student activism can help students place themselves in the university and in the world. It can also have the effect of leading students to look off campus after first looking on campus. As students in the past forged connections with other students and other groups, those learning about such movements will see their connections to students in other countries, to other young people, and to other groups in their communities. Historians can teach about student activism in classes at all levels—graduate courses, upper division classes, survey classes, high school classes, and elementary schools.

My own experience has been teaching a senior seminar on the history of student activism, an upper level course on the 1960s, and the United States history survey from 1877 to the present. The survey, an introductory level class that fulfills a university requirement, presents particular difficulties and opportunities. However all of the courses include a mixture of students who may be more or less receptive to a discussion of student activism.[17]

I teach at the University of Southern Maine (USM), a public university where many students are the first in their family to go to college, many are older students returning to school, and many are enrolled part time. There is some political activism on campus but most students in my classes are not connected with it and are generally unaware of it. In all of the classes it is important for students to find out about past and present student activism on their own campus. Guest speakers, from Students Against Sweatshops for example, and student newspapers from the 1960s and 1970s, make the subject more immediate. Students Against Sweatshops has been especially effective at combining concern with international and campus issues. The group has pressed universities to ensure that clothing (especially for sports) purchased on campus is purchased from companies guaranteeing decent working conditions for their employees. Increases in parking fees also perk up interest in activism. So do wars and disasters.

The first night of the senior seminar, after discussing what the point is of such a capstone experience, the final requirement for their major, and finding out what the students think about the subject, I show part of the film "The Way We Were."[18] It is a surprising film and in its own way a good portrayal of campus radicals in New York in the 1930s. The romance between two depression era students—working class radical Barbara Streisand and wealthy but literary Robert Redford—mixes with political discussion of class, capitalism, the rise of fascism, and finally the moral dilemmas posed by McCarthyism. It sets up many of the issues of the class, including that of cultural representations of campus life and the construction of individual and collective memory.

We then turn to reading and discussion of the history of higher education based on Helen Lefkowitz Horowitz's discussion of the history of different campus cultures.[19] Students write a brief paper on what cultures or subcultures can be found at USM. Their first response is sometimes that there is no campus culture, by which they mean that students just come and go. After looking around the campus and interviewing other students and staff, however, they do find parallels to the reading, especially with the description of the "outsiders," those who do not fit into traditional campus groups like fraternities and sports. We move then to the question of who controls the university—"Who Rules?" This is often a new question (like asking who decided they all have to take a language other than English, or who sets the parking fees) and elicits considerable interest. There are many texts they could read. However, I have them read chapters from Thorstein Veblin's *The Higher Learning in America*.[20] Most students find it barely readable, but Veblin's ideas about the role of businessmen in controlling education seem quite modern. Students report back to the class on who rules USM namely, who is on the board of trustees and how they got there, who isn't on the board and why not, what role students play as tuition payers, what is the connection with the state legislature and governor, who is the president of the university and what does he do? A positive aspect of this assignment is that the university administration becomes aware that students are asking questions.

We then return to the student movement of the 1930s, and students read a contemporary account by a then Columbia University student James Wechsler, and two historians' interpretations.[21] Wechsler's experience as editor of the college newspaper points out the importance of the campus press in student political activity. The expulsion of another student editor, Reed Harris, from Columbia (for his having the temerity to challenge collegiate football) shows a fear of free speech and free press that has been a characteristic of administrative responses to student protest. In an editorial, Harris called college football a "racket" and suggested that players be hired and paid outright instead of receiving hidden subsidies. The student activism of that period reveals connections with the past and with other groups like unions, civil rights groups and farmers. The role of the students at City College of New York (CCNY) argues against explanations of student activism based on students' elite status (and time and money). That movement also shows connections between U.S. students and those in other countries. The "Oxford Pledge" of 1933, for example, in which British students swore never to fight "for King and Country," was picked up by U.S. students as a pledge not to support the United States government in any war it might conduct (except perhaps in case of invasion).[22]

Students in the 1930s who were against both war and fascism were torn in a way that may seem familiar to students who oppose war and who condemn individual terrorism and state terrorism. The fact that many who took the Oxford pledge later did fight "for king and country" does not eliminate the value of knowing that such a refusal is an option. Those who watched the British and United States governments "preemptively" invade Iraq in the spring of 2003 could know that patriotism has not always been defined by obeying orders.

This case study also sets up the research assignments for the rest of the course. The first paper/oral report is a study of student activists as represented in a cultural text. The second is a study of a student movement in a country other than the United States. These two work together to take the students and the student movement beyond the campus and beyond their country. The culture is tied in with the class reading of a novel portraying student activism or about an incident related to it. One semester we read about Mexican students in *Calling All Heroes* by Paco Ignacio Taibo ll. In another semester we read about South African resistance in *My Son's Story* by Nadine Gordimer. In the future we will read *The Lion and the Iroko: A Play* by Chinyere Grace Okafor, who portrays students as part of the opposition to the Nigerian government.[23]

For this assignment students can examine films, novels, political speeches, monuments and public art, and music. Students may focus on the United States, other countries or both, and represent any time period. In practice, students have generally selected music and films, including "Biko," "The Big Chill," "Running on Empty," and "The White Rose."

Moving to the 1960s we can draw on new and comparative scholarship, as well as memoirs and first hand accounts. Vania Markarian's discussion of debate about the Mexican student movement traces the development of discourse and analysis of that movement over the last forty years, since 1968. In some ways it is similar to that in the United States and other countries as official and unofficial, academic and activist voices look for new ways to "speak of 1968."[24]

Martin Klimke's essay on the connections between the 1960s movements in Germany and the United States[25] adds a transatlantic perspective that breaks down boundaries within scholarship about students and movements in general. His use of theories about the origins and developments of social movements and Markarian's use of analysis of language to understand such movements offers students models for understanding how change occurs and the role students can play in social transformation, that is, changing the world. Similarly, sociologist Doug McAdam's *Freedom Summer* presents a combination of committed scholarship and methodology analyzing participation in the civil rights movement that students find useful and opens up ways of looking at movements.[26]

Primary sources include interviews, published documents, and documents and other material on the Internet.[27] For a comparative view, in addition to their paper, students each select a country discussed in *1968: The World Transformed* edited by Carole Fink, Philipp Gassert, and Detleff Junker.[28] Unfortunately, good books on student activism have gone out of print.[29]

Finally, to reinforce the point that student politics is both local and international, students read Elena Poniatowska's account of the Mexican government's suppression of the Mexican students in 1968.[30] We combined the discussion with two guest speakers, one our Latin American historian, the other a mathematics professor from Chile whose first-hand account of growing up under the government of General Augusto Pinochet caught the students attention a way the books did not.

Speakers who talk about their own experience in the 1960s also work well in the upper division class on the 1960s and the introductory level United States history survey. Students by now have often heard Vietnam military veterans speak, sometimes in history classes. However, except for some whose parents, or now sometimes grandparents were involved in the civil rights movement or antiwar movements, the voice of student activists is new to them. A combination of a Catholic pacifist, a member of the October League, a Marxist group that focused on organizing the working class, who worked in a factory in New Orleans, and a woman who went from sixties activism to working with a shelter for battered women in Maine, offers students a view of the diversity of the movements they read about in books. One of the weaknesses of much writing about the 1960s is, ironically, or perhaps not, its lack of inclusiveness, and its segmentation. Some monographs and overviews do attempt to show links among movements, for example, Sara Evans in *Personal Politics: The Roots of Women's Liberation in the Civil Rights Movement and the New Left*.[31] Two books that can add different ways of looking at student activism are *Seeds of the Sixties* by Andrew Jamison and Ronald Eyerman, and *Catholics and American Culture: Fulton Sheen, Dorothy Day, and the Notre Dame Football Team* by Mark S. Massa.[32] One important aspect of looking at periods like the 1950s during which students appeared to be apolitical, is that we can see that politics can take different forms. For example, discussion of Rachel Carson and *Silent Spring,* her path breaking 1962 study of the impact of DDT, shows that environmental concern predates the the creation of Earth Day in April 1970. Since the 1970s, interest in the environment and ecology has been especially strong on campuses. Students can see the connection of on campus efforts to conserve energy and national and international political work.

Documentary films like the "Eyes on the Prize" series, "Freedom on My Mind," "Berkeley in the Sixties," "The War at Home," "America Coming Apart," and, somewhat problematically, "The Sixties," are useful in a variety of classes. At the same time, for the survey course, the autobiographies of Anne Moody, for the civil rights movement, and Ron Kovic, for a Vietnam verteran's view of the antiwar movement, provide voices from the 1960s that the students can read and compare.

One of the most common themes of recent writing about the sixties and the legacy of student movements of that era has been the idea that "the personal is the political," that issues of individual life, whether about sexuality or child care, access to education or choices of majors, are relayed to social attitudes and institutions. Some accounts of student activism focus on a split between those who emphasized culture and individual change and those who emphasized structure and group change. But the desire for both cultural and structural change has been deeply embedded in student dissent. Caught between the end of World War II and the beginning of the cold war, a student at the University of Wisconsin, wrote on behalf of the "Pogo For President" campaign:

> A vote for Pogo is a vote for Life and for one's self. A vote for any politician is a vote for government, and what it is for: fear, coercion, regimentation, war, death. . . . When economic exploitation, social and moral coercion, sexual misery leave the streets, when freedom has meaning for the individual and is not a word which stimulates him to slaughter those who have less of it, then it will be because we spontaneously from below made it so.
>
> Peace is not legislated. Governments are for the birds. Vote for Pogo, or, better yet, don't vote.[33]

Some student activists would disagree with the rejection of voting and politics, but the desire for an individual role in bringing about change, and the need to have those individual voices heard, ties together the movements of students around the world and gives them strength.

Notes

1. James D. Ross, "Rain of Terror," *The New Republic* 205:18 (October 28, 1991): 10–13.
2. *New York Times*, 13 August, 2003, p. 6; BBC News, "Clemency Urged For Iranian Students," August 5, 2003 http://newsvote.bbc.co.ik/mpapps/pagetools/print/news/bbc.co.uk/1/hi/world/middle_east/312 (accessed 5 September 2003).
3. See for example the Web site of the All Burma Students League which includes an english text of a history of the student movement. http://absl.myip.org/absl_HTML/Burma/studentsMovement.htm (accessed 5 September 2003).

4. Peter Dreier, "The Myth of Student Apathy," *Nation* 266: 12 (April 13, 1998): 19.

5. Kelly McCollum, "Myanmar Expels 5 U.S. Students for Anti-Government Activity," *The Chronicle of Higher Education,* September 1998, A 76.

6. "The War: Death of a Human Shield", *Seattle Weekly,* March 19–25, 2003.

7. I have taught these particular courses at the University of Southern Maine since 1987. I also included student activism in courses I taught at other universities. These courses have all been influenced by ideas of colleagues and the work of many scholars and activists. There is also a larger body of scholarship on the role of public schooling on the elementary and secondary level and the connection to social control and Americanization. A classic is Samuel Bowles and Herbert Gintis, *Schooling in Capitalist America* (New York: Basic Books, 1976). Student activism in high schools and elementary schools deserves more attention. The role of young students in the Civil Rights movement is a case in point.

8. There are obviously exceptions including the work of Philip Altbach, Richard Flacks, and others cited later in this essay. On activism on campuses in the United States see Philip Altbach, *Student Politics in America* (New York: McGraw-Hill, 1974) and Willis Rudy, *The Campus and Nation in Crisis: from the American Revolution to Vietnam (*Madison, NJ: Fairleigh Dickinson University Press, 1996). There is also a larger body of scholarship on the role of public schooling on the elementary and secondary level and the connection to social control and Americanization. A classic is Samuel Bowles and Herbert Gintis, *Schooling in Capitalist America* (New York: Basic Books, 1976).

9. Raymond Wolters, *The New Negro on Campus: Black College Rebellion of the 1920s"* (Princeton, NJ: Princeton University Press, 1975).

10. For example, see John A. Andrew, *The other side of the sixties: Young Americans for freedom and the rise of conservative politics* (New Brunswick, NJ: Rutgers University Press, 1997).

11. For example, David Kennedy's Pulitzer prize winning, *Freedom from Fear: The American People in Depression and War, 1929–1945* (New York: Oxford University Press, 1999).

12. For discussion of similar avoidances in treatment of the 1960s see Bruce Shulman, "Out of the Streets and Into the Classroom? The New Left and the Counterculture in the United States History Textbooks," *The Journal of American History*, March 1999, 1527–1534, and Van Gosse, "Consensus and Contradiction in Textbook Treatment of the Sixties," *The Journal of American History* (September 1995), 658–669.

13. For discussion of the impact of the Port Huron statement see Tom Hayden and Dick Flacks, "The Port Huron Statement at 40," *The Nation. (*5 August 2002); http://thenation.com/doc.mhtml (accessed 20 August 2003), Hayden and Flacks do note that a character in the feature film "The Big Lebowski" claims a role in writing The Port Huron Statement.

14. The film "Mississippi Burning" is perhaps the best example of this. Supposedly about investigation into the murder of civil rights workers, James Cheney, Andrew Goodman, and Michael Schwerner, the film makes them and their colleagues in the movement invisible and gives a key role to the FBI. On the other hand "Ghosts of Mississippi" does offer a more realistic portrayal.

15. "May 4th, 1970—General Information," http://www.kent.edu/KSU/May4/welcome.htm (accessed 20 August 2003).

16. For a discussion of the history of campus cultures, see Helen Lefkowitz Horowitz, *Campus Life: Undergraduate Cultures from the End of the Eighteenth Century to the Present* (Chicago: University of Chicago Press, 1987).

17. The senior seminar, "Student Activism in Historical Perspective," attracts students interested in that subject but also students who need a seminar at a particular time.

18. Sydney Pollack, producer, "The Way We Were" (Columbia Pictures, 1973).

19. Horowitz, *Campus Life.*

20. Thorstein Veblin, *The Higher Learning in America* (New York: B. W. Huebsch, 1918).

21. James Wechsler, *Revolt on the Campus* (New York: Covici Friede, 1935); Robert Cohen, *When the Old Left Was Young: Student Radicals and America's First Mass Student Movement 1929–1941* (New York: Oxford University Press 1993); Eileen Eagan, *Class, Culture, and the Classroom: The Student Peace Movement of the 1930s* (Philadelphia: Temple University Press, 1981). Cohen has also put on line his essays and documents about the Thirties' students on the web site of the New Deal Network, a collaboration of the Franklin and Eleanor Roosevelt Institute (FERA) and the Institute for Teaching Technology at Columbia University/ /Teachers College.

22. See student newspapers of the period, for example, "War Against War," editorial, Brown *Daily Herald* 22 March 1933; Columbia *Spectator* 3 April, 1933.
23. Paco Ignatio Taibo ll, *Calling All Heroes;* Nadine Gordimer, *My Son's Story;* Chinyere Grace Okafor, *The Lion and the Iroko: A Play* (Ibadan, Nigeria: Kraft Books, 1996).
24. Vania Markarian, "Debating Tlatelolco: Thirty Years of Public Debates about the Mexican Student Movement"; see below.
25. Martin Klimke, "Between Berkeley and Berlin, San Francisco and Frankfort: The Student Movements of the 1960s in Transatlantic Perspective;" see below.
26. Doug McAdam, *Freedom Summer (*New York: Oxford University Press, 1988). For the almost all white students, it also raises a question for them of what they would have been or would be willing to do.
27. Two good collections are Judith Clavir Albert and Stewart Edward Albert, *The Sixties Papers: Documents of a Rebellious Decade (New York: Praeger, 1984)* and Alexander Bloom and Wini Breines, *Takin' It to the Streets (*New York: Oxford University Press, 1995).
28. Carole Fink, Philipp Gassert, Detlef Junker, ed. *1968: The World Transformed* (German Historical Institute and Cambridge University Press, 1998).
29. Modern technology comes to the rescue here. For example, students can locate at Columbia the interviews done for Ron Frazer, ed. *1968: A student generation in revolt* (New York: Pantheon Press, 1975).
30. Elena Poniatowska, *La Noche de Tlatelolco* (Mexico City: Ediciones Era, 1971); English translation, *Massacre in Mexico* (Columbia MO, University of Missouri Press, 1989).
31. Sara Evans, *Personal Politics: The Roots of Women's Liberation in the Civil Rights Movement and the New Left* (New York: Knopf, 1997). For a more recent discussion , see Ruth Rosen, *The World Split Open: How the Modern Women's Movement Changed America* (New York: Viking, 2000).
32. Andrew Jamison and Ronald Eyerman, *Seeds of the Sixties* (Berkeley: University of California Press, 1994; Mark S. Massa, *Catholics and American Culture: Fulton Sheen, Dorothy Day, and the Notre Dame Football Team* (New York: Crossroad Publishing Company, 1999.
33. "Pogo For President," University of Wisconsin *Daily Cardinal* 30 October, 1952.

CHAPTER 2

Debating Tlatelolco

Thirty years of Public Debates about
the Mexican Student Movement of 1968

VANIA MARKARIAN

Can the Mexican student movement of 1968 offer any guidance to those who are now looking critically at their society, either in Latin American or in U.S. campuses? Journals, newspapers, pamphlets, and books published in Mexico between 1968 and 2000 reveal that successive generations of Mexicans have learned various lessons from the student movement, reinterpreting it in accordance to their specific needs at a given moment. A revision of the last thirty years of public debate shows how actors and ways of talking of these events have changed over time, slowly reaching beyond the narrow circles of former leaders and activists to center the attention of wider sectors of the citizenry. If anything, this revision indicates that, as long as there are social actors willing to root their aspirations for social and political change in history, the achievements and effects of the student movement will remain open to further interpretation.

The first one to grasp this conclusion was probably the Mexican government, which wanted the popular imagination to remember 1968 as the year of the Olympic Games. After all, preparations for the first Olympics to be celebrated in a Latin American country had taken a long time and vast resources. But, instead of athletes, images of students protesting in the streets fill our minds when we think about 1968 in Mexico. In fact, the student movement of 1968 is today one of the most powerful Mexican political myths. Every political actor refers to these events in order to legitimize his or her voice in Mexican politics. Past and present volley back and forth in the political game: narratives of the events of 1968 support present-day political positions, which, in turn, act upon these narratives.

The "night of Tlatelolco" epitomizes public references to this year. The night of October 2, 1968, gunmen of the Mexican repressive forces killed several men, women, and children participating in a student rally in Tlatelolco Square in Mexico City. Thirty years later we are still learning what exactly happened that night: how many people died, who gave the orders, and who shot. But whereas the investigation of these issues has been extremely slow and difficult, public debates have only increased in these past three decades.

Until the 1960s, the government of the Partido Revolucionario Institucional (PRI) had been clearly popular—even though not thoroughly democratic—thanks to several decades of economic growth, civilian rule, and international peace. Most of the Mexican citizenry agreed that their country had created its own path towards economic development and political stability in Latin America. Official labor and peasant organizations provided the regime with a popular base, which resulted in the creation of a corporate state. The scarce efforts to express dissent were systematically subdued by the government and its allies. Sooner or later, the structures of the PRI ended up absorbing or eliminating every attempt at articulated protest. In the 1960s, however, the perceived end of the long period of "stabilizing growth" gave rise to the claim for a more pluralist political scene to debate the new dilemmas facing Mexican society. It soon became obvious that there was widespread resentment with the authoritarian style of the governing elite.[1]

All this discontent erupted in the mobilization of secondary school and university students in Mexico City, which rapidly secured support throughout the urban middle classes in the country. Since they took to the streets in July 1968, the students attracted public attention by criticizing the current political regime, rather than with specific claims involving superior education. Even before the October 2 massacre, repression against the students who took to the streets was intended to stop criticism of the long-lasting government of the PRI. In the period immediately after October 1968 and until 1970, during the last years of the presidency of Gustavo Díaz Ordaz, the government harshly repressed student mobilization and silenced public debate about it.

The day after October 2, 1968, government spokesmen offered the first official version of the events. Other officials repeated this version in the following months. Although they could not produce clear evidence to support their story, they all attested that "provocateurs" had fired shots at the army when they were approaching Tlatelolco Square, killing both students and soldiers. They also referred to the participation of "foreign forces," blamed intellectuals angered with the government for inducing the students to take to the streets, praised the response of the government, and concluded that there were no obstacles to the celebration of the Olympic Games.[2] A former student leader and a well-known writer collaborated with the government in spreading this version.[3] Mexican newspapers and journals reproduced it, paying almost no attention to other opinions.

Foreign media, however, devoted lengthy pages to the opinions of the few student leaders who were not jailed, published declarations by leftist groups, and interviewed several dissident intellectuals.[4] The resignation of writer Octavio Paz from his post as Ambassador to India was probably the most significant gesture, since it seriously damaged the image of reconciliation that the Mexican government was selling to the world.[5] Although these dissident voices could not agree either on a precise explanation of what had happened on October 2, mainly differing in how many dead and injured there had been, all of them coincided in characterizing the student rally as nonviolent and rejected the extraordinary violence displayed by the government. In the two years immediately following October 1968, however, these voices were clearly marginal in Mexican politics. The official truth was repeated endlessly whenever the issue of the student movement was brought up in public.

The inauguration of president Luis Echeverría in 1970 changed the terms of public discussion of these events. He aimed at getting rid of the accusation of being responsible for government repression (as Minister of Interior during the Tlatelolco massacre). He released student leaders from prison and met lingering demands in the universities, increasing government resources for higher education. But Echeverría also continued to repress the opposition and failed to investigate abuses by the repressive forces.[6] This position, however ambiguous, opened up a space to protest government repression of the student movement of 1968.

Unlike the pro-government books and pamphlets that appeared before 1970, the most important publications of this new period openly opposed the official truth. In 1970 and 1971, writers, journalists, and essayists (Carlos Monsiváis, Octavio Paz, Elena Poniatowska, LuisGonzález de Alba) denounced repression and referred to what had happened in Tlatelolco as a watershed in Mexican politics that had revealed the true nature of the current regime.[7] From then on, testimony and written pieces became the main genres to deal with 1968.

Many student leaders and activists recently released from jail used 1968 as a way to explain their political positions. Some saw in the continued repression of political opposition a reason to embrace guerrilla movements, both urban and rural. Others began to participate in the new political spaces opened up by the ruling party with the specific aim of suppressing dissidence among students and intellectuals. In between these two extremes, many went back to their activism in universities or began to collaborate with peasant and working-class organizations.[8] All these options showed that the former members of the student movement had different ideas on how to resume their involvement in politics. But for all of them, 1968 was the main reason for renewed political commitment; they all focused on this year to account for the course of their political involvement.

Government repression defined their political experience. Despite this emphasis on government brutality, there were no consistent attempts to investigate what had exactly happened on October 2. Those who presented themselves as the victims of repression could not identify specific culprits or name the alleged hundreds of dead in Tlatelolco. Instead, they kept repeating distressing images and metaphors of death.[9] They blamed the authorities and the regime, but could not offer any supporting evidence for their accusations, beyond their own imprecise testimonies.[10] The importance of testimonial authority disregarded the expression of opinions legitimized on other bases, such as academic analysis or research. Public discussion of the student movement was therefore confined to former leaders and leftist activists, more worried about their own internal issues than about including other types of approaches to understanding 1968.

José López Portillo, who succeeded Echeverría as president, avoided polemics and urged Mexicans to leave the past behind, forgetting all controversies and accusations.[11] But the tenth anniversary of the movement offered a new opportunity to talk about 1968. Some took advantage of the anniversary to publicly attack the portrayal of the movement presented by the former leaders and activists; they asked for documentation and investigation to replace personal testimony.[12] In 1978, in fact, a small number of essays and academic works addressed 1968 from a more analytical point of view. In general terms, all these works referred to the student movement as a significant historical event, emphasizing its call for democracy and its resistance to the authoritarianism of the government. Although these works did not appeal to testimonial authority but to the need for analysis and research, their authors were, once again, former leaders and other activists closely related to the student movement. In a similar way, only leftist groups participated in the rallies commemorating the tenth anniversary of the movement.[13] Debating about 1968 was restricted to, in the words of Carlos Monsiváis, the "ghettos" of the left.[14]

In the 1980s, the range of participants in public debates about the student movement of 1968 widened. The broad network of organizations that arose as a result of the inefficiency of the government in dealing with the 1985 earthquake in Mexico City made everybody recall the mobilizations of 1968.[15] In 1986–1987, a new student conflict opened up public discussion about the 1968 movement, and its similarities and differences with current events. Although the protesters targeted now university authorities and not the political regime, some of the new leaders claimed 1968 as their inheritance, and some former leaders felt that their struggle was being continued by the Mexican youth.[16] More generally, the now aged leaders and activists of the 1960s took the opportunity to rethink their past under a new light; they argued that the legacy of the 1968 movement was a valuable experience of self-organization before governmental arbitrariness.[17]

At the same time, political opposition to the PRI government could finally organize at the national level, making democratic liberties the center of its campaign. The drafters of the manifesto of the new coalition considered the 1968 student movement part of their political background. Many former student activists joined the new party.[18] With their incorporation into a political movement of national scope, their memories and opinions about the 1968 student movement reached a greater audience.

Closely associated with the extended claim for democratic reforms in the country, 1968 was proving politically powerful. It was already a foundational myth for several generations participating in Mexican politics. Starting in the mid-1980s, a shared set of beliefs and explanations favorable to the student movement enabled the enlargement of spaces and actors involved in discussing the events of 1968.[19] This understanding became common knowledge about 1968—open defense of the reaction of the government was now clearly marginal. Born out of the testimonies and writings of the previous years, this common knowledge had much larger repercussions.

Testimonial genre continued to be the privileged way of talking about 1968, and there were few analytic approaches.[20] The most common style was now a nostalgic, personal, and quotidian form of testimony.[21] Instead of the previous politically-informed accounts by former leaders and intellectuals, anonymous voices began to tell their own versions of this past, in which the main novelty was the remembrance of the 1960s not only as the age of political commitment, but also as the flourishing time of counterculture.[22] They coincided with leaders and intellectuals, however, in considering current political changes as the positive outcome of the student mobilization of 1968.[23] The political content of this shared knowledge was milder, with continuous references to democratic liberties and almost no remnant of the earlier radical and revolutionary language. The extreme version of this new, sometimes apolitical, reading of the movement was a widespread interpretation in New Age terms, with strong emphasis on its spiritual content.[24]

Together with the democratic vindication of the movement, there was another important innovation in the public debate about 1968, especially regarding government repression. Up to this moment, none of the former protagonists had precisely identified the culprits and documented casualties. It was not until the late 1980s that public references to 1968 were framed into a discourse that called for investigation of these and other repressive acts. These demands were made in the name of the human rights of the victims and as a condition of democratic change in the country.

In other Latin American countries, human rights organizations had denounced government repression since the beginning of the 1970s. Although governments consistently refused to investigate allegations and repressed denouncers, these organizations became reliable sources of information for the international community. But the transnational network developed in this period was focused on countries under openly authoritarian governments. With an elected civilian government and an international position respectful of human rights, Mexico did not attract their attention. In the late 1980s, negotiations of a free trade agreement with the United States and Canada led the Mexican government to take extra care of its international image. At the same time, once Argentina, Chile, and Uruguay made their transitions to democracy, the transnational human rights network began to look at other countries. As a result, the number of Mexican human rights groups grew from four in 1984 to 200 in 1993.[25]

On the twenty-fifth anniversary of the events of 1968, the language of human rights shaped the public debate about student mobilization and governmental repression. This is revealed in the foundation of a Truth Commission, which was the first attempt to create an independent organization to investigate and document the actions of all the participants involved. However, without any government support and very limited resources, it could not achieve its goals.[26] But it articulated a new way of coping with the recent past, where knowledge and denouncement prevailed over speculative accusation and political diatribe. Simultaneously, a group of ex-leaders and activists promoted the creation of a public space in the city to honor those who had died in October 1968. The monument, a series of plaques with the names of the twenty casualties they could clearly identify, was inaugurated with the biggest rally ever in commemoration of October 2, 1968.[27]

Although neither the Truth Commission nor the monument could meet the expectations of their promoters, falling short in their search of evidence, they showed a deep change in the ways Mexicans dealt with 1968. They made accountability an unavoidable condition for real democracy in Mexico. In these two initiatives, the student movement represented something bigger than the antecedent of current democratic movements, just as the deaths of October 2 represented more than the martyrdom of the youth or the revelation of an authoritarian system. With this new language, 1968 was the main symbol of every act of violence and abuse that had not been investigated—only knowing the truth could prevent government abuse.[28]

For example, the insurrection started in Chiapas in January 1994 under the banner of indigenous rights came to reinforce this new discourse about 1968, not because of its radical content, but due to the reaction of the government. When the army began to brutally repress the insurrection, many brought up the specter of Tlatelolco, asking for "truth and justice" and demanding a thorough investigation of the role of the armed forces in the 1960s and 1990s.[29]

The majority of the commemorations of the thirtieth anniversary of the student movement referred to democracy, human rights, and truth telling. This emphasis made 1968 increasingly appealing to wider sectors of the Mexican population. In part, this trend reflected the fact that the "1968 generation" had reached leading positions in Mexican politics and society. But at the same time that their political experience was becoming the object of public respect, many former activists and members of younger generations contested the idealized democratic content of the 1968 student movement and wondered why nobody was able to name the alleged hundreds of dead. They argued that truth telling and investigation were the responsibility of everybody.[30]

It is still too early to evaluate how the past two years have affected public discussion of the student movement of 1968. With the end of more than seventy years of PRI-dominated government, official silence has loosened, revealing the existence of new sources and materials that will surely improve our understanding of these events.[31] But this opening is only part of the change. On the anniversary of October 2 in 2000, then President-elect Vicente Fox paid his first homage to the dead. Those who had always commemorated this anniversary could not agree on specifics and, for the first time in many years, organized two different rallies.[32] If the new official voices do not belong to those who had legitimized their political participation in 1968, the latter still have to learn how to oppose a government that is not controlled by the PRI. How to speak of 1968 in a country that is trying to change its political structures and culture is the challenge of this new time.

Notes

This chapter began as a much longer piece for Professor Pablo Piccato in the program on Latin American history at Columbia University. It was published in Spanish in the Mexican journal *Anuario de Espacios Urbanos* (2001). I am thankful to Professor Piccato for his initial interest in the topic and his final comments to the paper, as well as to my friends Claudine Leysinger and Ashli White for their careful reading and useful suggestions. I would also like to acknowledge the comments and suggestions of the editors of this volume.

1. See Leslie Bethell, ed., *Mexico since Independence* (New York: Cambridge University Press, 1991), 352–60.
2. For these official versions see Sergio Aguayo Quezada, *1968: Los archivos de la violencia* (Mexico City: Editorial Grijalbo, 1998), 131–35 and 268–69; and Ramón Ramírez, *El*

32 • Vania Markarian

movimiento estudiantil de México, julio-diciembre de 1968 (Mexico City: Ediciones Era, 1969), 93–139.

For the role of the student Sócrates Amado Campos Lemus and the writer Elena Garro, see Jorge Volpi, *La imaginación y el poder: Una historia intelectual de 1968* (Mexico City: Ediciones Era, 1998), 327–61.

4. See Ramírez, *El movimiento estudiantil de México*, 369–404; and Aguayo, *1968*, 287–92. For the alienation of the intelligentsia from the regime, see also Leslie Bethell, ed., *Mexico since Independence*, 361.

5. See Volpi, *La imaginación y el poder*, 369–80. See also exchange of letters between Paz and the Mexican Foreign Office in Octavio Paz, "Un sueño de libertad: Cartas a la cancillería," *Vuelta* 256 (March 1998), 6–14 and 65.

6. For a smart contemporary analysis of the Echeverría administration, see Claude Bataillon, "El nuevo estilo de Echeverría," *Excélsior*, January 25, 1975. For different positions about their releasing among imprisoned student leaders, see Raul Alvarez Garín et alter, *Los procesos de México 68: Acusaciones y defensa* (Mexico City: Editorial Estudiantes, 1970).

7. See Carlos Monsiváis, *Días de guardar* (Mexico City: Ediciones Era, 1970); Octavio Paz, *Posdata* (Mexico City: Siglo XXI, 1971); Elena Poniatowska, *La noche de Tlatelolco* (Mexico City: Ediciones Era, 1971); and former student leader Luis González de Alba, *Los días y los años* (Mexico City: Ediciones Era, 1971).

8. On guerrilla involvement, see the open letter reproduced in Leopoldo Ayala, *Nuestra verdad: Memorial del movimiento estudiantil popular y el dos de octubre de 1968* (Mexico City: Joaquín Porrúa, 1989), 59–65. On the conservative swing, see Volpi, *La imaginación y el poder*, 421–23; and Bethell, *Mexico since Independence*, 366; see also personal testimony by Emery Ulloa in *Excélsior*, March 28 to 31, 1985. On the other kinds of activism, see, for instance, Roberto Escudero and Salvador Martínez Della Rocca, "Mexico: Generation of 68," *NACLA Report on the Americas* 12:5 (September–October 1978), 8–19.

9. For examples if this metaphoric language see Marco Antonio Campos and Alejandro Toledo, eds., *Poemas y narraciones sobre el movimiento estudiantil de 1968* (Mexico City: Universidad Autónoma de México, 1996). Among the 39 poems and short stories in this compilation, 33 dated back to the period 1968–1978 and 29 referred directly to October 2 with expressions like "the killing of the innocents" (Revueltas), "the funeral night" (Ramírez), "the black bliss" (Guillén), "the stone mirror" (Becera) or simply "the night," "the massacre" and "Tlatelolco."

10. Attempts to sustain charges against President Díaz Ordaz in November 1971 showed how difficult it was to deal with a reluctant judicial system. For this event, see E. Poniatowska, "El movimiento estudiantil de 1968," *Vuelta* 1:7 (June 1977), 24.

11. See José López Portillo, *El Ejecutivo ante el Congreso, 1976-1982* (Mexico City: Secretaría de Programación y Presupuesto, 1983). Despite López Portillo's call, the appointment of Díaz Ordaz as Ambassador in Spain reopened the debate about his role in 1968. See *Excélsior*, October 2 and 3, 1978. For other measures related to the events of 1968 during the López Portillo administration, see Bethell, *Mexico Since Independence*, 376

12. See, for example, Eduardo Lizalde, "¿Hemos aprendido algo del 68?," *Vuelta* 2:23 (October 1978), 8–11; and Carlos Monsiváis, "Prólogo," in Sergio Zermeño, *México, una democracia utópica: El movimiento estudiantil del 68* (Mexico City: Siglo XXI, 1978), xxii–xxiii.

13. For analytical works, see, for instance, Zermeño, *México, una democracia utópica*; José Revueltas, *Mexico 68: Juventud y revolución* (Mexico City: Ediciones Era, 1978). For a first attempt to evaluate these and other analytic approaches to 1968 see Susana García Salord, "Aproximación a un análisis crítico de las hipótesis sobre el movimiento estudiantil de 1968," *Cuadernos Políticos* 25 (July–September 1980), 71–84. On the tenth anniversary of the movement, see *Excélsior*, October 2 and 3, 1978.

14. Carlos Monsiváis, "Del ghetto a la explanada: La transición de la izquierda," *Viva* 4 (September 1988), 18.

15. Once again, Monsiváis and Poniatowska became the chroniclers of the event. See Carlos Monsiváis, *Entrada libre: Crónicas de la sociedad que se organiza* (Mexico City: Ediciones Era, 1987); and Elena Poniatowska, *Nada, nadie: Las voces del temblor* (Mexico City: Ediciones Era, 1988).

16. See David Aylett, "No es lo mismo veinte años después," *Vuelta* 13:152 (July 1989), 49–52; Juan Gutiérrez, "El movimiento estudiantil en la UNAM: Testimonios," *Cuadernos Políticos* 125 (January–June 1987), 28; and Mario Ruiz Massieu, "Principales diferencias entre el movimiento estudiantil de 1968 y el del CEU (1986-1987)," *Universidad de México* 43:453 (October 1988), 25–27.

17. See for instance Ayala, *Nuestra verdad*, 7; and Gilberto Guevara Niebla, *La democracia en la calle: Crónica del movimiento estudiantil mexicano* (Mexico City: Instituto de Investigaciones Sociales-UNAM, 1988), 167–85.

18. On the foundation of the Partido de la Revolución Democrática see its official web site (http://www.cen-prd.org.mx), and Jorge G. Castañeda, *Utopia Unarmed: The Latin American Left After the Cold War* (New York: Alfred A. Knopf, 1993), 153–64. On former activists' participation, see Ayala, *Nuestra verdad*, 31–32.

19. In her analysis of theatrical works, Jacqueline Bixter proposes a similar chronology, pointing out that "the memories of Tlatelolco remained relatively unstaged until the 1980s." Jacqueline E. Bixter, "Re-membering the past: Memory-Theatre and Tlatelolco," *Latin American Research Review* 37:2 (2002), 121.

20. Among these analytic approaches see Gilberto Guevara Niebla, *Las luchas estudiantiles en México* (Mexico City: Editorial Línea, 1986); and Salvador Martínez Della Rocca, *Estado y universidad en México (1920–1968): Historia de los movimientos estudiantiles de la UNAM* (Mexico City: Joan Boldó y Clement Editores, 1986).

21. See, for instance, Raul Alvarez Garín and Gilberto Guevara Niebla, *Pensar el 68* (Mexico City: Cal y Arena, 1988); Ayala, *Nuestra verdad*; and special issue of *Nexos* 121 (January 1988). This change in style resembles the decline of poetic and novelistic treatment of the events of 1968 in the early 1980s, when drama became gained importance to address the issue of Tlatelolco. Bixter explains that "This difference among genres suggests that the theatre, with its ability to maintain an eternal present, is a more effective medium in keeping the memories of Tlatelolco alive." Something similar could be said about the new forms of testimony when compared to those produced by former leaders and intellectuals. See Bixter, "Re-membering the past," 124.

22. Different organizations and journals sponsored public discussions and published the results. See for instance María Romero Valenzuela et alter, *Hoy maestro, ayer joven del 68* (Mexico City: Casa de la Cultura del Maestro Mexicano, 1990); and Daniel Cazés, ed., *Memorial del 68: Relato a muchas voces* (Mexico City: La Jornada Ediciones, 1993). The clearest association between political protest and counterculture was Paco Ignacio Taibo II, *68* (Mexico City: Joaquín Mortiz, 1991). For an intelligent analysis of the reasons why this association was not common in previous years, see Eric Zolov, *Refried Elvis: The Rise of the Mexican Counterculture* (Los Angeles: University of California Press, 1999).

23. Most of these former students (leaders, activists and onlookers) endorsed the new political coalition opposing the PRI. See Cazés, ed., *Memorial del 68*, 9; and Taibo II, *68*, 14–15, 53 and 115.

24. See Antonio Velasco Piña, *Regina: El 2 de octubre no se olvida* (Mexico City: Jus, 1987; Grijalbo, 1997). There are several Web sites maintained by the fans of this novel, who call themselves "reginos" or "reginistas."

25. See Margaret E. Keck and Kathryn Sikkink, *Activists Beyond Borders: Advocacy Networks in International Politics* (Ithaca, NY: Cornell University Press, 1998), viii–ix and 110–14.

26. See Aguayo, *1968*, 13; and notes of the secretary of the Truth Commission, Taibo II in *La Jornada*, September 24, 1998.

27. See Raul Alvarez Garín, *La estela de Tlatelolco: Una reconstrucción histórica del movimiento estudiantil de 1968* (Mexico City: Grijalbo, 1999); and *La Jornada*, October 3, 1998.

28. This language was also important during the transitions to democracy in countries where transnational human rights organizations had played a relevant role since the early 1970s. Initially, it expressed a reaction of the Latin American left to the direct experience of governmental repression. The demise of the socialist regimes in Europe in the late 1980s bolstered this change. See Castañeda, *Utopia Unarmed*, 237–66.

29. See, for instance, Aguayo, *1968*, 13–14; and expressions of Luis Morales Reyes in *La Jornada*, September 29, 1998.

30. See for instance Carlos Tello Díaz, "1968: El legado," *Nexos* 249 (September 1998); Martha Brant, "A Secret History," *Newsweek*, September 28, 1998; and Jorge Casteñeda, "The Decisive Mistery," *Newsweek*, September 28, 1998.
31. See for instance Julio Scherer García and Carlos Monsiváis, *Parte de guerra, Tlatelolco, 1968: Documentos del General Marcelino Barragán* (Mexico City: Aguilar, 1999); and Carlos Montemayor, *Rehacer la historia: Análisis de los nuevos documentos de 2 de octubre de 1968 en Tlatelolco* (Mexico City: Planeta: 2000).
32. See *La Jornada*, October 3, 2000. In 2001, Fox became the first acting president ever to officially pay homage to the 1968 student movement, while there was a big popular rally both in commemoration of October 2 and against the current government. See *La Jornada*, October 3, 2001. More recently, in July 2002, the government responded to long-standing claims to open secret official files, while former President Echeverría was summoned to testify about governmental repression in 1968 and later events—the first time ever that a high ranking official has been made accountable for alleged crimes. The accusers, a group of former student leaders, expressed their hope about the actions of the judicial system, but there are still no verdicts. See *La Jornada*, July 3, 2002.

CHAPTER 3

Between Berlin and Berkeley, Frankfurt and San Francisco

The Student Movements of the 1960s in Transatlantic Perspective

MARTIN KLIMKE

"You, Mr. Senator, and your like, are just a bunch of criminal bandits. I have certainly not come here today to serve any of your dirty purposes." With these words, Karl-Dietrich Wolff, the former head of the *Socialist German Student League* (Sozialistischer Deutscher Studentenbund, SDS), proudly addressed Senator Strom Thurmond, chair of the Senate Internal Security Subcommittee, on March 14, 1969. "The least thing I could do here [. . .] is bring the message that the victories of the movement in the United States are considered our victories, that the repression against the radical movement in the United States which is being stepped up is repression against us. The economic and political interdependence of our societies has made international solidarity more than just a moral duty to speak up for the oppressed anywhere. [. . .] We know that we are not alone."[1] Wolff, who was subpoenaed to the hearing after a speech at George Washington University, the "official" reason being a visa irregularity, turned it into a political happening and simply left when he had had enough. As Philip Carter wrote in the *Washington Post*: "Der Zirkus, which is German for circus, played briefly before the Senate Internal Security Subcommittee yesterday, but closed abruptly when its star performer stalked out of his act and into the Capitol's long history of showbiz. The sudden exit [. . .] made him the first witness ever to walk out of an open session of the subcommittee."[2]

Wolff's appearance before the United States Senate subcommittee can be seen as symbolic for the interconnectedness of the German and American student movements of the 1960s. However, it is not only indicative of this close relationship, but also an expression of the transnationality of the sixties' revolt. The relationship between the German Socialist Student League (Sozialistischer Deutscher Studentenbund) and the American Students for a Democratic Society movements of the 1960s exemplify the international dimension of protest during that decade. The American Students for a Democratic Society and the German Socialist Student League are both incidentally abbreviated SDS.

Historicizing the Sixties

Due to the rise of grassroots movements critical of globalization and in particular, recent international outpouring of protest against the war in Iraq followed by the emergence of the catchphrase of world public opinion as the "second global superpower," the international dimension of protest movements has gained the attention of a broad audience even outside academic circles.[3] The display of worldwide disapproval with U.S. actions in numerous countries in the spring of 2003 evoked images of anti-war demonstrations in the 1960s, which have ever since that decade been able to capture the public imagination. In trying to come to terms with the 1960s themselves and its protest movements, however, historians are often blessed by an exceptional dilemma. In addition to their own research, they also face an abundance of contemporary witnesses who have been dominating the debate ever since and continue to supply their mostly illuminating accounts of those years. Unfortunately, active or passive involvement in the historical events described combined with an ongoing political utilization and supposedly scandalous media coverage of the 1960s often times stand in the way of a critical historiographical analysis of this decade. Over thirty years later, the revolt of the younger generation and its historical consequences are thus still unusually controversial. Parliamentary debates, an increasing wave of new books and a fundamental public controversy over the actual legacy of the sixties exemplify this situation.[4] Although historians are pressing to overcome the stalemate between alternate recollections of former activists and their adversaries, they only seem to be at the beginning of a historical investigation of the legacies of protest within the individual countries during the 1960s.[5]

In Germany as well as in the United States, the sixties are therefore slowly beginning to move from an era mostly characterized by individual recollection to one of historical reflection and reconstruction.[6] As archives gradually open and time passes, historical scholarship has begun to take on the task of examining that decade and especially the protest movements in greater detail, acknowledging their extreme diversity and contradictoriness and deconstructing the mythology that has evolved around it; a precondition for any serious historical evaluation and balanced interpretation of the decade's legacy.[7]

As a consequence, the urge to assess from an international perspective the underlying reasons for movements that shattered established orders and radically questioned traditional values virtually simultaneously in France, West Germany, Italy, Japan, the United States and many other parts of the world has been progressively increasing. The questions posed by the temporal coinciding of all these protest movements, their similarities and differences, and in consequence, their possible mutual influences have been raised in historical scholarship, but have not been answered satisfactorily with regard to the underlying causes for and a thorough analysis of this phenomenon of global unrest. Recent studies illustrate the attempt to examine the global aspect of this phenomenon, yet a systematic and empirically solid study attempting to understand how it was possible for political activists from different geographical, economical, political and cultural frameworks to construct a common perception of their protest is still a desirability.[8] A closer look at two student movements of the 1960s with long-lasting legacies in their respective countries analyzing their mutual perceptions, cooperation and exchange thus seems to be a promising starting point to approach this phenomenon.

The Student Movement in the United States and West Germany

At the beginning of the sixties there were only a few signs of an emerging student movement in the United States or in West Germany.[9] The Students for a Democratic Society (SDS), which was to become the biggest and most influential student organization of that decade in the United States, was forming very slowly as a youth organization of the Old Left. It gradually drifted away and eventually also split organizationally and theoretically from the Old Left in the wake of the "Port Huron Statement" of 1962, which became a key document for the formation of the SDS and its breakaway from Old Left ideology. The Port Huron Statement rejected the cold war consensus and, drawing on the ideas of a New Left mainly developed in Great Britain by C. Wright Mills, provided a program for a multiple-issue organization, which would use students and intellectuals as agents for social change with universities as their basis.[10]

The American SDS was also involved in the civil rights movement and worked closely with the Student Nonviolent Coordinating Committee (SNCC), but also started its own projects to fight domestic racism and poverty.[11] The publicity and importance of the Freedom Summer and the rise of the Free Speech Movement in 1964 additionally fueled its membership. However, only the escalation of the war in Vietnam was able to transform the American SDS into the engine of a mass student movement. This, together with an increasing militancy in the civil rights movement, further broadened the New Left's basis and politicized more and more students, inspiring them to more active political engagement. Furthermore, the war in Vietnam seemingly connected the domestic struggles to other anti-colonial and liberation movements in the Third World and also fostered active student resistance and anti-war demonstrations on campuses all over the United States in 1967. This was nurtured by an adaptation of the ideas of Herbert Marcuse, Franz Fanon and other theoreticians on the Left. The year 1968 then proved to be a watershed for the American SDS and the New Left in terms of their eventual demise: the continuing departure from the organization's original pledge to nonviolence, a growing radicalization and the dominance of revolutionary theories, along with the influence of international and domestic events and their interpretation ultimately tore the organization apart.[12] During the following years, the organization lost its coherency and with it its mass basis, dispersing into various ideological factions and splinter groups.

The largest student organization on the Left in West Germany in the 1960s, the German SDS, followed a very similar path during that decade.[13] The organization, originally associated with the Social Democratic Party (SPD) in West Germany, also had to cut its ties in the early sixties after a period of ideological alienation and estrangement.[14] Having achieved its institutional independence, the German SDS sought a new theoretical stance and was attracted to the theories of the upcoming New Left as well. It similarly engaged in the university reform debate, pursued the democratization of the university, and refused any political utilization or economic interference with the strict independence of the academy. It was only when students at the Free University of Berlin saw this democratic and progressive ideal severely threatened by various incidents that they started to protest openly, unconditionally demanding the implementation of free speech on campus in 1965.[15]

The German SDS only rose to mass movement status, however, in June 1967, after a demonstrating student was killed by the police and protest erupted nationwide. It had already adopted the issue of the war in Vietnam and interpreted it in a larger anti-imperialist scheme, thus connecting their anti-war protest to anti-colonial and Third World liberation movements. The student organization also tried to work together with other domestic protest movements during the 1960s in Germany, such as the Easter March campaign and the rising opposition against the emergency law legislation.

Political tactics of strategic provocation, such as sit-ins and various other forms of protest, as well as an amalgamation of the ideas of George Lukacs, Herbert Marcuse and Che Guevara's focus theory put forward by Rudi Dutschke (one of the intellectual forerunners of German SDS) profoundly influenced the German movement. Just as the American movement, it peaked in 1968 and disintegrated shortly after, dissolving its main organization in 1970.

Even this brief outline demonstrates that the protest movements in West Germany and the United States reveal many structural similarities and ideological affinities. They have therefore already been the subject of various comparative historiographical accounts.[16] Nevertheless, it has not yet been attempted to trace their contacts, mutual perceptions and transatlantic connections and interactions systematically, and in an empirically solid way.

When thoroughly investigating the relationship between the German and American SDS throughout the sixties, one is rather surprised by the richness of sources and broad range of connections that can be unearthed by an analysis of media coverage on as well as personal interaction and intellectual affinities between the two. On the American side, the coverage of the German student movement in the *New Left Notes* (NLN), the publication of the American SDS, from 1966–1969 reveals an increasing awareness of a shared struggle and the emergence of a collective, international group identity between the German and the American SDS. Although the coverage of the European student movement was at first rather cautious and very sporadic, the years 1967 and 1968 saw a change from mere acknowledgment to open solidarity and desired cooperation. Attention mounted sharply after the shooting of Rudi Dutschke and the spectacular uprisings of students and workers in Paris in May of 1968, which fostered extensive reporting of the actions in Europe.[17] The Inter-organizational Secretary of the SDS, Carl Davidson, made this clear when he hoped that "the recent dramatic struggles of the European New Left students will change some of our [the American SDS] isolationist attitudes." For him, global cooperation was even more attractive in the case of West Germany due to the presence of U.S. troops there and the fact that "a variety of programs [. . .] could be developed, co-coordinating international actions around Draft-resistance, desertion, or attacks on the CIA, NATO, and other military alliances." Apart from that, Davidson stressed the similarities of the West German student movement with the American one:

> Of all the advanced capitalist countries, the New Left in West Germany (SDS) faces conditions most similar to our own: a dominant ideology of anti-communism, basic unity between supposedly opposing parties

in parliament, a neo-Nazi upsurge similar to Wallace, manipulative mass media, and an apathetic public submissive to authority. German SDS began much like us, as a breakaway student group from the Social Democrats. [. . .] A few years ago, the presence of some American New Left radicals in Berlin influenced the German radicals into adopting 'new' forms of opposition, quite familiar to us: sit-ins, mass rallies, and counter-institutions.[18]

Likewise stressing its international awareness, American SDS discussed the German movement at its 1968 National Convention and included it in its resolutions:

We recall as well that it was a year ago this week that a member of German SDS was murdered by German police while his organization was protesting the Shah's presence in Bonn. The fight for tyranny is international because tyranny is international. Your fight against the Shah, the fight of German SDS against Kiesinger, of the French against deGaulle, of the Japanese against SATO—these are a few of the current fronts of a single war. We are your allies and brothers.[19]

Other reports on the German student movement further emphasized their strong affiliation, sometimes only by describing the German movement as "learning from the American movement" or "just as the American SDS."[20] This indicates that parts of the American movement were becoming increasingly of their inspirational role and influence, and in return tried to intensify the relationship to a closer cooperation on equal terms.

Another available source of information for the American New Left was the established press in the United States, which naturally presented a very different picture of the German student movement. The general U.S. press never lost sight of the geographical and political position of West Germany, so that cold war considerations often overshadowed its coverage. The situation in West Berlin, one of the centers of the student protest, was perceived as particularly tense and as a serious concern for American foreign policy. The fear was that East Germany, and, in turn the Soviet Union, were welcoming the student unrest, even secretly supporting it, and that in consequence these riots would disturb the relationship between the United States and West Germany.[21] In addition, the seemingly anti-American elements of German student protest were perhaps the most important aspect in the whole mainstream coverage of the German student movement. Newspapers and periodicals that reported on events in Germany strongly emphasized this point.[22] All of this reveals a high degree of awareness of the seriousness of the situation not only as representing a student riot or massive social protest, but also as having consequences on the international political scale, one of whose focal points was Berlin.

Apart from the implications for United States foreign policy that the press drew from the German student movement, the comparison to domestic events was apparent.[23] The U.S. press not only saw close similarities between the two movements, but also viewed the actions of protesting the war in Vietnam as especially important for the German movement.[24] It observed that the war was able to bring the two movements closer together because they could identify with a common cause for protest, something which race relations and university reform had not provided to that extent. That this process subsequently led to further connections between the United States and German SDS did also not go unnoticed in the press, which even commented upon the transfer of U.S. protest slogans to the German youth or solidarity demonstrations in the United States.[25]

Conversely, when examining the coverage of events in the United States in the German press, the picture is disproportionately more differentiated, manifold and complex. The leftist German media for example, among others the publication of the German SDS, the *Neue Kritik*, focused on particular issues and acknowledged a common cause as far as New Left ideology and opposition to the war in Vietnam were concerned. However, it also elevated exclusive U.S. problems such as race relations to its agenda. It presented a plethora of information on events in the United States and openly discussed practical experience gained there as well as new ideas that were being developed across the Atlantic. A cross-section of the leftist media in Germany therefore illustrates a high degree of awareness and cultural, ideological and practical identification of the German student movement with its U.S. counterpart.

In the early sixties, the German SDS can be seen as not only drawn to New Left philosophy from Great Britain, but also observing developments on the American Left, where the writings of C. Wright Mills had a particular impact.[26] The ideas developed by Mills thus found their way to Germany, influencing the German SDS with regard to its own position in the structure of West German society.[27] A phase of heightened awareness of the theoretical and practical approaches of the New Left in the United States set in as early as 1963.[28] From then on, coverage of the U.S. protest movements and especially their demonstration techniques (which were also proposed as a guideline strategy for the German SDS and provoked a fierce debate within the organization) followed.[29] Particularly the events in Berkeley in 1966 and 1967 often served as a frame of reference for the German SDS as far as protest strategies and their results were concerned.[30]

However, by far the most coverage involved opposition to the war in Vietnam, which can thus be seen as the most important single issue that connected the two movements. Interestingly enough, for the German movement this war not only exemplified another imperialist conflict in which its own federal government was somehow entangled through its alliance with the United States, but it was also seen as an embodiment of a re-arising fascist threat creeping through an imperialist U.S. policy. United States war techniques, strategy, reasons and justifications given for fighting were constantly seen against the background of National Socialism.[31] From that angle, the war in Vietnam became a war that was also fought within West Germany against potential authoritarian tendencies in the still relatively young West German republic. The impulse caused by this parallel had special consequences for the German student movement and its radicalization, although it was also vital on a European and global level. Moral outrage, political analysis and a close ideological affinity for the U.S. opposition against the war were therefore combined with a particular feeling of historical guilt resulting from German history.[32] This historical encumbrance nurtured the drive and the pressure to take action even more.

The established German press also served as a readily available source of information for the German students with respect to the U.S. movement.[33] The university reform debate, the Free Speech Movement and other events at U.S. campuses were the object of intense coverage.[34] The transfer of protest techniques, strategies and concepts of counter-institutions were seen as an open embodiment of U.S. influence and a transfer of that phenomena to the German setting, in which representatives of the U.S. SDS also actively took part.[35] As in the United States, cold war politics overshadowed press coverage in Germany. The German press often branded the student movement at home and in the United States as having been infiltrated by Communist agitators, thus making them threats to the established cold war status quo. The press was especially aggressive when it saw possible consequences for West Germany itself, such as the protection of West Berlin or the stationing of U.S. troops in West Germany. Considering all this, one comes to the conclusion that the established German press also saw striking parallels between the two student movements as far as their New Left roots, their protest techniques and strategies and even their issues were concerned, which it very often saw transferred to Germany. It also very alertly watched all developments in the United States, therefore acting as an extremely rich transatlantic channel of information.

In addition to the media coverage in both countries, the German and the U.S. movements also had a plethora of personal and institutional contacts which they could rely on. Both organizations enjoyed a steady, institutional relationship that began well before the sixties through their common membership or affiliation with organizations such as the International Union of Socialist Youth (IUSY), but also established direct contacts through personal channels. Already in the early sixties, Tom Hayden and other members from the early American SDS were acquainted with Michael Vester from the German SDS, whose 1961–1962 stay was sponsored by the Fulbright exchange program.[36] Equally searching for a theoretical base in the rising New Left movement, they not only engaged in productive intellectual exchange of ideas but also in organizational cooperation. As Hayden acknowledged, Vester, who was present at the Port Huron conference, was "instrumental in the adoption of our present stand on the German question" and strongly pointed to their common ideological stance, out of which mutual information, cooperation and solidarity developed over the years.[37] It was Michael Vester, who had a decisive influence on the introduction of the American New Left to the German student movement. Through his demand for the transfer of ideas mainly practiced in the United States by the civil rights and anti-war movement to Germany, he supplied a theoretical framework for the notion of nonviolent civil disobedience and teach-ins to a German audience that would soon come in touch with these new forms of protest through events at the Free University in Berlin, thereby placing them in a larger agenda of a New Left ideology. Thus, his writings are largely responsible for the introduction of what historian Wini Breines has termed "prefigurative politics" to West Germany, meaning the effort to create and prefigure in lived action and behavior the desired society, the emphasis on means and not ends, the spontaneous and utopian experiments that developed in the midst of action while working toward the ultimate goal of a free and democratic society.[38]

In the years ahead, this understanding of politics would become a decisive feature of the German student movement, when public conventions or rules were strategically violated or ridiculed to capture the attention of the public, all of that in preparation for a long term, broad based social and cultural change.

Yet another example of this personal, transatlantic exchange was Karl-Dietrich Wolff, president of the German SDS from 1967–1968. Wolff spent a year in America as a high school student and after his return to West Germany closely followed events of the leftist movements in the United States. At the Vietnam Congress in West Berlin in 1968 (also a peak of transatlantic cooperation with representatives from various U.S. protest movements) he then established further contacts, which were the basis for his lecture tour through the United States and Canada in February/March 1969, during which he stressed the need for an "International Revolutionary Alliance." As mentioned at the beginning, he was subsequently subpoenaed to a hearing of the Senate Internal Security Subcommittee, where he was asked to elaborate on the connections between the German and U.S. movement.[39] Similar contacts can be traced in abundance for people from both sides, who were despite their geographical distance very much informed about each other's events and perceived the movements in the different countries essentially as one. Particularly interesting examples that challenge the assumption of transatlantic diffusion as a one-way street are the experiences of Patty Lee Parmalee and Elsa Rassbach, who were American activists living in Berlin and were familiar with both protest movements. They, like other activists in Berlin or West Germany, were widely involved in activities of the German movement, but also injected their own issues, such as GI-organizing and Black Panther solidarity.[40]

Another aspect facilitating these personal contacts were the close intellectual affinities of the two movements. Besides the common New Left roots stemming from the British New Left and C. Wright Mills, the German-born philosopher Herbert Marcuse not only provided through works such as *One-Dimensional Man,* a significant intellectual inspiration for the two movements, but also actively engaged in efforts to connect them institutionally.[41] Marcuse was part of a whole generation of German emigrants who had a particular influence on the development of the protest movements in Germany as well as in the United States. Having escaped the National Socialist persecution, many emigrants went into exile in the United States and from there exerted a decisive influence on the emergence of the American New Left.[42] They had loosened themselves from the old dogma of the workers being the sources of revolutionary change early on and found the interest of the young generation with their theories on human alienation in modern society caused by anonymous institutions as well as an analysis of the early writings of Marx. In Germany, the reception of these emigrants was predominantly through U.S. channels and only started having a decisive influence on the German SDS in the mid-sixties, long after the return of the members of the Frankfurt School Max Horkheimer and Theodor Adorno.[43] Marcuse, as the most influential representative of these emigrants can thus be seen as another important intellectual link between the two movements and as a personal embodiment of the impact of the Frankfurt School on the American left. He and the other emigrants, who only partially returned to West Germany, developed a radical critique and rethinking of capitalism which was taken up by the young generation of the 1960s. As Kurt Shell described this intercultural exchange:

> The impact of the 'Frankfurt School'—as illustrated by the person Marcuse—was almost as profound on the American New Left as it was on the German; a strange case, without precedent in American history, of essentially metaphysical German theories affecting a mass populace in America. It may, in this instance, be perhaps as valid to speak of the 'Germanizing' of American youth [. . .] but because of the rediscovery of these ideas after World War II *via* America and loaded with a specifically American change it seems justified to accept it as an example of 'American' influence.[44]

As becomes apparent, an empirical illustration of the interconnectedness between the student movements in West Germany and the United States provides fertile ground for a further exploration of the internationality of sixties' protest. To analyze this phenomenon, historians of the 1960s' student movements in Europe have hitherto argued that these should be seen and investigated as social movements, using methodological tools and theorems provided by sociology to analyze them.[45] However, when considering the evidence presented above, existing explanatory schemes circling around theories from social movement research do not seem to be sufficient. Different cultural frameworks, misperceptions and resistance, as well as the complex processes of acculturation or creolization are all too often neglected by these approaches.[46] In addition, they ignore the international historical framework of the cold war as well as intercultural processes before the 1960s. Several leading social movement scholars themselves have, as a consequence, already voiced substantial doubts about the comprehensiveness and persuasiveness of these theories with regard to sixties' protest.[47] Therefore, to escape the trap of overstretching the social movement approach, it seems appropriate to broaden the analytical perspective by taking into account transnational structures and relations.

Reflections for Further Research

The second half of the twentieth century was characterized by an increasing international exchange of economic, social, political and cultural ideas. With regard to the analysis of international relations, the field of "diplomatic history" has recently been trying to account for these phenomena with historiographical models that transcend the nation state, in other words, could "internationalize" historical approaches.[48] Especially groundbreaking in this regard has been the influential shift away from state-centered activities and the proposal of a "cultural approach to diplomatic history," which is mirrored in the works of Akira Iriye, Frank Ninkovich, Jessica-Gienow Hecht and others.[49] The inclusion of social and cultural factors into the history of foreign relations has been made fruitful for many studies. Undeniably, it also contributed to an explicit shift from theories of one-sided "cultural imperialism" to processes of mutual intercultural transfer.[50] Following from this "cultural turn," concepts that include both processes of cultural transfer and comparative perspectives, as well as theoretical frameworks of a "transnational" or "intercultural" historiography have been advanced.[51]

In the context of the case study at hand, a closer look at the relationship between West Germany and the United States applying this more comprehensive perspective is particularly enlightening. The multifarious political, economic, and cultural exchange between the two countries during the cold war early on reached an incredible intensity due to the specific situation of occupation, economic support, re-education and political dependency after 1945.[52] These intercultural processes have in recent years been revaluated and more complex theories of "Americanization"[53] and "Westernization" have been introduced into the debate, which can also be of great value for the analysis of the student movements.[54] Accordingly, in the first decade after World War II, U.S. "cultural diplomacy" decidedly aimed at a democratization of German political culture, in other words an "Americanization from above."[55] The years after that, reaching from 1955 to 1965, can, however, be viewed as a starting point for a "grassroots Americanization," where official political goals are complemented and even replaced by an immense cultural influence on West German society and the political landscape.[56] However, with the increasing actions of the civil rights and Free Speech movements, U.S. prestige among the young generation gradually began to change. It became increasingly clear that the general discontent among the younger generation, which had already transcended national boundaries, had been swelling ever since the fifties.[57] What added to that dissatisfaction among the younger generation in West Germany was the legacy of the German past and the after-effects it still had on the young republic, which in their perception had not successfully mastered its legacy.[58] In addition, the notion that even the United States, which had been viewed as a democratic model, guiding spirit and leader of the supposed free world was waging an ever escalating and questionable war in Southeast Asia led many to revolt against what was believed to be a cynical version of democracy.[59]

By that time, similar feelings of disillusionment concerning the United States that had already developed within that country, found their way to Europe, where they fundamentally challenged the previous image of the United States among parts of the young generation. Hence, the split perception of the United States was one of the dominating concepts for the New Left in West Germany because it vehemently clashed with previous images.[60] As Richard Pells wrote with respect to the European perception of America in the 1960s:

> America might be racist and repressive, but it also supplied the leaders and the troubadours of the revolution: Malcolm X and Bob Dylan, Angela Davis and Joan Baez, the Students for a Democratic Society and the Jefferson Airplane. A young person living in Austria, Holland, or Italy could denounce the imperialist in the White House and the Pentagon while at the same time learning from the media how to emulate the adversarial style of the American counterculture and the tactics of the civil rights and antiwar movements in the United States.[61]

Since most of those counter-cultural items originated, or had strong roots in the United States, it is hard to brand their import as simply anti-American.[62] The anti-Americanism it included mainly consisted of a critique of the official U.S. government, thus understanding itself as predominantly anti-imperialism and as such being a further expression of intense mutual relations and an additional degree of American cultural influence. In other words, it was an anti-Americanism of "With America against America," as it has been aptly labeled in recent studies.[63] These ambiguous images were part of the intercultural, transatlantic network and exchange between the two movements. West German and European students selectively adopted, modified and used American counter-cultural imports, thereby turning them into their own.[64]

Therefore, future research on the student movements should follow the lead in current historiography of transcending the nation state and not only dedicate itself to comparative analysis, but broaden the approach towards an international history which is *multicultural* as well as *multi-dimensional* and reconsiders sixties' protest in its global context.[65] For the case at hand this would mean taking into account not only the protest movements themselves, the intercultural transfer of ideas and social practices between them and their respective domestic repercussions, but also the international framework of the cold war in which they developed and operated. In addition to extending the analysis of U.S. cultural influence into the late 1960s, this would involve a closer look at the reactions student or youth protest prompted on various governmental levels, e.g., with respect to U.S. institutions in West Germany or United States foreign policy planning, as has already been demonstrated with respect to the policy of "détente."[66] To evaluate the significance U.S. officials attached to the student protest, the examinations of U.S. cultural diplomacy efforts also need to be extended into the 1960s. A further analysis of the long-term effects of American cultural diplomacy at the receiving end of this "fourth dimension" of American foreign relations could then enable us to assess in how far postwar American elites with respect to West Germany succeeded in creating what Oliver Schmidt has labeled a "civil empire of co-optation," where its limits were, and how, or if, it was transformed during that decade.[67]

Because, as far the U.S. and West German student movements are concerned, their common bond which had been cultivated through their countries' official relations, emigration and exchange even before the sixties was also a product of German-American associations after World War II. Out of this historical constellation a transatlantic counter-alliance between the two movements was eventually created.[68] This "imagined transnational community of protest" and counter-elite positioned itself against the official free world policies of their own countries in the cold war, whose governments had to and did react to this challenge in various ways.[69] The transnational experience thus had an essential influence on the emergence and formation of the two student movements. As a result, these movements then played a significant role in paving the way for a substantial change of the domestic social and cultural systems. At the same time, this Americanization process further strengthened, as an expression of an increased cultural globalization, the rise of a global consciousness, thereby shattering so-called geopolitical realities of the cold war.

Today's transnational protest movements must therefore despite their idiosyncrasies be connected to this historical context and the historical development of a cultural internationalism which intensified drastically during the second half of the 1960s and the following decade, as is reflected in the rise of international, non-governmental organizations concerned with the preservation of fundamental human rights, nuclear disarmament or environmental issues.[70] As Margaret Keck and Kathryn Sikkink have elaborated in *Activists Beyond Borders* with respect to that growth:

> The new networks have depended on the creation of a new kind of global public (or civil society), which grew as a cultural legacy of the 1960s. Both the activism that swept Western Europe, the United States, and many parts of the world during that decade, and the vastly increased opportunities for international contact, contributed to this shift. With a significant decline in air fares, foreign travel ceased to be a privilege of the wealthy. Students participated in exchange programs. The Peace Corps and lay missionary programs sent thousands of young people to live and work in the developing world. Political exiles from Latin America taught in U.S. and European universities.[71]

When Karl-Dietrich Wolff was subpoenaed to testify before the Senate Internal Security Subcommittee, on March 14, 1969, the interconnectedness of the two student movements and the international system their respective countries were placed in as allies was all too clear to him and to his questioners. Being pressed to elaborate on the comparability and connections between the German and U.S. SDS, Wolff lashed out against the, in his view, imperialist complicity of the two governments, making it very clear that he considered the protest movements of the 1960s as unrestrained by national borders:

> As I said before, you do not see that there are problems in our society which are the same in West Germany and in the United States or at least very similar and you do not see that we are up to debate about them now and that we are up to realize that our interests are the same.

You see, you have been conspiring for a long time. We do not need to conspire. And our efforts to create an internationalist consciousness has [sic] only started [...].[72]

How and to which degree this other cold war alliance composed of students could succeed in this aim, and in which way this contributed to a change in their respective societies and the post-war world order at large, remains the topic of future historical research not only on the transnationality, but indeed ultimately, on the global dimension of the sixties' revolt.

Notes

1. "Testimony of Karl Dietrich Wolff. Hearings before the Subcommittee to Investigate the Administration of the Internal Security Act and other Security Laws of the Committee on the Judiciary," United States Senate, Ninety-First Congress, First Session, March 14 and 18, 1969, U.S. GPO (Washington, 1969): 7.

2. Philip D. Carter, "Thurmond Presides at Senate Circus," *Washington Post*, 15 March, 1969, A4.

3. Patrick E. Tyler, "Suddenly, it's U.S. and rest of the world," *New York Times*, February 17, 2003.

4. As Todd Gitlin noted: "The interesting, genuinely divisive question is which sixties to embrace and which to criticize." in ibid., "Afterword," in Stephen Macedo, ed., *Reassessing the Sixties. Debating the Political and Cultural Legacy* (New York: W. W. Norton, 1997), 290. For an illustration of the ongoing debate on the consequences of that decade in Germany see: Paul Berman, "The passions of Joschka Fischer. The surprising origins of liberal interventionism," *New Republic* (August 27 / September 3, 2001): 39–59; Susan Neiman, "Germany remembers the Sixties," *Dissent* (Summer 2001): 18–21; Wolfgang Kraushaar, *Fischer in Frankfurt* (Hamburg: Hamburger Edition, 2001); Gerd Koenen, *Das rote Jahrzehnt. Unsere kleine deutsche Kulturrevolution 1967–1977* (Köln: Kiepenheuer & Witsch, 2001).

5. Wilfried Mausbach, "Historicizing '1968'," in *Contemporary European History*, II, I (2002): 177–87.

6. Various reports on the available secondary literature and archival guides have been published in recent years: Franz-Werner Kersting, "Entzauberung des Mythos? Ausgangsbedingungen und Tendenzen einer gesellschaftlichen Standortbestimmung der westdeutschen '68er'-Bewegung," in Karl Teppe, ed., *Westfälische Forschungen* 48 (Münster, 1998), 1–19; Wolfgang Kraushaar, "Der Zeitzeuge als Feind des Historikers? Ein Literaturüberblick zur 68er-Bewegung," in ibid., *1968 als Mythos*, 253–347; Christoph Jünke, "Den Ursprung historisieren? Ein Literaturbericht zum 30. Jubiläum der Revolte von 1968," in *1999. Zeitschrift für Sozialgeschichte des 20. und 21. Jahrhunderts* 16 / 2 (2001): 159–84; Philipp Gassert and Pavel A. Richter, *1968 in West Germany. A Guide to Sources and Literature of the Extra-Parliamentary Opposition* (Washington DC, 1998); Thomas Becker and Ute Schröder, ed., *Die Studentenproteste der 60er Jahre. Archivführer–Chronik-Bibliographie* (Köln, 2000). For the sixties in the U.S. see David Farber and Beth Baily, eds., *The Columbia Guide to America in the 1960s* (New York: Columbia University Press, 2001).

7. From the booming literature on the sixties in the U.S. see David R. Farber, ed., *The Sixties: From Memory to History* (Chapel Hill: University of North Carolina Press, 1994); Jürgen Heideking, ed., *The Sixties Revisited: Culture, Society, Politics* (Heidelberg: Winter Verlag, 2001); Alexander Bloom, *Long Time Gone: Sixties American Then and Now* (Oxford; New York: Oxford University Press, 2001). For Germany see Peifer, Elizabeth. "1968 in German Political Culture, 1967–1993: From Experience to Myth." Doctoral Dissertation, University of North Carolina, Chapel Hill, 1997; Ingrid Gilcher-Holtey, ed., *1968—Vom Ereignis zum Gegenstand der Geschichtswissenschaft* (Goettingen: Vandenhoeck & Ruprecht, 1998); Axel Schildt, et al., eds., *Dynamische Zeiten. Die 60er Jahre in den beiden deutschen Gesellschaften* (Hamburg: Christians, 2000).

8. George Katsiaficas, *The Imagination of the New Left. A Global Analysis of 1968* (Boston: South End Press, 1987); Ronald Fraser, *1968: A Student Generation in Revolt* (New York: Pantheon Books, 1988); Carole Fink, et al., eds., *1968. The World Transformed* (Cambridge, UK; New York: Cambridge University Press; Longman, 1998); Arthur Marwick, *The Sixties. Cultural Revolution in Britain, France, Italy and the United States c.1958–c.1974* (Oxford, UK; New York: Oxford University Press, 1998); Gerard J. DeGroot, ed., *Student Protest. The Sixties and After* (London: Longman, 1998); Ingrid Gilcher-Holtey, *Die 68er Bewegung: Deutschland, Westeuropa, USA* (München: C.H. Beck, 2001).

9. For histories of the student movement in the U.S. see Kirkpatrick Sale, *SDS* (New York: Random House, 1973); Todd Gitlin, *The Sixties. Years of Hope, Days of Rage* (New York: Bantam Books, 1987); James Miller, *Democracy is in the streets. From Port Huron to the Siege of Chicago* (New York: Simon & Schuster Inc., 1994); Terry H. Anderson, *The Movement and the Sixties. Protest in America from Greensboro to Wounded Knee* (New York: Oxford University Press, 1995).

10. For the British New Left that was of crucial importance to the German and American SDS see: Michael Kenny, *The First New Left. British Intellectuals After Stalin* (London: Lawrence & Wishart, 1995). See also Kevin Mattson, *Intellectuals in Action. The Origins of the New Left and Radical Liberalism, 1945–1970* (University Park, PA: Pennsylvania State University Press, 2002).

11. Jennifer Frost, *An interracial movement of the poor: community organizing and the New Left in the 1960s* (New York: New York University Press, 2001).

12. Numerous detailed accounts of the year 1968 have been written, e.g., Jules Witcover, *The Year the Dream Died: Revisiting 1968 in America* (New York: Warner Books, 1997); David Caute, *The Year of the Varricades. A Journey Through 1968* (New York: Harper & Row, 1988); Tariq Ali and Susan Watkins, *1968—Marching in The Streets* (New York: The Free Press, 1998).

13. Recent scholarship has just begun to take on the task of a systematical and, indeed, historical analysis of the student movement: Pavel A. Richter, "Die Außerparlamentarische Opposition in der Bundesrepublik Deutschland 1966 bis 1968," in Gilcher-Holtey, ed., *Gegenstand der Geschichtswissenschaft*, 35–55; Michael Frey, "Die voluntaristische Wende—Die Entwicklung des SDS 1966 / 67" (Master's Thesis, University of Bochum, 2001); Gilcher-Holtey, *68er-Bewegung*; For the most exhaustive works on German SDS from the former activist's perspective: Tilman Fichter and Siegward Lönnendonker, *Macht und Ohnmacht der Studenten. Kleine Geschichte des SDS*, 2nd ed. (Hamburg: Rotbuch Verlag, 1998); Lönnendonker, Siegward, Bernd Rabehl, and Jochen Staadt, eds. *Die antiautoritäre Revolte. Der Sozialistische Deutsche Studentenbund nach der Trennung von der SPD* (Wiesbaden: Westdeutscher Verlag, 2002).

14. For a concise overview of the history of the German SDS from 1946 to the beginning of the 1960s, see Willy Albrecht, *Der Sozialistische Deutsche Studentenbund (SDS), Vom parteikonformen Studentenverband zum Repräsentanten der Neuen Linken* (Bonn: Dietz, 1994).

15. Jens Hager, ed., *Die Rebellen von Berlin: Studentenpolitik an der Freien Universität* (Köln: Kiepenheuer & Witsch, 1967).

16. Most recently Michael Schmidtke, *Der Aufbruch der jungen Intelligenz. Die 68er-Jahre in der Bundesrepublik und den USA* (Frankfurt/New York: Campus Verlag, 2003); Ingo Juchler, *Die Studentenbewegungen in den Vereinigten Staaten und der Bundesrepublik Deutschland der sechziger Jahre. Eine Untersuchung hinsichtlich ihrer Beeinflussung durch Befreiungsbewegungen und—theorien aus der Dritten Welt* (Berlin: Duncker & Humblot, 1995); Jeremy Peter Varon, *Bringing the War Home: The Weather Underground, the Red Army Faction, and the Revolutionary Violence in the Sixties and Seventies* (Berkeley: University of California Press, 2004); Claus Leggewie, "1968—Ein transatlantisches Ereignis und seine Folgen," in Detlef Junker et al., ed., *Die USA und Deutschland im Zeitalter des Kalten Krieges*, vol. 2, 2 vols. (Stuttgart: DVA, 2001; publication by Cambridge University Press forthcoming 2004), 632–43; Philipp Gassert, "Atlantic Alliances: Cross-Cultural Communication and the 1960s Student Revolution," in Jessica Gienow-Hecht and Frank Schumacher, eds., *Culture and International Relations* (New York: Berghahn Books, 2004).

17. *New Left Notes*, 15 April 1968, 1; *New Left Notes*, 22 April 1968, 4 f.; *New Left Notes*, 29 July 1968, 4, 7–8; Out of this series in the New Left Notes, a book on the European Movements

finally emerged, in which the German movement is analyzed in detail: Barbara Ehrenreich and John Ehrenreich, *Long March, Short Spring, The Student Uprising at Home and Abroad* (New York, 1969), 23–50.

18. *New Left Notes*, 10 June 1968, 11.
19. Ibid., 24 June 1968, 4. The resolution is also revealing because of its factual errors. The student, Benno Ohnesorg, was killed on June 2, 1968 during a protest demonstration against the Shah in Berlin (not in Bonn) and was a regular student at the Free University and not an active and vocal member of German SDS.
20. Ibid., 29 July 1968, 4, 7 f.
21. "West Germany had earned a reputation as America's strongest ally in Europe. Now things are changing. Street riots are becoming a commonplace. There is political turmoil. And anti-Americanism is growing. [. . .] Reds on the other side of the Berlin wall are quietly helping out the students and other radicals of the APO with money and professional advice." In "Uproar in Germany, too: Extremists on the march," *U.S. News & World Report*, 3 June 1968, 44.
22. "Berliners attack an anti-U.S. Group," *New York Times*, 20 August 1967, 7; "Clashes mark end of parade in Berlin," *New York Times*, 18 May 1969, 10.
23. *Time Magazine* called the beginning of the German student movement in June 1967 a "rerun from Berkeley." In "West Germany: A case of *Kulturkrankheit*," *Time Magazine*, 30 June, 1967, 28; *The New York Times Magazine* observed: "A group of liberal students, borrowing such methods as sit-ins and hunger strikes from the Free Speech Movement at the University of California, were demanding that the university grant more academic freedom and democratize the entire educational process." In *The New York Times Magazine*, 28 April 1968, 115.
24. "Germany: Rudi's Ructions," *Newsweek*, 26 February 1968, 42; Philip Shabecoff, "The Followers of Red Rudi Shake up Germany," *The New York Times Magazine*, 28 April 1968, 115.
25. *Newsweek* called this transfer of protest slogans "a fine display of cross-cultural influences" with reference to the slogan "Burn, baby, burn." during shoutings at the attack of the Springer building in April 1968 "West Germany: The Sword Unleashed," *Newsweek*, 22 April 1968, 37; For solidarity demonstrations see Martin Arnold, "Burning of a Nazi Flag in Protest Stirs Clash at Rockefeller Center," *The New York Times*, 18 April 1968, 14.
26. Hannes Friedrich, "Voices of Dissent," *Neue Kritik* 9 (1962): 37-39; Michael Vester, "Schöne neue Welt?," *Neue Kritik* 14 (March 1963): 3–8.
27. Manfred Liebel, "Die Rolle der Intellektuellen in der Bundesrepublik," *Neue Kritik* 18 (November 1963): 5–8, here 5; Dieter Rave, "Die Rolle der Intelligenz in der kapitalistischen Gesellschaft," *Neue Kritik* 19 / 20 (December 1963): 3–5; Michael Vester, "Das Dilemma C. Wright Mills," *Neue Kritik* 27 (December 1964): 20–23.
28. Michael Vester, "Die Linke in den USA," *Neue Kritik* 17 (July 1963): 6–14.
29. Günter Amendt, "Die Studentenrevolte in Berkeley," *Neue Kritik* 28 (February 1965): 5–7; Michael Vester, "Die Strategie der direkten Aktion," *Neue Kritik* 30 (June 1965): 12–20.
30. Reimut Reiche, "Studentenrevolten in Berkeley und Berlin," *Neue Kritik* 38 / 39 (October / December 1966): 21–27; Lothar Hack, "Am Beispiel Berkeley: Rigider Funktionalismus und neue Unmittelbarkeit," *Neue Kritik* 41 (April 1967): 36–52; See Wolfgang Kraushaar, "Die transatlantische Protestkultur, Der zivile Ungehorsam als amerikanisches Exempel und als bundesdeutsche Adaption," in Heinz Bude, *Westbindungen: Amerika in der Bundesrepublik* (Hamburg: Hamburger Edition, 1999), 257–84.
31. Jan Myrdal, "Vietnam und die kommenden Kriege," *Neue Kritik* 42 / 43 (August 1967): 32–41; Christian Geißler, "Nürnberg und Vietnam," *Konkret* 10 (October 1965): 14–15. See also Harold Marcuse, "The Revival of Holocaust awareness in West Germany, Israel and the United States," in Fink, *A World Transformed*, 421–38.
32. Wilfried Mausbach, "Auschwitz und Vietnam: West German Protest Against America's War During the 1960s," in Andreas W. Daum, et al., eds., *America, the Vietnam War, and the World: Comparative and International Perspectives* (New York: Cambridge University Press, 2003); A.D. Moses, "The State and the Student Movement in West Germany," in Gerald J. DeGroot, *Student Protest: The Sixties and After* (London: Longman, 1998), 139–49, here 143; Philipp Gassert and Alan Steinweis, eds., *Coping with the Nazi Past: West German Debates on Nazism and Generational Conflict, 1955–1975* (New York, Berghahn Books, forthcoming 2004).

33. For the connections between the German and American media see: David Braden Posner, "Transatlantische Verschränkungen: Deutsch-amerikanische Medienbeziehungen in der Nachkriegszeit," in Junker, *USA und Deutschland*, vol. 1, 899–908.
34. Sabine Lietzmann, "Die protestierende Generation," *Frankfurter Allgemeine Zeitung* 115, 19 May 1965, 2; Petra Kipphoff, "Außenseiter der Gesellschaft," *Die Zeit* 44, 29 October, 1965, 22 f.
35. Günter Zehm, "Droht die Gegen-Universität," *Die Welt* 161, 14 July 1967, 2; Stefan T. Possony, "Die Studenten-Unruhe in den USA" *Die Welt* 162, 15 July 1968, 2.
36. Academic exchange programs undoubtedly did their best to provide an institutionalized opportunity for transatlantic rapprochement. See Ulrich Littmann, *Partners, Distant and Close: Notes and Footnotes on Academic Mobility Between Germany and the United States of America, 1923–1993* (Bonn: Deutscher Akademischer Auslandsdienst, 1997).
37. Tom Hayden to Michael Vester, undated (probably 1963), in BV Referat Ausland, Okt. 64– 65, SDS, C1 Archiv "APO und soziale Bewegungen," Otto-Suhr-Institut für Politik- wissenschaft, FU Berlin (hereafter quoted as Archiv APO). The presence of Michael Vester in the U. S. and even at the Port Huron conference has been acknowledged (Sale, *SDS*, 48; Miller, *Democracy is in the streets*, 107,123), but his role as a prime example of cross-cultural diffusion of ideas has not yet been sufficiently evaluated.
38. Wini Breines, *Community and organization in the New Left, 1962–1968: The Great Refusal*, 2nd ed. (New Brunswick/London: Rutgers University Press, 1989), xiv.
39. *Testimony of Karl Dietrich Wolff*, 28, 8 ff.
40. Patty Lee Parmalee, "SDS and SDS—Eine Amerikanerin in Ost und West," *Beiträge zur Geschichte der Arbeiterbewegung* 43, 1 (2001): 86–108; Elsa Rassbach, "Aktivistin gegen den Vietnamkrieg," in Ute Kätzel, *Die 68erinnen. Portrait einer rebellischen Generation* (Berlin: Rowohlt, 2002), 60–79.
41. Herbert Marcuse, *One-Dimensional Man: Studies in the Ideology of Advanced Industrial Society.* (Boston: Beacon Press, 1964); Ibid., "Das Problem der Gewalt in der Opposition," in Wolfgang Kraushaar, *Frankfurter Schule und Studentenbewegung: Von der Flaschenpost zum Molotowcocktail 1945–1995*, 2 vols. (Hamburg: Rogner & Bernhard, 1998) vol. 2, 272– 75, here 272; John Bokina and Timothy J. Lukes, *Marcuse: From the New Left to the Next Left* (Lawrence, KS: University Press of Kansas, 1994).
42. Jost Hermand, "Madison, Wisconsin 1959–1973: Der Einfluß der deutschen Exilanten auf die Entstehung der Neuen Linken," *Exilforschung*, 13, 1995, 52–67; For a detailed autobio- graphical account see ibid., *Zuhause und anderswo. Erfahrungen im Kalten Krieg* (Köln: Böhlau, 2001), 101–70.
43. Claus-Dieter Krohn, "Die Entdeckung des 'anderen' Deutschland in der intellektuellen Protestbewegung der 1960er Jahre in der Bundesrepublik und den Vereinigten Staaten," *Exilforschung* 13 (1995): 16–52, 30; also Claussen, Detlev, Oskar Negt, and Michael Werz, *Keine Kritische Theorie ohne Amerika* (Frankfurt/Main: Neue Kritik, 1999). On the impor- tance of the Frankfurt School for West Germany see Wolfgang Clemens Albrecht, et al., eds., *Die intellektuelle Gründung der Bundesrepublik. Eine Wirkungsgeschichte der Frankfurter Schule* (Frankfurt/New York: Campus, 1999).
44. Kurt L. Shell, "The American Impact on the German New Left," in A.N.S. Den Hollander, ed., *Contagious Conflict: The Impact of American Dissent on European life* (Leiden: E.J. Brill, 1973): 30–49, here 39 f.
45. Ingrid Gilcher-Holtey, "Mai 68 in Frankreich," in ibid., ed., *Gegenstand der Geschicht- swissenschaft*, 11–34, 12; Ibid., *Die Phantasie an die Macht": Mai 68 in Frankreich* (Frank- furt: Suhrkamp, 1995); Doug McAdam and Dieter Rucht, "The Cross-National Diffusion of Movement Ideas," *Annals of the American Association of Political and Social Science* 528 (July 1993), 56–74.
46. For a closer description of the idea of these amalgamation processes that has been labeled "creolization" see Rob Kroes, *If You've Seen One You've Seen the Mall. European and Ameri- can Mass Culture* (Urbana: University of Illinois Press, 1996), 162–72.
47. For example Donatella Della Porta, "Zwischennationale Diffusion und Transnationale Strukturen," in Gilcher-Holtey, *Gegenstand der Geschichtswissenschaft*, 149; Dieter Rucht, "Die Ereignisse von 1968 als soziale Bewegung: Methodologische Überlegungen und einige empirische Befunde," in ibid., 130.
48. Akira Iriye, "The Internationalization of History," *American Historical Review* 94, 1989, 1– 10; For an overview of this approach with respect to American history see Thomas Bender,

ed., *Rethinking American History in a Global Age.* (Berkeley: University of California Press, 2002).

49.   Ibid., "Culture," *The Journal of American History* 77 (June 1990): 99–107; See also ibid., "Culture and International History," in M.J. Hogan and T.G. Patterson, eds., *Explaining the History of American Foreign Relations* (Cambridge: Cambridge University Press, 1991), 214–25; also ibid., *Cultural Internationalism and World Order* (Baltimore: Johns Hopkins University Press, 1997).

50.   For a detailed illustration of this development see Jessica Gienow-Hecht, "Academics, Cultural Transfer, and the Cold War—A Critical Review," *Diplomatic History* 24, 3 (Summer 2000): 465–95." For an overview of books see Robert Griffith, "The Cultural Turn in Cold War Studies," *Reviews in American History* 29.1 (2001): 150–57. An excellent example of a successful application of these methodological ideas is Daniel T. Rodgers, *Atlantic Crossings—Social Politics in a Progressive Age* (Cambridge, MA: Belknap Press, 1998).

51.   Johannes Paulmann, "Internationaler Vergleich und interkultureller Transfer. Zwei Forschungsansätze zur europäischen Geschichte des 18. bis 20. Jahrhunderts," *Historische Zeitschrift* 267, 1998, 649–85; Jürgen Osterhammel, Geschichtswissenschaft jenseits des Nationalstaats. Studien zu Beziehungsgeschichte und Zivilisationsvergleich (Vandenhoeck & Ruprecht: Göttingen, 2001), 7–72; Ibid., "Transnationale Gesellschaftsgeschichte: Erweiterung oder Alternvative?," *Geschichte und Gesellschaft* 27 (2001), 464–79. For an extremely valuable collection of essays picking up this approach see Harmut Kaelble et al., eds., *Transnationale Öffentlichkeiten und Identitäten im 20. Jahrhundert* (Frankfurt/New York: Campus, 2002). For a good illustration of similar methodological innovations from the field of political science and their incorporation into a common agenda see Ursula Lehmkuhl, "Diplomatiegeschichte als internationale Kulturgeschichte: Theoretische Ansätze und empirische Forschung zwischen Historischer Kulturwissenschaft und Soziologischem Institutionalismus," *Geschichte und Gesellschaft* 27 (2001), 394–423. Also Fuchs, Eckhardt, and Benedikt Stuchtey. *Across Cultural Borders: Historiography in Global Perspective* (Lanham, MD: Rowman & Littlefield, 2002).

52.   Junker, *USA und Deutschland*, 2 vols., passim. Considering the depth of this relationship, the question has already been asked if it is still justified to talk about *inter*-national relations. See Thomas A. Schwartz, "The United States and Germany after 1945: Alliances, Transnational Relations, and the Legacy of the Cold War," *Diplomatic History* 19 (1995), 549–68.

53.   Axel Schildt, *Zwischen Abendland und Amerika. Studien zur westdeutschen Ideenlandschaft der 50er Jahre* (München: Oldenbourg, 1999); Alf Lüdtke, Inge Marßolek and Adelheid von Saldern, eds., *Amerikanisierung. Traum und Alptraum im Deutschland des 20. Jahrhunderts* (Stuttgart: Steiner, 1996); David E. Barclay and Elisabeth Glaser-Schmidt, eds., *Transatlantic Images and Perceptions. Germany and America since 1776* (Cambridge: Cambridge Univ. Press, 1997); Philipp Gassert, "Amerikanismus, Antiamerikanismus, Amerikanisierung," *Archiv für Sozialgeschichte* 39 (1999): 531–61.

54.   Historiography dealing with American influence on West Germany under this heading has mostly focused on the 1950s, and only rarely explored the exchanges of cultural lifestyles and practices in the following decade. For the works of the research project "Westernization" at the University of Tübingen see representatively Anselm Doering-Manteuffel, *Wie westlich sind die Deutschen? Amerikanisierung und Westernisierung im 20. Jahrhundert* (Göttingen: Vandenhoeck & Ruprecht, 1999); Ibid., "Westernisierung. Politisch-ideeller und gesellschaftlicher Wandel in der Bundesrepublik bis zum Ende der 60er Jahre," in: Axel Schildt et al., *Dynamische Zeiten*, 311–41.

55.   Axel Schildt, "Vom politischen Programm zur Populärkultur: Amerikanisierung in Westdeutschland," in Junker, *USA und Deutschland*, vol. 1, 955–65, esp. 958.

56.   Kasper Maase, " 'Halbstarke' and Hegemony. Meanings of American Mass Culture in the Federal Republic of Germany during the 1950s," Rob Kroes, et al., ed., *Cultural Transmissions and Receptions. American Mass Culture in Europe* (Amsterdam: VU University Press, 1993), 153–70; Ibid., "Establishing Cultural Democracy: Youth, 'Americanization', and the Irresistible Rise of Popular Culture," in Hannah Schissler, ed., *The Miracle Years. A Cultural History of West Germany, 1949–1968* (Princeton: Princeton University Press, 2001), 428–50. See also Uta Poiger, *Jazz, Rock and Rebels: Cold War Politics and American Culture in a Divided Germany* (Berkeley: University of California Press, 2000).

57.   Richard Pells, *Not like us: How Europeans have loved, hated and transformed American culture since World War II* (New York: Basic Books, 1997), 285.

58. A.D. Moses, "The State and the Student Movement in West Germany," in DeGroot, esp. 143; Jeffrey Herf, *Divided Memory: The Nazi Past in the Two* Germanys (Cambridge: Harvard University Press, 1997), 334–50.

59. Knud Krakau, "Zwischen alten Stereotypen und neuen Realitäten: Westdeutsche Bilder der USA, in Junker, *USA und Deutschland*, vol. 1, 920–31.

60. David B. Morris, "Auf dem Weg zur Reife: Amerikabilder in der westdeutschen Öffentlichkeit," in Junker, *USA und Deutschland*, vol. 2, 761–74, here 767 f.

61. Pells, *Not Like Us*, 286.

62. Allerbeck also points to the fact that students in West Germany and the U.S. protested against the clash between traded and practiced values in their societies, and were thus convinced in believing they had to defend 'true' American, resp. democratic values. Klaus Allerbeck, *Soziologie radikaler Studentenbewegungen, Eine vergleichende Untersuchung in der Bundesrepublik und den Vereinigten Staaten* (München: Oldenbourg, 1973), 207–13; See also Krakau, *Westdeutsche Bilder*, 931. For the use of American mythology and traditional values in the American movement see: Dominick Cavallo, *A Fiction of the Past: The Sixties in American History* (New York: St. Martin's Press, 1999), here 11–13, 251–55.

63. Philipp Gassert, "Mit Amerika gegen Amerika: Antiamerikanismus in Westdeutschland," in Junker, *USA und Deutschland*, vol. 2., 750–60, here 754 f.; Jürgen Horlemann and Reinhard Strecker to the U.S. ambassador to the Federal Republic of Germany, 26 February 1966, in Collection Wolfgang Nitsch, FU WS 1965 / 66, Archiv APO; This view is also confirmed by the recollections of former activists: Krippendorff, Ekkehart. "Die westdeutsche Linke und ihr Bild von den USA," in Willi Paul Adams and Knud Krakau, eds., *Deutschland und Amerika, Perzeption und historische Realität* (Berlin: Colloquium Verlag, 1985), 39–46, here 43–46.

64. As has been concluded, any "Americanization" of Europe would always be accompanied by a process of europeanizing American culture. See Gassert, *Amerikanismus, Antiamerikanismus*, 550; also Rob Kroes, *If You've Seen One*, XI; Pells, *Not Like Us*, XV.

65. For the establishment of the categories see Jeremi Suri, "The Significance of the Wider World in American History," in *Reviews in American History* 31 (2003: 1–13), here 8.

66. Ibid., *Power and protest: global revolution and the rise power of detente*. (Cambridge, MA: Harvard University Press, 2003).

67. Coombs, Philip Hall, and Council on Foreign Relations. *The fourth dimension of foreign policy; educational and cultural affairs*. (New York,: Published for the Council on Foreign Relations by Harper & Row, 1964); Schmidt, Oliver. "A Civil Empire by Co-Optation: German-American Exchange Programs as Cultural Diplomacy, 1945–1961." PhD diss., Harvard University, 2000; Bu, Liping. *Making the World Like Us: Education, Cultural Expansion, and the American Century, Perspectives on the Twentieth Century,* Westport, CT: Praeger, 2003; Schumacher, Frank. "Propaganda, Ideology and Alliance Management: The United States and West Germany, 1949–1955." In *The Cultural Turn. Essays in the History of U.S. Foreign Relations,* edited by Frank Ninkovich and Liping Bu, 29–52. Chicago: Imprint Publications, 2001; See also Junker, *USA und Deutschland*, vol. 1, 601–45.

68. Gilcher-Holtey recently made the case for "transnational counter-public sphere" (*Gegenöffentlichkeit*) created by the protest movements of the 1960s, but again fails to acknowledge the specific historical pre-condition necessary for the blossoming of such: a *lingua franca*, common cultural ground based on historical ties and various forms of formal and informal exchange, as well as a favorable international setting. See ibid., "Der Transfer zwischen den Studentenbewegungen von 1968 und die Entstehung einer transnationalen Gegenöffentlichkeit," in Kaelble, *Transnationale Identitäten*, 303–26.

69. On the concept of transatlantic elites see Felix Philipp Lutz, "Transatlantische Netzwerke: Eliten in den deutsch-amerikanischen Beziehungen," in Junker, *USA und Deutschland*, vol. 2, 665–74, here 665 ff; For the idea of imagined communites see Benedict Anderson, *Imagined Communites. Reflections on the Spread and Origins of Nationalism*, 2nd ed. (London: Verso, 1991).

70. Akira Iriye, *Cultural Internationalism*, 156 ff.; Ibid., *Global Community: The Tole of International Organizations in the Making of the Contemporary World*. (Berkeley: University of California Press, 2002), 65, 113 ff.

71. Margaret E. Keck and Kathryn Sikkink, *Activists Beyond Borders: Advocacy Networks in International Politics* (Ithaca, NY: Cornell University Press, 1998), 14f.

72. Testimony of Karl Dietrich Wolff, 22.

Students in Unions—
Rethinking the University

Students in Unions—
Rethinking the University

CHAPTER 4

Unionizing for a More Democratic and Responsive University

ANITA SETH

On 19 September 2003, four thousand workers at Yale University ended a two-and-a-half-year campaign for a fair contract, winning back subcontracted jobs, increasing wages, and nearly doubling pensions. The strike included dramatic actions by unlikely participants, beginning with an overnight sit-in by eight retired workers at the Yale Investments Office who demanded (and got) a meeting with Yale's Endowment Manager David Swensen, and ending with thirteen Latino temporary replacement workers, escorted by managers across a largely African American picket line in the center of campus, deciding to join the strike. Strikes are nothing unusual at Yale, but rarely have they been so short and successful.[1] At a time when many workers were forced to accept take-backs, the unions at Yale pulled off a stunning victory while striking for less than a month. The reasons for their success included an aggressive campaign to support organizing rights for other Yale workers, and an ambitious alliance with local activists, church leaders, and politicians, aimed at making the university a better corporate citizen in New Haven.

The campaign at Yale was also able to draw strength from an unusual coalition taking shape within the national labor movement, which aims to reverse declining union strength by dedicating greater resources to organizing new groups of workers and pooling resources to take on large companies or to build union density by geographical area.[2] Informally dubbed the "New Unity Partnership," the coalition came to life the weekend before strike's end as carpenters, Teamsters, health care workers, and textile workers poured into New Haven by the thousands for a march that shut down the city for the afternoon. AFL-CIO president John Sweeney took an arrest in a mass civil disobedience with other national labor leaders and more than 150 rank-and-file union members.[3] The Yale drive is a microcosm of this new organizing philosophy, both in the extent of community organizing that has accompanied the contract fight, and the intense cooperation between two international unions, the Hotel and Restaurant Employees International Union (HERE) and the Service Employees International Union (SEIU).

The movement growing in New Haven is nothing less than a fight to preserve the vitality and integrity of universities and unions, two of the basic building blocks of democratic society. Graduate teachers and researchers at Yale have played an integral role in this fight. Universities now face a crisis on several fronts. First, decreasing government funding has led university administrators to place increasing weight on economic criteria in evaluating academic research. Second, increasing corporatization is eroding freedom of speech and the intellectual community on campus. Third, universities have increasingly cut themselves off from the life and problems of the communities in which they are located and the larger society as a whole. Confronting these trends will require both organization of academic workers on a national scale, and strong local alliances between these teachers and researchers and others in their communities.

The Importance of Democratizing Universities

The Graduate Employees and Students Organization (GESO) has fought for more than a decade to win union recognition for more than two thousand graduate teachers and researchers at Yale, organizing well before receiving official federal sanction to do so. Even since the 2000 ruling by the National Labor Relations Board (NLRB) that extended employee protections to graduate students at private universities, Yale's president and provost have repeatedly expressed their determination to fight unionization efforts in the courts.[4] GESO has therefore chosen a locally focused strategy, building strong alliances with Yale's two recognized unions, HERE Locals 34 & 35, and with the two thousand workers at the Yale-New Haven Hospital who also seek union recognition. The March, 2003 one-week walkout marked a significant moment for the alliance, as graduate student employees, including a group of research scientists, joined members of the existing unions on the picket lines for the first time.

The academic organizing movement has exploded over the last decade, spurred by decision-making at universities that is increasingly indistinguishable from the corporate boardroom in its lack of democracy and relentless pursuit of profit. That there is a crisis in the academic labor market is by now common knowledge—an awareness due in no small part to organizing efforts. Grim statistics about the academic job market and the corporatization of universities fill the pages of professional association journals and *The Chronicle of Higher Education* and are increasingly common fare in more popular magazines and major daily newspapers.[5] The editorial boards at the *New York Times* and even the *Wall Street Journal* have written in support of graduate employees' efforts.[6]

But there is more at stake with the changes in the university than the future job prospects of aspiring academics. GESO's alliance with the other Yale unions has helped us to contextualize the casualization of our labor as part of a larger economic process through which corporations extract increasing profits at the expense of their workers through downsizing and subcontracting.[7] Because of universities' central place in an information economy, the patterns of employment and economic decision making within the academy have larger ramifications for many other workers.

Equally urgent is the question of what role universities will play in our society. Will scientific and medical advances be available to a broad section of the public, or be restricted to a wealthy few? Will education be considered a basic right for all, a public good, or a rare privilege? It is no accident, for example, that corporatization of higher education has been accompanied by a rise of private schooling and decreasing public commitment to fund education at all levels.

Expanding corporate involvement and influence in research and the devaluing of teaching through innovations like distance learning and on-line courses both undermine the control of teachers and researchers, while emphasizing the profit potential of our work. Yale is at the forefront of both these trends.

The Patent and Trademark Act Amendments of 1980 (better known as the Bayh-Dole Act) allowed universities, for the first time, to patent discoveries that had been supported with public money. The result has been a sharp increase in the number of patents issued to universities, more than two thousand each year by the mid 1990s. Supporters of the legislation argue that it has made a growing number of discoveries available to the public and encouraged private investment in research at universities. But with the federal government providing more than 60 percent of the funding for academic science research, it is hard to escape the impression that Bayh-Dole has in fact made universities a conduit for converting public money into private profit.[8]

The consequences of such corporate partnerships have come under scrutiny at Yale with a controversy around d4T, a crucial anti-retroviral drug used to treat AIDS. In the spring of 2001, the international humanitarian group, Doctors Without Borders, launched a campaign to make d4T available more cheaply in South Africa. Although d4T was originally invented at Yale using primarily government money, Yale granted an exclusive license to Bristol Meyers Squibb to produce the drug, which generated more than $2 billion in sales under the brand name Zerit. At the time of the campaign, Yale had received over $120 million in profits from Zerit.[9] As part of the campaign, GESO circulated a petition that was signed by over six hundred Yale graduate students and medical staff calling on Bristol Meyers Squibb and Yale to release the patent to the drug. One of the signatories on the petition was the inventor of the drug, Dr. William Prusoff, bringing into sharp relief scientists' lack of control over the results of their work in the current corporatized university environment. Under public pressure, Yale released the patent shortly thereafter.

If scientific discoveries are the most obvious and hotly contested sources of potential profit at universities, distance-learning technologies provide an opportunity to increase revenues in other fields as well. In fall 2002, a distance-learning venture (AllLearn) jointly backed by Yale, Oxford and Stanford began offering ten-week enrichment courses. Although AllLearn is a non-profit company, one does not have to look far to see a potential future of greater corporatization. In June 2002, the *Chronicle of Higher Education* reported that the for-profit on-line educational consortium Universitas 21 "plans to offer its first *product*, a master's degree, through-out Asia in early 2003."[10] Later in the article we learn that it "should cost about $7,500 and take about 18 months to complete." A Merrill Lunch study estimates the potential international education market outside the United States at $111 billion per year. It is not surprising that the first degree available from Universitas 21 is an MBA. This is the logical endpoint to the trends of downsizing departments and casualizing academic labor: a faceless inter-action over a computer in which the only courses offered are those with large market demand among a global elite who can pay for them, with educational value reduced to an assessment of "credible academic brand names."[11]

Unfortunately, it seems that many leaders within the academy are more inclined to celebrate corporate models than to consider the dangers of such trends. Yale President Richard Levin has repeatedly referred to universities as "engines of economic growth." In a May 2001 speech with that title at Tsinghua University, he made clear his fully market-driven view of how the academy should set its priorities.[12] The speech celebrated the tradition of a broad-based liberal arts education as the perfect training for today's business leaders. In this view, academic freedom and critical thinking are valuable insofar they meet a corporate agenda for quick response in a cut-throat world. In Levin's laudatory description of universities as "America's primary basic research machine" there was no acknowledgement of the ethical issues involved with the privatization of important scientific knowledge. Of the "active long-term projects with great economic potential" his first example was mapping the humane genome.

Levin's speech in China fits into a larger vision for Yale as a global university. Globalization provides a central focus for the humanities at Yale, just as huge investments in biomedical research do in the sciences. At the core of these plans is the Center for the Study of Globalization, founded in 2001. Through a fellows program, the Center gathers potential leaders from around the world to be mentored by Yale faculty and to develop networks among themselves. The Center will also host "Track II" diplomatic negotiations to bring together opposing sides of political conflicts for informal discussion. Such an elite focus is not surprising given the model that Yale now provides to the international community: one of a wealthy institution with little internal democracy and a feudal relationship with the surrounding city.

But even proponents of corporate models for education occasionally admit the fundamental incompatibility between the search for profit and the educational mission. While celebrating the structure of American scientific funding for providing "a virtual free market in ideas," Levin has acknowledged that it is precisely the lack of market pressures that makes scientific inquiry possible: "Universities, in their unending, unadulterated search to know, are uniquely situated to undertake such long-term research without worrying about its commercial application and payoff—a luxury that profit-seeking private industrial firms cannot afford."[13] Left unanswered is what happens as the public space for basic research and inquiry erodes. This is the space where organized teachers and researchers can and must intervene. Today's generation of young academics stand on the frontlines of a battle to maintain universities as invaluable repositories for democratic and non-corporate values.

The Fight for Free Speech

Yale has become famous not only as a university where scholars conduct world-class research, but also as an institution unparalleled in the academy for its disregard and contempt for its workers and its surrounding community. The union fight exists at the nexus of this contradiction, fueled by the vision of academic excellence based on respect for, rather than at the expense of, human dignity. The systemic disrespect for workers at Yale was noted immediately by a consultant hired (and less than a year later, dismissed) by the university administration at the beginning of the most recent round of contract negotiations. The consultant suggested that fundamental change would be needed to turn around a "highly adversarial and dysfunctional relationship" (with one manager quoted describing the university's labor strategy as "somewhere between union containment and union avoidance"), and recommended that Yale "manag[e] its own employees as if they were capable of independent thought."[14]

The administration's resistance to unions has gone so far as to undermine the basic values that should be at the core of university teaching. The administration has adopted a portrayal of union activity as outside of and even antithetical to the university's educational mission. This was evident in the letter sent by the Dean of Yale College to undergraduates leading up to the March 2003 walkout. After assuring students that their classes would continue normally in spite of a teaching assistant (TA) strike, he continued: "Undergraduates will be expected to meet their academic responsibilities as scheduled. Students should understand that they are free to cross a picket line to meet their academic responsibilities."[15] Graduate students' decision to boycott classes in support of that strike was characterized by several administrators and faculty as anti-intellectual.

Most troubling has been the attack on union speech and the use of police presence to limit free association. In September 2002, constables at the Yale-New Haven Hospital (YNHH) arrested eight union members for leafleting at the entrance to the building where they worked and charged them with first-degree criminal trespass, carrying a sentence of up to one year in prison. The NLRB had already upheld unfair labor practices charges against the hospital for police harassment of its own workers. This time, the hospital administration argued, because the workers were employees of the University, they were within their rights to arrest them.[16] Although the hospital eventually dropped the charges and the City of New Haven stripped YNHH constables of their arrest powers, abuses of police power to harass union members and supporters has continued. Just weeks after these incidents at the Hospital, two undergraduates were detained by Yale University police for handing out pro-union leaflets to parents outside of a Parents' Weekend panel.[17]

Private security guards (in March, their uniforms and cars declared them to be literally "Pinkertons") appeared at the entrances to Yale buildings and drove around campus during the 2003 strikes. During the September strike, GESO members were detained repeatedly when entering Yale buildings with pro-union signs. One member in the history department, wearing a sign that read "Stand up for Change at Yale," was stopped while entering the university medical center for an appointment. In response to a written complaint, the medical center director defended the policy of barring people wearing signs from entering the building because of its alleged "potential for disrupting the provision of health care."[18] Several other graduate students wearing pro-union signs or distributing union leaflets were stopped by police and threatened with arrest at the entrances of academic buildings and in the library. In another case, a rank-and-file union organizer in the chemistry department was stopped in his building by Yale police after talking to colleagues about the union, detained for more than a half-hour in the central hallway of the building, and told that it was illegal to conduct union business on Yale property.

Reconnecting to the Community

In his 1955 history of Yale, George Wilson Pierson described campus upheavals of the 1920s, when students protested against trustees on the Yale Corporation who "seemed more concerned for financial stability than educational morale, more interested in buildings than in books," and who "[w]orst of all . . . were strangers."[19] The basic issues remained unchanged in the fall of 2001, when Reverend W. David Lee, an alumnus of the Yale Divinity School and pastor of the Verrick AME Zion Church in New Haven, petitioned for candidacy to become a trustee on the Yale Corporation. Backed by a coalition of local clergy, community groups, and unions, Lee gathered signatures from more than four thousand Yale alumni to win a place on the ballot. His campaign focused on the need for a community-based voice on the corporation, and he pledged to make himself accountable to students and residents of New Haven.

In spite of support from the local community, political leaders, and many alumni for Lee's election bid, the response of the Yale administration was swift and harsh. The Association of Yale Alumni nominated only one candidate to oppose Lee, rather than the usual five or six. Their choice, architect Maya Lin, whose projects include the Vietnam War Memorial and the Women's Table at Yale, seemed calculated to divide the sympathies of liberal alumni. Trustee Kurt Schmoke, who, legend has it, engaged in a hunger strike in support of labor struggles while a law student, led the official attack on Lee's campaign. In a June 2002 letter, after the conclusion of the election, Schmoke complained that Lee's campaign had tainted the alumni election process and proposed reforming the system to prevent such a threat in the future. A coalition of wealthy alumni ran full-page ads in the alumni magazine and sent out mailings criticizing Lee's "relative youth" and "lack of professional distinction." More unbelievably, they attacked Lee for being "beholden to special interests," a reference to his ties to the Yale unions. Many students, alumni and community groups would point out the irony of this charge, given the array of corporate interests represented by sitting trustees.[20] In the face of such institutional hostility, Lee lost the election.

Just as Yale's governing board has no room at its table for a leader of the local community, its vision of New Haven almost entirely overlooks the city's current residents. The contrast of Yale's wealth and New Haven's poverty has long been a sensitive topic for those on both sides of the university walls. One in fifty New Haven residents are incarcerated, and one in five live in poverty.[21] Educational testing scores in the public schools are the lowest in Connecticut.[22] As New Haven has lost the manufacturing base that once provided the bedrock of the economy, residents have been left with low-paying service jobs, or no jobs at all. Yale, like many other universities, has become the economic hub for a de-industrialized city as well as a generator of wealth in the national and international information-based economy. Today, one in four jobs in New Haven is at Yale University and Yale-New Haven Hospital.

The Yale administration's plans for economic renewal in New Haven revolve around the development of a biotech industry. In spite of rosy predictions that sound suspiciously like Reagan-era trickle-down economic theories, the $1 billion of investment in biotech so far has not generated many jobs or significant tax revenue for the city. Because many successful companies leave New Haven after taking advantage of development incentives, biotech provides only 1.6 percent of the city's tax base, and only 400 jobs.[23] Furthermore, university officials are vague about how a few high-tech jobs will translate into economic benefit and needed employment for the city's more than hundred thousand residents. Yale's profoundly undemocratic vision for economic development stretches beyond jobs into policies for real estate investment, housing and policing that are aimed at gentrifying the downtown area. Skyrocketing housing prices and the controversial proposed conversion of publicly-subsidized housing units into luxury apartments have prompted the local weekly newspaper to ask, "Whose Livable City Is It?"[24]

The Connecticut Center for a New Economy (CCNE), a non-profit organization affiliated with the Yale unions, has been building an organized base across New Haven's neighborhoods to demand greater democracy in local economic development plans. As teachers and researchers within the university, GESO members have found that we can play an important role, working together with members of the community, in encouraging Yale to act more responsibly and to play a positive role in the social fabric of New Haven.

The work of CCNE has brought the unions together with community leaders to demand a new social contract between the Yale administration and New Haven. The planks of the proposed contract include improving access to Yale jobs for New Haven residents, expanding employee home-ownership programs, and increasing Yale's financial contribution to the local budget. Although Yale is New Haven's largest property owner, it pays less tax on its growing number of commercial properties in New Haven than it does to New York City.[25] A fair share contribution would begin to address the revenue shortfall that New Haven experiences because of Yale's tax exemption on more than $1 billion dollars of property.

The Yale administration has responded to these critiques by stressing its direct and indirect economic contributions to New Haven, and by pointing to the payment-in-lieu-of-taxes (PILOT) program, under which Connecticut taxpayers make up a portion of what Yale would owe in property taxes through an annual grant to the city. However, in spite of millions of dollars of advertising and the efforts of Yale's Office of New Haven and State Affairs, city residents appear unconvinced by Yale's declarations of its largesse. In July 2003, the Board of Aldermen passed a resolution calling on Yale to voluntarily make up the difference between the PILOT payment and what it would owe in property taxes (about $12.5 million) and initiating an investigation into the possibility of repealing a special tax exemption held by Yale and several other Connecticut universities.

The issue that perhaps most galvanized the union-community alliance was debt collection practices at YNHH. In the spring of 2003, CCNE published a report, which found that the hospital was employing unusually aggressive tactics in going after poor patients who were unable to pay their bills, including wage garnishment, property foreclosure, and adding court costs to patients' bills.[26] Between 1994 and 2003, YNHH filed liens on more than nine hundred homes in New Haven owned by hospital debtors.[27] In spite of a $37 million dedicated "free bed fund" to provide free care to the indigent, many poor patients who might have been eligible for such aid had not been informed about its availability. State officials got involved as well, with the Connecticut Attorney General bringing charges against YNHH for misuse of free bed funds and the Connecticut legislature passing a new law cutting the maximum interest on hospital debt in half, to five percent.

Beyond Tenure

Because the problems that we face can seem monumental, it is important for graduate employees to realize the considerable power we hold. Even at a university with an endowment like Yale's, tuition and research grants make up 42 percent of the annual operating budget. Without us, much of the teaching and research simply do not occur. Unionization, by providing an institutionalized voice that is backed by the economic power of our labor as teachers and researchers, provides academics the opportunity to protect our futures, while pressuring universities to live up to their educational mission.

The structural changes that will come through increased union density in the academy are only a small part of the difference we will make. Even more important are the qualitative, personal transformations that occur through academic organizing. In my experience at Yale, it is rank-and-file GESO organizers who most tenaciously hold on to a stubborn idealism about what the academy can be, and who are most willing to take risks to safeguard the intellectual community.

The labor movement has two powerful lessons to offer academics: the necessity of collective action to secure personal freedom and the importance of respecting our work. Unionization encourages us to throw out the myth of the cloistered scholar and the illusion that we can individually win our right to a voice through hard work, brilliance, and a recognized, secure position within the university (tenure). We realize that we will not secure academic freedom through personal dedication or bravery (although there is plenty of room for these), but will have to reclaim it through organization and collective action. By supporting each other and engaging with the *entire* community around us, we help create space where academic debate can thrive and scholars can afford to take risks in their work.

Even more importantly, unionization puts us back in touch with the truth that intellectual work is indeed *work* and should be respected as such. How many times have I heard (or even said) that what we do as academics is really mostly fun, just sitting around reading books? Who among us has not had our moments of thinking, "I can't believe that they pay me for this!" But these kinds of attitudes denigrate the very thing that is most valuable about the academy—the opportunity it provides to do interesting and rewarding work in an atmosphere of respect and dignity. These are precisely the things that are most endangered within a capitalist economy. To downplay their value is to surrender to evaluating our work in market-driven terms and to fail to appreciate the crucial role universities play in safeguarding democracy. Worst of all, when we become convinced about the worthlessness of our own work, we are unwilling to fight for it and put ourselves more readily in the service of those in power.

Universities need to be public spaces where the needs of human beings come before the pressures of the market. Although some faculty worry that unionization could institutionalize the corporatization and casualization of the academy, my experience in GESO has instead encouraged me to think about the social importance of my teaching and research. For us to impart the humanistic values and ideas that lie at the heart of education to our students, we need to recover those ideas for ourselves. Today's academics face a market-driven logic that discounts intellectual work as unimportant and views education as mere job training and credentialing. By taking seriously the work we do and developing strong alliances with fellow workers and residents in New Haven, GESO is training a new generation of socially-engaged young scholars with a strong vision for a transformed academy.

Notes

The ideas and analysis presented here have emerged from hundreds of conversations and meetings that are scarcely represented in the footnotes. I owe a special debt to David Sanders, who has challenged me to clarify my thinking over hours of patient organizing. I'd also like to thank Jesse Lemisch for his comments on an earlier version of this chapter.

1. For example, the 1984 strike in which clerical and technical workers won their first contract lasted for ten-and-a-half weeks. The 1995–1996 contract fight involved two one-month strikes. For the history of labor struggles at Yale, see Cary Nelson, ed., *Will Teach for Food: Academic Labor in Crisis* (Minneapolis: University of Minnesota Press, 1997), especially John Wilhelm, "A Short History of Unionization at Yale," 35–43; and Toni Gilpin et al., *On Strike for Respect: The Clerical and Technical Workers' Strike at Yale, 1984-85* (Urbana: University of Illinois Press, 1995).
2. "Breaking Ranks with the AFL-CIO," *Business Week*, 15 September 2003.
3. New Haven Register, "10,000 Yale strike supporters rally in New Haven," 14 September 2003.
4. See for example, President Richard Levin's statement of November 1, 2000 in which he urges the NYU administration to appeal the NLRB ruling on graduate teaching assistants. Available at http://www.yale.edu/opa. GESO and the workers represented by District 1199 of the SEIU at Yale-New Haven Hospital have both asked the administration for card-count neutrality agreements. For documentation of the weaknesses in the NLRB election process, see Human Rights Watch, *Unfair Advantage: Workers' Freedom of Association in the United States under International Human Rights Standards*, August 2000.
5. Much of the work highlighting these changes comes out of the unionization movement itself. See for example, *Casual Nation* (Coalition of Graduate Employee Unions, 2000), available at www.cgeu.org; and *Casual in Blue: Yale and the Academic Labor Market* (GESO, 1999); *Postdoc Crisis* (GESO, 2002), both available at http://www.yaleunions.org/geso. Also, Gordon Lafer, *Organizing Graduate Students* (New York: Foundation for the Study of Independent Social Ideas, 2001).
6. The *New York Times* editorial of Nov. 25, 2000, argued that, "American graduate programs, the envy of the world, are not so fragile they cannot coexist with unions, or provide workers the rights they enjoy elsewhere in the economy." The *Wall Street Journal* on the one hand supports the claim that graduate teachers and researchers are underpaid employees, but on the other, questions the principle of unionization. The editorial uses the plight of graduate employees as a launching point to attack on tenure. See, "Class Struggle," 22 March 2002.
7. For an eloquent formulation of the larger context, see David Montgomery, "Planning for Our Futures," in Steven Fraser and Joshua B. Freeman, eds., *Audacious Democracy: Labor, Intellectuals, and the Social Reconstruction of America* (Boston and New York: Houghton Mifflin, 1997).
8. By contrast, in 1997, industry provided 7% of funding for academic research and development (Council on Governmental Relations, "The Bayh-Dole Act: A Guide to the Law and Implementing Regulations," September 1999). For a more critical view of corporate influence in academic science, see Eyal Press and Jennifer Washburn, "The Kept University," *The Atlantic Monthly*, March 2000.
9. "GESO Pressures University to Make AIDS Drug Available," *The GESO Voice*, April 2001; and "Yale Researchers Respond to Global AIDS Crisis," August 2001. Available at http://www.yaleunions.org/geso.
10. Michael Arnone, "International Consortium Readies Ambitious Distance-Education Effort," *Chronicle of Higher Education*, June 28 2002 (emphasis is mine). The consortium includes seventeen universities around the world, including the University of Virginia. University of Michigan and University of Toronto were both initially members of the consortium that have withdrawn their support.
11. Ibid.
12. "The University As an Engine of Economic Growth," May 2001. Available at http://www.yale.edu/opa/president. An earlier version of this speech, with the same title is published in Richard C. Levin, *The Work of the University* (New Haven and London: Yale University Press, 2003), 87–94.
13. *The Work of the University*, 90.

14. Restructuring Associates Inc., *Assessment of the Relationship between Yale University and HERE Locals 34 & 35*, January 2002. Available at http://www.yaleunions.org.
15. Letter from Richard Brodhead to students of Yale College, 21 February 2003.
16. The University and the Hospital have strenuously argued that they are separate institutions, in spite of significant overlap in their governing structures—a number of officers of the University, including Yale President Richard Levin, sit on the board of the Hospital. Property boundaries are even more unclear, as the Hospital and University share use of a number of buildings in the Medical School complex.
17. "Union Supporters Leaflet at Parents' Weekend Panel," *Yale Daily News*, 14 October 2002.
18. E-mail correspondence from Dr. Paul Genecin to Ashley Riley Sousa, 12 September 2003.
19. George Wilson Pierson, *Yale: The University College, 1921–1937* (New Haven: Yale University Press, 1955), 78–79. I am grateful to Michael Mullins for bringing this passage to my attention.
20. For a list of Trustees and their affiliations, see www.yaleinsider.org. In July 2003, union researchers uncovered evidence of a troubling correlation between members of the Yale Corporation and Yale Investment Committee, and the companies in which Yale chose to invest money. Of the twenty people on the Investment Committee between 1995 and 2003, at least six were themselves or had family members heading up companies in which Yale invested, a fact not disclosed in Yale's public filings with the federal government. For details of one case, see "Trade Unions Call for Yale Investments Probe," *Financial Times*, 29 June 2003.
21. Both figures are from 2000. According to the Connecticut Department of Corrections, 2800 of the state's almost 18,000 prisoners in January 2000 were from New Haven. Poverty figures come from census data.
22. Connecticut Center for a New Economy, *Schools, Taxes and Jobs*, 2002.
23. Connecticut Center for a New Economy, *Incubating Biotech: Yale Prospers, New Haven Waits*, July 2001.
24. *New Haven Advocate*, August 8–14, 2002.
25. *Schools, Taxes, and Jobs*, 9.
26. Connecticut Center for a New Economy, *Uncharitable Care: Yale-New Haven Hospital's Charity Care and Collection Practices*, March 2003.
27. Connecticut Center for a New Economy, *"Yale, Don't Lien on Me,"* September 2003.

CHAPTER 5

What Is a University?
Anti-Union Campaigns
in Academia

KIMBERLY PHILLIPS-FEIN

Though I've had the conversation hundreds of times, I'm always a little bit nervous when I'm waiting outside a classroom. I peek in to make sure the class isn't over yet. I make sure that I have my cards. In this moment when I'm waiting for the conversation to begin, what I'm about to do always seems, just for a minute, daring, like a step into a new world.

Once the door opens, anything might happen. I will ask, right away, about some of the most intimate aspects of another person's life—money, childcare, health insurance, power, respect. I am not talking to a friend. I have, at this point, no personal relationship with the teacher behind the door. Yet I have learned more about graduate school from these conversations than I could ever know from my experience alone. I have listened to graduate students talk about the mechanics of credit card debt and the second jobs that they take on to pay it off. People have told me about all kinds of health problems. I have heard about being a single mother and facing the disdain of a department chair, and about what it feels like to be a new mother and teach a course with a newborn in a basket by the desk. A single mother has told me of the disdain of her department chair, and a new mother has described teaching a course with her newborn in a basket by the desk. People have confided in me about the power their advisors casually and genteelly wield. And I feel at times that I have learned as much about the anxieties and evasions of the academic life from the people who have turned away from me—too busy, shy or afraid to talk.

The door opens. Students trickle into the hallway. Almost always some linger behind to ask a last question or make an appointment for office hours. When they leave, ten or fifteen minutes later, the teacher starts to pick up her stuff, and just then, at last, I knock on the open door.

"Hi," I say. "My name is Kim. I am a teaching assistant in the history department. I'm here to talk to you about the union."

By the time this chapter is published, teaching and research assistants at Columbia University will have been organizing a union (Graduate Student Employees United [or GSEU]—Local 2110 UAW) for four years, the amount of time it would take one of the undergrads we teach to graduate from college. The group of student workers includes both graduate and undergraduate teaching and research assistants. We work in a wide variety of jobs. Teaching assistants (TAs) hold discussion sections, meet with students one-on-one during office hours, work on undergraduate writing and grade examinations; they are often responsible for final undergraduate grades. Lab assistants for science courses help first and second year students survive physics, chemistry, computer science and biology, leading hands-on experiments and guiding students through lab reports. Research assistants (RAs) do basic scientific research. They carry out experiments, write grants, and run laboratories in physics, astrophysics, molecular biology, chemistry, computer science and other fields of research. There are about 2000 people in our organizing drive, making it one of the largest ongoing in New York City.

The issues at stake in the Columbia organizing drive are similar to those that lead any group of workers to try to form a union. Wages are low and people often work second jobs while in school. The basic health plan is the same as that offered to undergraduates, and is keyed to college students and their health problems—not those of adults in their late 20s and early 30s. There is no childcare. When we began to organize, teaching assistants were often paid different amounts for doing the same work. If class enrollment is lower than expected, jobs can be taken away at the last minute. Positions are doled out in an arbitrary way. There is no neutral grievance procedure through which students can gain redress for problems on the job. Finally, graduate students are doing more and more work at Columbia—teaching all of the first and second year composition classes, about half of the courses in the prestigious Core curriculum, many foreign language classes, and serving as TAs in the majority of science courses and half of all social science and humanities classes, not to mention performing the brunt of daily work in the research labs.

Underlying these bread-and-butter issues at Columbia are larger concerns about the transformations taking place within the culture and economy of academic insitutions. Budgets for public universities have been cut back so sharply that some college students can't even take the courses they need to graduate. Meanwhile, private universities obsessed with cost-cutting refuse to hire full faculty, instead employing semester-by-semester adjuncts, post-docs and lecturers. The reason for the "job crisis" in academia is not so much a shortage of a demand for our labor as it is the transformation of tenure-track jobs into contingent teaching positions, which do not permit scholarship or even pay health benefits. Graduate student unions are one part of a larger movement that seeks to strengthen the collective weight of teachers and scholars in the academy, so that we can try to protect the values of learning and research and the material resources dedicated to education and scholarship, in an era when these are not always the primary concerns of administrators.

Graduate student employee unions are not new. The first ones were organized at public universities like the University of Michigan and the University of Wisconsin in the late 1960s and early 1970s. TAs throughout the University of California system organized in the 1990s, and several campuses in the University of Massachusetts system organized in the 1980s. But in more recent years, facing a job crisis in academia and a rising workload while in graduate school, student employees at private universities—including New York University (NYU), Penn, Brown, Cornell, Tufts and Yale—have started to organize unions. And while these campaigns have been similar in many ways to the earlier ones, the university administrations at these private universities have greeted the organizing campaigns with a new and surprising level of hostility. They have waged anti-union campaigns that are familiar in private industry, but unexpected at prestigious research institutions.

At Columbia, after we filed for a union election, the university hired a law firm known throughout industry for its expertise in union busting. Taking advantage of the Bush administration's conservative labor board appointees, the university's administrators—many of whom are liberal scholars—are currently seeking to overturn legal precedent, throw out our union election, and deny hundreds of thousands of teaching and research assistants across the country the right to form unions and collectively bargain. Our union election was held in March 2002. More than two years later, the ballots have not been counted. The university administration has justified its attempt to throw out our election by arguing that graduate students are not employees that unionization will destroy the intimate relationships between faculty and students, and that it will shatter the special privileges of the doctoral candidate. Implicit in this argument is the idea that the union will destroy the magic space of the academy, making it simply another corporate institution, divided by conflict. But the strategies that Columbia has used to fight the union have been borrowed from corporate

America, and the university's anti-union campaign makes it clear just how much it has become part of that world already.

From the outside, the Columbia campus looks like a castle, surrounded by a thick barricade, guarded by imposing gates. It radiates a breezy Beaux Arts classicism, where money and the great books meet. On the library and college buildings, the names of Greek philosophers are carved out in huge capital letters: HERODOTUS SOPHOCLES ARISTOTLE: to remind day-dreaming students why they are here. Great steps lead up to Low Library, the administration building, and undergraduates sprawl across them on sunny spring or autumn days.

The university looks different from a union organizer's perspective. Hidden rooms become uncovered and visible. Labor that is usually silent becomes part of the university's story. Most of the time, students and faculty move through campus alone. Going to one course and then the next, to particular offices and special library cubicles, each student or professor follows his or her unique schedule. In their own lives as well, they pursue lonely missions, rising up the steps of Low Library, in search of an elusive foothold in the professional middle class. From the standpoint of an organizer, though, the university seems regimented and powerful, teaching work being done in one classroom after another, streams of students swinging around the campus in synchronized motion, one class hardly admitted before the next year's applications flood in. The thousands of people who work for Columbia bring the university into being every day, and suddenly our capacity to shape the institution appears greater than we could have imagined, wandering through the library stacks.

Teaching and research assistants at Columbia began to organize in the late summer of 2000. That year, the National Labor Relations Board (the federal agency that handles union organizing) recognized graduate student employees as workers with the right to organize, as a result of a union election at New York University. Teaching and research assistants in the University of California system had recently won legal recognition after years of organizing. At the same time, the broader political situation seemed friendly to a union campaign. The stock market was starting to tumble from the dizzying heights of the Internet boom, and the memories of the World Trade Organization (WTO) demonstrations in Seattle lingered over the campus.

We began by holding meetings at the West End, a local pub that was once a haunt of beat poet Jack Kerouac's. The meetings started small but grew quickly. A few of us went downtown and met with organizers from the United Auto Workers (UAW), the union that the teaching assistants at NYU joined and the union which has represented Columbia clerical workers for twenty years. We came back up and had more public meetings—fifty people came to the first, and still more to the second. It seemed that people were saying things they had never said before, expressing dissatisfaction in a way that had power to it. We voted to affiliate with the UAW, a natural decision for us given the union's history in academic labor and on Columbia's campus.

Intellectual work in general, and graduate school in particular, is fiercely isolated and often lonely. It is also intensely competitive, especially given a job market in many fields that resembles the waterfront during the Great Depression—literally hundreds of people clamoring for a few spots. Most of the time, the problems of graduate school seem like they are one's own fault. Not able to write an A paper after grading piles of blue books? Can't find a spot to meet with your students when you don't have an office? Your advisor demands you put in eighty-hour weeks at the lab? Paid half of someone else doing the same work? In the lazy wealth and interior luxury of the university campus, it is hard not to feel that nearly every problem reflects your own deficiencies—surely real scholars would be able to surmount these petty difficulties!

The first few months of organizing felt like waking up. Most of the work we did in those early days was grassroots organizing: we would find teaching and research assistants, usually in classrooms and labs, and talk to them about the union. These conversations gave people information and a chance to ask questions, but they were also the first step in building a union, for the network of bonds and connections that is created through grassroots organizing is the union's greatest strength. People do not join the union out of abstract principle, nor do they commit to it out of blind hope. The choice to stand with others can only be made when there is another person standing in front of you, asking you to join with him or her. Those connections make it possible for people to take the risks that they must take to win. In a lived, daily way, organizing expresses a new vision of academia. It allows people the perspective to see, in a concrete way, that graduate students are bound by common needs, not competition; that the crisis our profession faces is one that no individual can change alone; and that the stress we all face in graduate school can be changed, could be eased, but not through anything that any one of us could do differently or better or more originally or intelligently. Graduate students in History and Physics alike face a poor job market and a proliferation of non-tenure-track jobs; teaching assistants in French and Chemistry both lack decent health insurance for their spouses. Admitting that there are deep problems in our common situations, no matter how difficult, is easier than laboring forward into a fantasy. Graduate school then becomes something to take seriously, not to be endured for the sake of a faraway future that might not come.

It still seems counter-intuitive, almost taboo, to say it, but objectively speaking, in terms of the cost-of-living and the median income in New York City, most graduate students at Columbia are poor. In 2000, at the close of a decade when the stock market sent Columbia's endowment soaring, we earned a minimum stipend (and the majority were at the minimum) of $13,000 for nine months, to live in the most expensive city in the country. (The minimum stipend now is $17,000. The university increased stipends shortly after we began organizing—even granting a retroactive raise to the beginning of that academic year—and has since granted a series of raises to make sure that Columbia keeps up with stipends at unionized NYU.) Although most fellowships forbid graduate students to work outside the university, most do, or else they go into debt or receive financial assistance from family members or from a spouse.

There are many compensations for the financial realities of graduate school: the pleasure that most grad students take in academic and intellectual work, the sense of borrowed prestige that comes from attending a well-known university, the flexible schedule, and the promise of a future professional career. What is more, precisely because graduate school is financially insecure and the rewards are ephemeral and distant, most people who attend it have a solidly middle-class background. They went to good undergraduate colleges and made a choice to take a less lucrative position for the moment. They are not, in other words, used to thinking of themselves as poor. I remember talking to many TAs and RAs who pointed out that we aren't like sweated, minimum-wage workers. That's true—we aren't. But at the same time, graduate students who are not receiving major subsidies to their income struggle financially—which is expecially problematic given that academic jobs that pay a decent salary are so hard to get. Some professors, maybe even some students, feel that poverty is appropriate for the graduate student: It stimulates him or her to work and complete the degree. But the opposite is true. It is depressing and hard to scramble for money, and what it primarily makes you feel is that what you're doing must not be very important—after all, it isn't worth much. The sense of schizophrenic desperation that comes from not having enough money and at the same time being supposed to *not care* about it was one of the forces that propelled our organizing drive in the early days, even though it took a lot of time and organizing before many of us could articulate this in a straightforward way—so deep is the sense that academic work is not really legitimate work at all.

We organized through the winter and early spring of 2001. In the spring, we participated in a forum attended by hundreds of graduate students who cheered the union. We obtained a majority of grad employee signatures on union cards (at that time, we were focused on organizing TAs), and we filed the cards at the National Labor Relations Board (NLRB). It was our statutory right to have a union election within forty-five days. That's when Columbia began to fight back.

The cornerstone of Columbia's campaign against the union has been its legal challenge to the right of graduate students at private universities to form unions. When Columbia learned that teaching and research assistants were organizing, it hired Proskauer Rose LLP, a prestigious New York law firm that advertises seminars on such topics as "The New Union Drive: Understanding and Protecting Against the New Union Tactics" on its Web site. Proskauer Rose—which Yale and New York University had also employed to fight graduate student unions—went through legal gymnastics to try to stop our campaign. The university demanded extensive hearings to try to prove that we were students, not employees, and therefore did not have the right to form a union. Administrators argued that teaching is a degree requirement at Columbia, which is simply not true—students who pay tuition receive PhD's without ever teaching a course. They claimed that we hardly work for the school at all, saying that we don't teach stand-alone classes (which is also not the case). To be an "employee," one must work for a wage, under supervision, and provide a meaningful service. Columbia could not deny that we were paid; they could not claim we were independent contractors. The heart of the university's argument was that graduate students do not provide services to the university: The teaching and research work we do is *only* training, a service the university provides for us.

The university could not stop the election from going forward. But once the election was held, Columbia promptly appealed, preventing the ballots from being counted. As of today's date, two years after the election, the ballots are impounded, as the union waits for the NLRB to decide whether or not the people who work in labs and grade Columbia's undergraduates provide a meaningful service to the school.

The university's campaign was not limited to the courts. The administration mounted an extensive propaganda campaign against the union, telling graduate students to vote no, citing partial and misleading information, and using the power of faculty members to try to persuade students not to organize. In the weeks leading up to the election, all graduate students received letters from the university president, the provost and the dean of the graduate school seeking to convince them to go out to the polls and vote against the union. These letters, which are standard in industrial anti-union campaigns, were filled with innuendos, half-truths and flat-out inaccuracies that would have been deemed unacceptable in any normal academic context.

To take one example, the letter from Provost Jonathan Cole, sent February 22, 2002, three weeks before the union election, was six pages long. Despite the widespread student activism in support of the union, the letter warned that the "UAW" was seeking to further "national labor policy by casting students as employees," and that "the unfortunate casualty of this conflict could very well be the quality of graduate education at the nation's best universities." Ignoring thirty years of bargaining history at public universities, Cole claimed that student unions "don't achieve better economic results," and warned that "an industrial model—one that is bureaucratic, formalized and legalistic" could come to replace the friendly, collaborative relationship between students and faculty. Not mentioning top-notch public universities that have unionized, like Berkeley, Madison and UCLA, the letter suggested that unions would "distort" the academic process and that "the long-term result could well be a decline in the value of a graduate degree at Columbia." At the end of the letter, Cole reflected on his own graduate student career—a "time that was full of anxiety," but that nonetheless was "punctuated by time spent in public protests against the war in Vietnam and marches for civil rights." Shoring up his radical credentials, he ended by mentioning his father, a professional actor, who "worked for the creation of a strong actors' union . . . for which he was blacklisted in the McCarthy period." His parentage aside, in the end, Cole returned to a rhetorical standby that his father might have recognized: "Unions that represent graduate students in the mode of industrial unions simply are a poor fit for what we seek to do in graduate education—and they are unnecessary."

While Cole's letter proclaimed the sanctity of the student-faculty relationship, the administration was encouraging faculty to manipulate that very relationship to get their students to vote no. After we filed for our election, Elizabeth Keefer, the university's general counsel, sent all faculty members an e-mail telling them that an advisor would be within his or her legal rights to inform graduate students that "he or she believes that it is likely that faculty-student relationships could suffer were teaching fellows to be unionized." Among the reasons might be that "faculty will have to treat their students as employees whom they supervise; that meetings between individual faculty and their teaching fellows may at times require the involvement of a union steward as a third party; that grades . . . could become the subject of a grievance or an unfair labor practice charge."

The language in Keefer's note seemed carefully chosen to coach faculty to tell their students to vote no without violating the National Labor Relations Act, which gives workers the right to organize without employer coercion—free from threats, promises or bribes, and punishment. Keefer did not cite a single case where any of the scenarios she had depicted had come true (unions do not bargain over grades). Yet by encouraging faculty to tell their students about their opposition to the union, letting them know they should express their vague apprehensions about the future, Keefer was urging Columbia faculty to engage in a highly questionable intellectual activity. She was asking them to suggest that a union would hurt faculty relationship with students in order to frighten graduate students into voting against the union. There is no way to know how many faculty members had such conversations with their students; there is no way to know how many of them remained within the perimeters of the law, which forbids explicit threats. But certainly many graduate students experienced these communications from their advisors as implicit threats, and felt that supporting the union openly could endanger their academic relationships, learning the lesson that political outspokenness can be dangerous to your career. Had the university administration been truly concerned with preserving the relationships between students and faculty, it would never have encouraged faculty to express their opposition to the union (and given them a nice list of reasons to fight it).

Many department chairs and faculty members took up the mantle of the anti-union campaign. Department chairs held departmental meetings where they spoke against the union. These meetings were held in the weeks leading up to the election. The points and arguments raised by administrators were often nearly identical, suggesting significant co-ordination. The dean of the Engineering School lobbied his students with e-mails expressing his personal opposition and lauding as "magnificent" an op-ed that ran in the *Columbia Spectator* by a student who described the union as "fascistic." The chair of the economics department sent e-mails to all students encouraging them to vote no. One professor in visual arts told her teaching assistants not to talk to a fellow student union organizer who visited a class. Another faculty member in the Spanish department told students that they would no longer be able to teach more than one class a semester—which many relied on financially—because of the union drive (the union, of course, had no input into this decision; the department and administration were responsible for it). An art history professor spoke at public forums against the union, saying that it might threaten the "fragile structure" of fellowships and funding at the university. At one public forum, the Dean of the Graduate School of Arts and Sciences said that he was afraid that with a union, "if we're pressed to the wall financially," the university would demand that students work additional hours, "Of course that's not a threat," he then said to the audience.

In communications about the union with graduate students, faculty members often repeated anti-union arguments seemingly without doing independent research or gathering information on their own. In protecting the status quo, standards of academic inquiry appeared to have been abandoned. For example, one boilerplate anti-union tidbit cited by an interim dean was that graduate students could be forced by the union to go on strike, and would be fined for not striking. The dean did not mention (and perhaps did not even know) that according to the UAW constitution, a strike may only be called by a secret ballot two-thirds majority vote of the workers who will strike, and that the UAW does not levy fines for crossing a picket line. Manipulating the UAW's position in favor of reforming H-1B Visas (a visa program which grants temporary work visas for skilled workers to employers, instead of to workers themselves) administrators sought to portray the UAW as anti-immigrant—even though after 9/11 the UAW was at the forefront of fighting to protect student visas, and has repeatedly advocated general amnesty for immigrants and an expansion of the number of green cards. This was especially nasty because it played on the fears and insecurities of international students regarding visa status. Finally, administrators raised the specter of the UAW meddling in academic affairs. "A union could compromise the ability of graduate students to make important educational decisions by shifting responsibility for deciding what is best to professional union agents who are unfamiliar with our university," wrote University President George Rupp. But with a union, student employees—not "professional union agents"—would decide what to bargain over, sit at the table with the administration, and vote on the contract. At other schools, unions have bargained over stipends, health insurance and workload issues—not how many classes to take, what should be taught, or when graduate students should take their oral examinations.

The administration at Brown University, advised by another anti-union law firm, ran an anti-union campaign that was remarkably similar to that at Columbia (graduate students at Brown voted on unionization in December 2001). The values of truth and inquiry were repeatedly cited to defend the administration's "right" to spread outright distortions and inaccuracies. Graduate students at Brown received a letter written by a faculty member in the Linguistics department, saying that she believed the union would "encroach" on "the role and responsibility of the faculty to determine all aspects of the undergraduate curriculum—who teaches and what courses are taught at Brown." She also wrote that "Brown as a university-college prides itself on training its graduate students to be free and independent thinkers and to be individualists—as students, scholars and teachers." With a union negotiating over health insurance and wages, she envisioned a push towards a "one size fits all" standard, resulting in a "de-emphasis on individuality . . . [and] a negative impact on the imagination and creativity that defines the Brown experience." Brown president Ruth Simmons, the first black woman president of an Ivy League institution, also wrote an impassioned plea to the graduate students at Brown to vote no, asking for their "help" in making Brown better. Graduate students had asked Simmons to make sure that the administration and the faculty did not get involved in

the union campaign—protecting the right of graduate students to come to a decision without intimidation from the faculty and without aggressive propaganda from the administration. Simmons responded that this would "be completely contrary to everything for which Brown stands," and that "while comfort may be found in silence, truth cannot dwell there."

Administrators justified the anti-union campaigns at Brown and Columbia, using the rhetoric of free speech, intellectual discourse and thoughtful exchange.[1] The union, by contrast, was supposed to stifle originality and individuality, depriving students of their right to speak for themselves. Yet the fact is that there was nothing original about the anti-union campaigns at Columbia and Brown. Not only were they similar to one another, they echoed the arguments the universities used to fight the organization of clerical workers in the 1970s and 1980s. During the graduate union campaign, Columbia cited unions as perfectly acceptable for clerical workers—just not for students. But when Columbia's clericals started to organize in the 1970s, the university president wrote to them, "The traditional model of industrial labor-management relations does not work well in the university context." The university ran an anti-union campaign against the clerical workers that used many of the same tropes as that against the graduate employees, asking why a union of autoworkers would want to represent secretaries. But today, Columbia's clerical workers have been union members for nearly twenty years, and the school is no worse off—on the contrary, clerical workers are paid more, have better benefits and more stability than they ever did before the union.

Not all faculty members at either Brown or Columbia campaigned against the union. Many were openly pro-union, and others took a principled, neutral stance and simply did not talk to their students about the union. Regardless of their own ideas about unions, they were at least respectful of their students' abilities to make a choice for themselves. Why might faculty members have supported the union, given the dire picture painted by the administration? While Columbia administrators waxed eloquent about the ways that a union would hurt graduate education, they appeared blind to the many ways that graduate education currently suffers from inadequate funding and poor health coverage. They did not say anything about the fact that many graduate students must work outside of the university. They said not a word about the proliferation of adjuncts—even at Columbia—or about the rising number of post-docs in the sciences and the increasing difficulty of getting a full-time, tenure-track job. The hard fact is that many graduate students and professors alike today find themselves facing an academic environment that is in many ways hostile to the work that they most want to do. The real threat to the ability of academics at all levels to do their work in a reasonable, collegial environment is the disappearance of public funding for higher education, and the profit-mindedness of private universities that hire part-time workers without benefits to teach undergraduate courses—not the efforts of graduate students to organize unions.

Another troubling aspect of the Columbia anti-union campaign was the role that an anti-union student organization played in the campaign. Nominally, the group was independent of the university. But the Dean of the Graduate School of Arts and Sciences was present at two early meetings (as one of the group's leaders told the *Chronicle of Higher Education*) and the university's anti-union consultant was copied on various e-mails. For employers in general, instigating "vote no" committees (as they're called in the literature) is a time-honored anti-union tactic. In his book *Confessions of a Union-Buster*, Marty Levitt, who worked for many years as a professional anti-union consultant, writes of writes of carefully interviewing employees to determine their suitability for "vote no" committee, marshalling anti-union sentiment. Nathaniel Shefferman, the first professional anti-union consultant of the post-World War II period, wrote in a memo, "Your only hope is your own employees." On university campuses anti-union students are well-organized and becoming more so. Despite their claims to be ad hoc committees of concerned students at particular schools, anti-union student groups have shared advice with similar organizations on other campuses, sent members to campaign against unions at other schools and used similar posters and campaign strategies.

The anti-union student group at Columbia—which seemed to have a handful of members out of a population of nearly 2000—ran a campaign that explicitly brought out some of the themes the university had to raise sotto voce. Taxes, for example, were a central element of the student anti-union campaign. "Considered the tax effects?" one flyer read. "Currently, the university does not report your stipend to the IRS. You can make whatever deductions you think are fair without leaving a paper trail. Under a union, your stipend would go through payroll and start being reported." Aside from being false (the stipend is considered income by the Internal Revenue Service, so you can't make whatever deductions you want, and the university would not have to process the stipend differently because of a union), tax evasion is not the most principled reason to vote against a union.

The anti-union students also embraced the theme of apathy. On the one hand, the union was supposed to be tyrannical; on the other, it was too democratic. "Sick of all this union talk?" a flyer said. "If we vote to unionize, next we'll have to vote on our bargaining committee, on contracts, on whether to strike. It will never stop." "APATHETIC?" another asked. "A union will only empower you if you take the trouble to go to meetings, follow negotiations, know the terms of the contract." Like the administration, the

anti-union group also sought to depict the union as anti-immigrant. But the deepest message of the anti-union student group was elitism. Graduate students should not see themselves as employees or workers—it was demeaning to join a union. "Fight for your rights as a Graduate *Student*," said one poster. Another asked: "Where would you like to send YOUR children? Columbia College or United Auto Workers College?" It concluded, "Vote No! Keep Columbia Graduate Students free of labor unions!"

Anti-union students often justified their actions by arguing that the Columbia union drive was run from the outside, by a gigantic third party dominated by greedy bureaucrats from unpleasant parts of the country who just wanted to get their hands on union dues (which are 1.5 percent of annual salary). Pro-union students were naïve dupes, students hoodwinked by bright promises and leftist politics. But no union campaign could get far without a large core of graduate student employees who are willing to devote an enormous amount of their time and energy to organizing—who don't take pleasure in thinking of themselves as "apathetic," and who can handle a meeting or two. When anti-union student groups attacked the union, they were destroying something that their colleagues, not "outsiders," sought and struggled to create. At times, anti-union student groups have liked to portray themselves as brave individualists, the real rebels, standing up against a tidal wave of unionization. But in truth, regardless of their individual intentions, they are doing work of which authority figures like the anti-union deans and administrators deeply approve, while students who support the union and campaign for it publicly sometimes must place their careers on the line. Anti-union students, despite their self-image as iconoclasts, never have to take any such risks.

The anti-union campaigns at Columbia, Brown, Tufts and Penn received relatively little notice outside of each particular campus, yet they were key moments in the history of the university and campus activism. The basic principles of an anti-union campaign, in the university or elsewhere, are simple. Anti-union campaigns depend upon instilling a sense of doubt, insecurity and fear in the working population. They seek to destroy the sense of solidarity and common purpose that makes it possible to seek meaningful change. They tell workers that they are foolish to think that they can ever accomplish anything by joining together, that they have no choice but to rely on people in power over them.

But while the academic anti-union campaigns were very similar to those in industry, there is something especially poignant about universities running such campaigns against their own students. While claiming to protect the bond between student and teacher, university administrations encouraged teachers to use their influence to prevent students from winning higher pay and better benefits and exercising power in their jobs and school. Professors and advisors exercise real power over graduate students' future careers. Threats of their disfavor carry tremendous weight in the minds and lives of graduate students. Ideally, during graduate school, the student moves from being a subordinate, a junior colleague, of his or her advisor, to entering as an equal into a community of scholars. By making graduate students afraid of the professional repercussions of contradicting their advisors, the anti-union campaign at Columbia interfered with this important process of intellectual and personal maturation, one that is, at least in theory, central to the meaning and purpose of graduate school.

Universities are not alone in drawing upon fear to fight unionization—not only workers' fear of those in power over them, like supervisors or employers, but also the fear that the union will ultimately destroy a fragile, yet precious social good. Most corporate anti-union campaigns invoke values of family and community, emotional bonds of sentiment and intimacy that would be violated by the explosive force and conflict of the union. In the university, as well, people sometimes talked about the union as though it threatened to unleash a destructive rage that would leave nothing in its wake. It was as though the union would annihilate all the most precious aspects of academic life. The truth, however, is that the union is built upon nothing but its members' trust and solidarity with one another. The conflicts that it expresses are there already, even though they are often silent or suppressed. Yet at the same time, even though it gives voice to real problems, the union is not a destructive force—its power comes from solidarity, which is the opposite of nihilism.

What is more, just as the deep love of family and the bonds of genuine community are not casually built or easily kept, the intellectual and academic values that Columbia cited in its anti-union campaign are not to be taken for granted. Originality, free thought, and independent inquiry—these are all difficult aspirations, hardly encouraged by our society at large. The university, like most social institutions, contains within itself warring forces and different political strains—conformity and individualism, hierarchy and equality. In my experience as a graduate student organizer over the past three years at Columbia, the many student workers who have had the hope to build the union have embodied the most truly challenging dimensions of the university. Unlike the administrators who purchased an expensive anti-union campaign, they have had the courage of purpose to believe that the collective achievements of scholarship and education are worth protecting—and worth fighting for—even in an age that offers scant rewards for such strenuous ambitions.

Notes

I would like to thank Beverly Gage, Maida Rosenstein, Greg Vargo and Maggie Williams for their comments on this article. I would also like to express my deepest gratitude to the women and men of Graduate Student Employees United, Local 2110-UAW and the UAW International Union. However, the views and interpretations in this article are mine alone, and should not be seen as an official statement of GSEU or of the UAW. I would also like to thank the History Department for its support, and to express my appreciation to the History faculty and administrators for never allowing the administration's anti-union campaign to affect relationships between History students and faculty in a negative way. Finally, I would like to thank Greg Vargo, for everything.

1. Not all the anti-union campaigns have been so high-minded. At Cornell University, where the union drive was defeated in an election held in October 2002 (Cornell agreed to let the ballots be counted), one faculty member from the Chemistry department stood up in front of a meeting of Chemistry students to denounce the union as a bunch of "evil dudes." Even though there was a Cornell physics student present addressing the Chemistry students, the faculty member said, "These guys want to get the money out of your pockets and take it back to Motown…These are the bent-nosed mothers who probably took out Hoffa." He exhorted the Chemistry students to turn out the no vote: "Goddamn wake up and stop listening to this crap." The reasons for the union defeat at Cornell go beyond the scope of this article, but these kinds of aggressive attacks from faculty members played a role in the loss. Not only the United Auto Workers has been the subject of such campaigns. At the University of Pennsylvania, president Judith Rodin waged a similar anti-union campaign against an organizing drive in which graduate students sought to join the American Federation of Teachers.

CHAPTER 6

Where Have All the Politics Gone?
A Graduate Student's Reflections

JOHN McMILLIAN

"Can we please keep this list-serve free of all blatantly political announcements? Whether you want your Mumia freed or fried, I'd like to keep this list-serve relevant to issues specific to history graduate students."

This was the indignant response I provoked during my second year of graduate school at Columbia University, when I used a list-serve that is shared by history graduate students to announce an upcoming rally to protest the impending execution of Mumia Abu-Jamal, a former Black Panther whose case remains a cause célèbre among the far left.

Although I'm mindful of the fact that no one wants their e-mail account used as a dumping ground for unwanted messages, the sharp tone of his reply caught me off guard. For one, I was surprised and disappointed that one of my Columbia colleagues would speak about a person on death row as if he were a strip steak, just so he could make a lame witticism. But I was also bewildered at the assumption that fueled his message. People had long used this very same discussion list to sublet apartments, find homes for pets, and announce various parties, and no one had ever complained. Yet here it was being suggested that political announcements are so irrelevant that they should never even be mentioned on our list-serve.

I awaited the avalanche of sharp rebuttals that would soon begin to rain upon this poor students' head. Before long, I was sure my inbox would be spilling over with the replies of dozens of students who would capably defend their craft, avow their partisanship, and insist on the intrusion of politics into academic life. But as it turned out, only a couple of plucky students bothered to dispute his extreme position. And balanced against this, several others even offered support for the idea of banning political expression on our list-serve. It was a disappointing day.

One might think that history graduate students, who operate in a liberal profession, who are heirs to a rich legacy of social activism, and who often wrestle with difficult questions about the relationship between selfhood and historical consciousness, might be well-suited for political action. And in fact, we *have* seen a recent push in this direction, as pockets of grad students at Columbia and elsewhere have begun agitating for graduate student unions. But generally speaking, social activism does not seem to be a prevailing trend at Columbia or at many other graduate history departments. To the contrary, it appears that the bulk of history students today approach their scholarship with something approaching political indifference. Although I suspect most grad students vote, have good ideas, and stay well-informed, I know only a few who intend to enter the professional arena in a consciously political way, or who charge their research and writing with an explicitly political agenda.

To wit: In the five years that I lived in Morningside Heights, I can think of only two examples of formal cooperation among leftist history students. The first was a short-lived Marxist reading group, which was greeted with general bemusement and was killed by a lack of interest around the time students finished Part One of *Capital*. The other instance—a notable one— was the formation of Graduate Student-Employees United (GSEU), an organization of teaching and research assistants that arose in response to our exploitation as academic laborers. But as of this writing, it remains to be seen whether GSEU will regain its momentum after a period of relative inactivity brought on by the University's appeal of a recent National Labor Relations Board (NLRB) decision that paved the way for grad student unions at private universities.

It seems likely that the discouraging political climate among history graduate students owes much to larger social trends. So long as we operate outside the context of a rising social movement, it is probably fanciful to hope that we could redefine the prevailing relations between politics and scholarship. Meanwhile, the hyper-competitiveness of the job market, which on the one hand leads grad students to relate to their professors with timidity and caution, and at the same time sets students clawing against one another whenever a new job opening comes about, does not exactly encourage free-wheeling political engagement.

But this has not always been the case. As a historian of the New Left, I've lately been exploring some of the ways that grad students of the 1960s tried to connect their scholarship with a larger set of political ambitions. This work has invited some wistful thinking about how things *could be* if today's grad students were to generate some of the optimism, energy, and sense of purpose of an earlier time.

To be sure, leftwing academics of the 1960s sometimes faced an unhealthy pressure to write immediately relevant scholarship that could be deployed by organizers; Marx's Eleventh Thesis was frequently invoked, and pressing political exigencies sometimes drew intellectuals away from their study carrels and into the streets. Nevertheless, today the historical profession is flush with scholars who cut their political teeth in the 1960s, who anchored their radical commitments in intellectual activity, and who self-consciously set out to build a corpus of work that would set us upon a path toward meaningful social change. Paul Buhle, founding editor of the New Left journal *Radical America*, crystallized this sentiment when he coined the idea that he and his movement comrades were "writing love letters to the future." Through a serious-minded and patient commitment toward building a radical "house of theory," he suggested, New Left grad students and young professors might one day offer aid and comfort to the movement's heirs.[1]

In the process, budding scholars also found a useful way to enrich their graduate student experiences. In a 1969 letter, then-Columbia history student Mark Naison evoked this as well. "All last year," he wrote,

I felt exhilarated about doing historical research and writing for *Radical America* because I felt that people were sincerely interested in learning. I saw a role for myself as a historian in relation to a growing, healthy movement. . . . I felt genuinely liberated from deeply ingrained compulsions and ambitions. I felt my work was serving an important purpose, and therefore, had few pangs of guilt that I was not a complete activist.[2]

History graduate students at Columbia also had a "Committee for a Radical History." A humorous flyer announcing one of their meetings illustrates how the group literally blended political protest and street theater with academic study.

THE COMMITTEE FOR A RADICAL HISTORY
will not be meeting Tuesday, November 14, so that its members may attend the Foreign Policy Association dinner (black tie)—with its guest of honor Dean Rusk—which will be held at the New York Hilton . . .

On Tuesday, November 21, there will be an informal spaghetti dinner (red shirt) and discussion at 309 W. 106th St. Apt. 5C, at 6:30 PM. All history graduate students are invited to attend.[3]

Whereas many New Left activists took to the hustings, the scholar/ activists I've studied also ran elaborate speakers' bureaus, sponsored internal education meetings, communicated through mimeographed bulletins and journals, devised curricula for free universities, and in 1969 formed a radical history caucus that challenged the leadership and direction of the American Historical Association (AHA)—all driven by a missionary impulse to turn much of the reigning scholarship on its head.[4] As a result, whole new avenues of scholarly inquiry have opened up. Revisionist scholars began taking into account the lives of ordinary people—slaves and freedmen, indentured servants, housewives, workers, children, Native Americans, immigrants, gays and lesbians, and other Americans who had long been ignored. In addition to uncovering a broader range of experience, scholars also experimented with new interpretive paradigms. Thirty years ago it was rare for historians to showcase a sophisticated awareness of the ways that race, class, gender and sexuality have shaped the lives of Americans; today it is de rigueur. What's more, as a result of New Left activism, academic culture has been liberalized in countless salutary ways, and the historical profession is no longer quite the gentleman's club it used to be. It's probably safe to say that this reordering of the scholarly enterprise is recognized as a positive development by almost everyone to the left of Lynne Cheney.[5]

So, we can be grateful that a considerable number of former activists have won positions of power and prestige within the academy. But it may also be worth asking whether the institutionalization of these radical impulses has carried some costs as well. Certainly it was a grim sign of the times when, in 1998, Princeton historian Sean Wilentz proclaimed in *Lingua Franca* that a petition drive against Bill Clinton's impeachment, signed by some 400 historians, was "the most important academic political effort in the last thirty years."[6] Was this really something to boast about? What does it say about the current climate when a bunch of historians' signatures on a failed petition—on behalf of Bill Clinton, no less—is thought to constitute an important political movement?

In spite of the apathy I've just described, there are some signs that graduate students are ready to recall a more hopeful and energetic time. The academic labor movement seems critical. In recent years, students at several leading campuses have gone on strike, formed unions, and won encouraging victories in the struggle against the shameful labor practices of modern universities. As contributors to this volume have shown, there remain pockets around the country where graduate student radicalism "of the sort pioneered during the late 1960s" is "alive and kicking."[7]

According to a history grad student who joined the University of Illinois (UI) Graduate Employees' Organization (GEO), "the idea of a political community" was a major source of inspiration for graduate student organizers. "What really excited me about GEO," he recalled, "was that it could be a political community, and we would be able to work with other political groups on campus, and make this campus just a better place, a more politically charged place, and a more democratic place."[8] In addition to opening up new social vistas, some activists reported that their political efforts had a beneficent impact upon their scholarship. Said another history student, "It only enriches your academic work to be constantly thinking about the factors that shape what you can study, how you can study it, [and] what you write. . . . Being an activist and bringing these issues to bear . . . has only made my academic work better."[9]

But much work remains to be done. Unionized campuses are still the exception rather than the norm, and wherever teaching assistant unions *have* emerged, they have been opposed by counter groups of graduate students who—despite all evidence to the contrary—would rather think of themselves as apprentices in some sort of postmodern guild than as workers with federally protected rights. The apathy and false consciousness that afflicts most graduate history departments is still a big problem.

The good news is that a previous generation of scholars has left us with a rich set of values and actions—by no means unfailing or unflawed—that nevertheless speak to some of the ways that we might embark upon our professional goals with a greater sense of political mission. Furthermore, those intrepid students who *are* beginning to adopt some of these approaches are finding that activism and scholarship can complement each other in surprising and healthy ways.

If today's history graduate students truly want to imitate their professors—as frequently seems the case—then we might start by becoming more unabashedly political, by enlarging our notions of academic citizenship, and by looking for new ways to pursue the twin ideals of scholarship and social justice. Otherwise, a future historian who examines grad student culture at the dawn of the millennium may well overlook the efforts of a minority of activist students, and conclude that pets, apartments and parties were all more "relevant . . . issues specific to graduate students" than politics.

Notes

This chapter was originally printed, in slightly different form, in *The Radical Historians Newsletter*, no. 81, December, 1999.

1. See McMillian, John, "Love Letters to the Future: REP, *Radical America*, and New Left History," *Radical History Review* 77 (Spring 2000), 23.
2. Mark Naison to Paul Buhle (Fall, 1969). *Radical America* Papers, Box 2, Wisconsin State Historical Society.
3. Linebaugh, Peter, "From the Upper West Side to West Episcopi," *New Left Review* 201 (September/October, 1993), p. 21. On November 14, 1967, some 3000 people protested Sec. of State Rusk's appearance in New York City; 46 demonstrators were arrested. See "War Foes Clash with Police as Rusk Speaks," *New York Times* (November 15, 1967), 1.
4. See Bell, Robert A., "The Changing Voice of Left History: New Left Journals and Radical American History," (PhD diss., University of Waterloo, 1999).

5. According to Cheney, former head of the National Endowment for the Humanities, too many of today's academicians "paint a grim and gloomy picture of the American past, one that emphasizes failure and makes it seem that most of the faults of mankind have here found their most fertile ground." See Cheney, Lynne V., "Politics in the Classroom is Nothing New," posted Saturday, January 1, 2000 *Wall Street Journal* publication date: January3,1996. [www.aei.org/news/filter.all.newsID.6027/newsdetail.asp]
6. David Greenberg, "All the President's Men," *Lingua Franca* (April, 1999), 5.
7. Mattson, Kevin and Patrick Kavanagh, "Graduate Student Radicalism," *AHA Perspectives* (November, 1999).
8. Vaughn, William. "From Sociality to Responsibility: Graduate Employee Unions and the Meaning of the University," *AHA Perspectives* (November, 1999).
9. Ibid.

SECTION **III**
Historians for Social Justice

CHAPTER 7

The Glass Tower
Half Full or Half Empty?

NANCY A. HEWITT

I began my activist career in fall 1969, at the same time as my undergraduate career, and I almost immediately came to the conclusion that the two were incompatible. During my first year at Smith College I was introduced to the anti-war movement, the Black Power movement, and feminism. I had certainly heard of these movements and read about them in the newspapers, but I had never participated in them nor had any of my immediate friends or family members. What people in my hometown in western New York did participate in was the war in Vietnam itself. Close friends of mine from high school were serving as foot soldiers in that war, and they would come back with slides of their adventures and tell us how important a victory over the Communists would be to our future security. The young men I knew who served in Vietnam were not mean and vicious; they were patriotic and well-meaning and sometimes scared. I continued to write to them and to pray for them to make it home safely, even as I became more and more convinced that they, and we, were in Vietnam for all the wrong reasons. Coming to the realization that I opposed the war was painful, and finding out that much of the red, white and blue history I had grown up with was wrong, wrenched me into a new consciousness without ripping me apart from friends and family.

It was students just a year or two older than I was, but with much more political experience, who took me to my first demonstrations, discussed the Vietnam War and its history with me, and introduced me to ideas about women's liberation. Having grown up in a town where supporting Hubert

Humphrey for President in 1968 was viewed as radical, I simply had not thought in the terms familiar to women who were active in Students for a Democratic Society (SDS), who followed the trials of Bobby Seale and the Chicago Seven, accused of conspiring to incite a riot at the 1968 Democratic National Convention in Chicago, with intense interest, and who proclaimed themselves sexually liberated. The presence of President Richard Nixon's daughter Julie on campus—she was a senior when I was a freshman—heightened the politicization of the Smith campus. So, too, did the killing of students at Jackson State in Mississippi and at Kent State in Ohio in spring 1970, which led to student strikes on campus as it did elsewhere across the country.[1]

During my first two years at Smith, I learned the history of U.S. engagement in Southeast Asia, was introduced to regional networks of anti-war activists by one of my older (sophomore) classmates, Carolee Colter, and became a self-proclaimed radical feminist. I quit wearing make up and bras, stopped shaving my legs and curling my hair, traded in my brown plastic frames for wire rims, and exchanged my skirts and blouses for blue jeans and baggy sweaters. Both in and out of classes, I joined debates on United States policies past and present, not only involving Southeast Asia but also Native Americans, African Americans, workers, and women. During my second year at Smith, a friend and I got permission to teach an undergraduate course, under the guidance of a faculty sponsor, on the history and anthropology of Native Americans. I was also involved in a coup in which another young student and I took over leadership of our house, denying the presidency and vice-presidency to more moderate and respectable upper class students. Yet for all my activism on campus and off, I felt like I was wasting my time, picking my way through the detritus of a Seven Sisters' education to find a few sparkling shards of meaning. I dropped out of Smith College at the end of my second year to pursue a career as an activist.

Within a year of dropping out I was living in Rochester, New York, near where I grew up, and working sixty hours a week at minimum wage jobs—night shift at Dunkin' Donuts was the highpoint. I tried to participate at least from time to time in local anti-war and feminist activities, but I was exhausted most of the time. Fortunately, the State University of New York at Brockport ran an urban outreach program behind an office supply store where I worked in spring 1973, and as a result I got back into college. At Brockport State, I discovered Women's Studies and Women's History (neither of which existed when I attended Smith) and completed my BA eighteen months later. Two of my history professors suggested I apply to PhD programs and become a professional historian, but I was still ambivalent enough about academia to try another route first.

Like so many others of my generation, I moved to Berkeley (California). I worked as a volunteer at the Women's Herstory Archives while hoping to launch a career as a community organizer. It was in Oakland that I first came to grips with the difficulties of supporting oneself as an activist and with the fact that a feminist organization could have less than progressive class, racial and generational politics. Indeed, from my perspective, the Women's Herstory Archives did not even represent good gender politics. The director, Laura X, appeared to make decisions without any consultation with those of us working in the archives; the promised training in how to establish local women's centers was never forthcoming; and our attempt to organize for better pay (actually *any* pay) and improved working conditions, was summarily quashed. Having been chosen—by pulling straws—to present the workers' views to Laura X, I was summarily fired from my unpaid position and removed from the building. The others were allowed to stay on and received a minimal stipend for the duration of the project. This underside of activism—battles over scarce resources, petty personality conflicts, guilt trips in the name of feminism—lacerated my ideals and inspired me to take the Graduate Records Exam and apply to doctoral programs in History.

The university might be a tower, isolated in many ways from the daily struggles of the disenfranchised; but it was the one place where I had always been encouraged to think, to challenge others and myself, and to act on my beliefs. Perhaps it would provide me once again with a space to explore new forms of activism. When I left Smith, I thought of college as a glass half empty, offering an education far removed from the brutal realities of everyday life. After my time at Brockport State, I hoped instead that it might be at least half full, providing me with opportunities to use my education to reach a wider community. Certainly in comparison to my experience in Berkeley, the glass tower seemed a better bet for me than the one other form of feminist institution building I had encountered.

Both when I applied to graduate school and during my six years in the PhD program at the University of Pennsylvania, I pursued research on women's activism and stayed minimally involved in political activities around feminist issues, local elections, and protests against police brutality (which were frequent in Philadelphia in the 1970s). A group of graduate students worked as volunteers at the Well Red Book Room, a lefty institution in West Philadelphia; and we met monthly to discuss the latest political debates among scholar-activists. A number of us also took teaching seriously as a political act and worked collectively to hone our classroom techniques and develop innovative ways to challenge students who sometimes seemed all too complacent. At Penn, my glass was overflowing intellectually, politically and personally. I felt like I had found a home, if only the kind of temporary residence that graduate school offers. What is more, I assumed that once I received my PhD and got a job, I would have more time for activism beyond the university. It seemed clear in 1980 that women's history and women's studies would remain marginal to the main purposes of academic institutions, thus allowing those of us teaching in these fields to have closer ties to the community than the university.

I thought, in fact, that it would be relatively easy to combine writing, teaching, and activism. I was writing about antebellum women's activism, including first wave feminism, specifically as a means of broadening the legacies on which contemporary feminists could draw. I certainly viewed teaching women's history and race, class and gender-conscious American history, as political work. But I also assumed that, whatever city I ended up in, I would get involved in grassroots feminist politics.

I was fortunate to get my first tenure-track job at the University of South Florida in 1981. There was a very active and activist faculty there, especially in the History Department. I was encouraged to develop an array of courses in women's history, and to teach at least one every semester. During my first several years at USF, both before and after tenure, I participated in and helped to organize teach-ins and protests related to U.S. policies in Central America, apartheid and divestment, U.S. militarism, and the (first) Gulf War. A group of faculty from History, Theatre, Women's Studies, International Relations, Anthropology, and Internal Medicine served as the steering committee for these events, working alongside student activists and with the support of the local community radio station, WMNF. I also joined a socialist-feminist reading group—we called ourselves Lust for Theory, after a *Socialist Review* cartoon from the early 1980s. That group included long-time activists from Tampa who were involved primarily in self-help health movements and programs to assist/empower abused women. At the same time, teaching in a state university that attracted many first-generation college students, I felt that what happened in my classes made a significant difference in many undergraduates' lives. Indeed, sometimes it seemed to make too much difference. When students came to me announcing they were contemplating a divorce or seeking words of wisdom after being sexually assaulted or anticipating that I was a lesbian and about to come out of the closet, I felt inadequate to the expectations I had set for them and myself. Fortunately, there were services available for most of these women in Tampa at the time, some at USF and some in the larger community and almost all initiated by local feminists. For a few years, it seemed like I had achieved some miraculous balance among teaching, research and activism. For alongside classes and campus and community activism, I had managed to write and publish three articles and a book and received tenure and promotion a full year ahead of schedule. The glass was not only full; it was running over. In fact, it was about to tip over.

What I had not prepared for, what most young women's history and women's studies faculty—and the vast majority of us were young—had not prepared for, was the incredible expansion of these fields in the 1980s and 1990s. Nor were we prepared for colleges and universities to respond so quickly to feminist demands for inclusion and change. The generation of feminist faculty just before mine had begun demanding courses, programs, changes in hiring and promotion practices; access to department, university, and professional committees and conferences; and institutional policies that promoted sex and race equity. We joined those campaigns, and they were enormously successful, indeed more successful in the university and in professional associations than in many other arenas in that period. We were thrilled with our achievements, but we rarely considered the toll it would take, or the ways it would channel our activism over the next twenty years.

At least by the mid-1980s, and earlier in some institutions, our claims for courses, programs, and departments in women's history and women's studies were heeded; our efforts to gain increased representation on department, university and professional committees and on editorial boards and at professional conferences succeeded; our demands that universities develop and implement affirmative action, sexual harassment, maternal (later parental) leave, and partner benefits resulted in significant changes at many institutions. Meanwhile, publishers who were once concerned that there wouldn't be a market for our books, started begging us for monographs, textbooks, readers, document collections, and anthologies. At the same time, our efforts to transform teaching via feminist pedagogy transformed classroom cultures and raised expectations about the kinds of support we would provide undergraduate and graduate students. And graduate students, new PhDs and new assistant professors in women's history and women's studies started pouring into colleges and universities. They all needed advisors, directors, mentors, letters of recommendation, readers for article and book manuscripts, and evaluations for tenure and promotion.

The incredible growth of women's history and women's studies and the increased institutional and legal sensitivity to gender issues changed my relationship to activism and that of many of my colleagues. Though we sometimes worried that the glass tower was still half empty, or had a false bottom, in terms of the demands on our time, we could not seem to keep it filled. In my first six years at University of South Florida, for instance, I served on three department search committees; served on and then chaired the university-wide Status of Women Committee; helped to write the university's sexual harassment guidelines; and, the year I received tenure, chaired the University Sexual Harassment Committee. Many of my male colleagues at South Florida, although not by and large those in the History Department, now saw me as wielding a bit more power than they had imagined or desired. But if the sexual harassment guidelines were my primary weapon, I was fighting with a glass sword: it looked fierce, but did not always fare that well in battle. And I had other battles to fight as well. In the same period, I served on the University's Affirmative Action Committee and the Women's Studies Council, gave talks to a variety of local women's organizations, participated in outreach programs for the Florida Humanities Council, and counseled students (for better and worse) on a range of issues from abortion to rape to divorce to sexual harassment. Still, I was fortunate. My senior colleagues, all men, were supportive; my first editor, Larry Malley at Cornell University Press, was a godsend; and the college administration, although problematic in many ways, allowed me to be tenured and promoted early.

Yet, I felt constantly poked and prodded by slivers of guilt over what I was not doing. Suddenly all the time that I might have devoted to community-based projects was being absorbed by university and professional projects. My experience at USF was not unique. Colleges, universities and historical associations all formed women's committees; many universities and departments sought to assure that at least one woman served on every hiring committee; program committees tried to create more gender-integrated panels at conferences; and editors recruited women and women's historians to serve on their boards. At the same time, the organizations initiated by women in the 1970s to put pressure on professional associations, like the Coordinating Committee for Women in the Historical Profession (CCWHP) and the Conference Group in Women's History (CGWH) continued on, to make sure that our agendas did not get co-opted once women were let into the organizational hierarchy. In addition, new women's studies programs and departments needed faculty to teach courses, serve on committees, and organize events on and off campus. When colleges and universities started writing sexual harassment guidelines, creating women's centers, establishing various kinds of grievance committees, diversity workshops, and curriculum integration projects, women, especially those whose research focused on women, were called on to provide the necessary expertise. I joined other feminist scholars in pushing the profession forward, serving on program committees, editorial boards, nominating committees, book and article prize committees; running curriculum integration workshops; participating in outreach programs to middle school and high school teachers; and working with public humanities programs and museums to increase awareness of women's history. I had only been in the profession for six years when I became U.S. editor of a new journal, *Gender & History,* launched in Great Britain. Within a decade, I was president of the CGWH and five years later vice-president of the International Federation for Research in Women's History. It was both exhilarating and exhausting to have such opportunities offered so early in my career, a career in which I thought I could remain on the margins of academe.

In 1992, I moved to Duke University and became a full professor. There the demands of campus and professional committees as well as journals, publishers and external organizations—foundations, funding agencies, etc—became even greater. My fancier letterhead assured that I would be asked to evaluate far more tenure and promotion cases for younger scholars in the field, who seemed to be multiplying exponentially. When the Duke Committee on the Sexual Harassment of Students faced a crisis in 1993, the provost asked me to step into chair the committee. I felt I could not refuse. Women's Studies and Women's History were more high profile at Duke than at USF, and this too created more administrative work and more complicated political divisions and personal conflicts. I was soon serving on the executive committee of both departments and as Associate Chair of History. In addition, the doctoral program at Duke was attracting a growing number of students in women's history, African American history and American social history.

There were benefits to being at a resource-rich institution, of course, and not only in terms of my own salary and research funds. Duke was endowed with beautiful grounds and offered abundant financial and intellectual resources for a variety of projects. Amazing faculty at Duke and neighboring institutions, most notably University of North Carolina, Chapel Hill, provided a new circle of colleagues whom I could join in political and scholarly ventures. The Southern Oral History Project at UNC, directed by Jacquelyn Dowd Hall, and the Behind the Veil Project on the Jim Crow South at Duke, managed by a team of faculty and graduate students, reached well beyond traditional academic endeavors to document issues in communities throughout the region. As a Duke faculty member, I was able to apply for Sawyer Seminar funds from the Andrew Mellon Foundation, which I was granted in 1995–1996, to run a year-long seminar that brought together activists, scholars of activism, and scholar-activists concerned with women's grassroots organizing. Graduate students Anne Valk and Kirsten Delegard along with members of the UNC Oral History Project and the Duke Institute of Public Policy helped plan and orchestrate events that year; and the outside speakers who joined us from Rwanda, Haiti, Zaire, Mexico and various parts of the United States were uniformly inspiring.

Still, much more than I had ever imagined, my activism has become university, rather than community, based. Without release time to direct the seminar and the lecture series that accompanied it, I was working harder than ever to balance teaching, including an increasing number of dissertation committees, administrative responsibilities, and professional service. I had almost no time to pursue my own research and writing, even though I was now at a major research university, or to engage directly in community-based activities.

Moreover, nagging institutional questions remained. Duke was filled with brilliant scholars, bright students, and vast resources, but the university struggled to claim an identity. Was it the Harvard of the South? Could it be? Should it be? Did I care? Was Duke a haven of racial toleration and diversity despite its southern heritage and the legacies of past discriminations? Could it serve the surrounding city, which was both darker and poorer than the university community? And what of all the local residents who worked at Duke but did not feel part of that community? Was it possible to teach inside those privileged walls—and there were literally walls around Duke's East Campus, where the History and Women's Studies departments re-sided—and still feel connected to a larger world of activism? Was being active within Duke enough?

I had a chance to step back from this swirl of issues and refocus attention on my own research through the gift of a fellowship from the Center for the Advanced Study in Social and Behavioral Sciences at Stanford University. For more than a decade I had been working on a book on Anglo, Black and Latin women's activism in Tampa, Florida, reshaping the arguments and interpretations to engage changes in the field of women's history. During the 1980s, attention to differences of race, class and region had transformed frameworks of analysis in women's history and women's studies. A study of community-based movements that explored women's efforts within and between native-born white and African American and racially and ethnically diverse immigrant neighborhoods in a single city promised to enrich our understanding of how activists forged identities, agendas and coalitions over time and across racial, ethnic and gender divides. It was work that I hoped would have some practical appeal, or at least application, to activists outside the academy as well as contribute to the ways scholars themselves analyzed activism historically. I was particularly concerned with trying to reimagine U.S. women's activism in more global terms while recognizing the racial, ethnic and class conflicts that fractured any sense of sisterhood within the United States.

When I returned to Duke in fall 1997, my energy for and interest in combining activism and academic life had been revitalized. Yet I quickly found both slipping away again. A series of battles in both History and Women's Studies over future directions and priorities absorbed enormous amounts of time and effort. I was swamped with graduate students, many of them unhappy with various aspects of the PhD program; and I wavered between supporting their demands and wanting them to focus simply on research, writing and completing their dissertations. My activist commitments and my scholarly engagement were already bleeding away, and I had only been back at Duke for three months.

When my husband Steven Lawson and I were recruited by Rutgers University that winter, we agonized over what to do and survived a tortuous process of offer and counter-offer. Despite the difficulties of that year, the decision to move to Rutgers in fall 1998 saved me. It brought me back to the public university system that nurtured me and that still gives me hope that activism and academics can be fruitfully combined. At Rutgers, a number of programs are focused on just the kinds of issues that have long intrigued me. The Rutgers Center for Historical Analysis sponsors not only academic programs but also teachers' institutes. The Institute for Research on Women, part of an expansive Institute for Women's Leadership (IWL), runs year-long seminars on themes that bridge not only disciplines but also the academic-community divide. Other units in the IWL, most notably the Center for Women and Global Leadership and the Institute for Women and Work, address contemporary social, economic and political issues through the resources of scholarship and intellectual exchange. The History Department also houses one of the top ranked women's history doctoral programs in the nation, a program that encourages attention to racial and global issues in the context of women and gender. And I am once again surrounded by students for whom an undergraduate education is not a given, but something to be prized. Of course, this does not mean that they are all dedicated to learning, but rather that far more than at Duke, I feel that the classroom is a political space, one where students' lives are being challenged and shaped in critical ways. Perhaps most important to me, there are students who remind me of myself in the 1960s and 1970s, young women and a few good men searching for ways not only to forward their careers but to change the world, or at least their little corner of it.

It is still difficult to balance pedagogy, politics, and publications, I am still over committed on campus and in the profession, but at Rutgers it seems possible to slowly divest myself of some of that institutional responsibility because there are so many other wonderful senior and junior women to share the burden. In addition, the intellectual opportunities at Rutgers are so rich that it has been easier to say no to requests for service on editorial boards, professional committees, and other outside invitations. Instead I can focus my attention on Rutgers University Press, on the Rutgers' Black Atlantic Project, on Rutgers' Institute for Research on Women, and on Rutgers' women's history program. Although this is still not quite the career I had imagined—still too heavy on institutional commitments and too light on community-based activism—I have finally found a situation in which I can make peace between my expectations and the possibilities surrounding me.

Like so many of my generation, I have tried to take advantage of the openings that exist without getting co-opted by the institutional structures from which they unexpectedly emerged. I still live in a glass tower, but one from which I can more clearly see the connections to a wider world. There is still plenty of broken glass out there, awaiting a misstep. For the moment, however, I am picking my way through and finding safe spaces to work.

Note

1. I once assumed that I, like many white students, had only paid attention to the killings at Kent State, but in a letter to my home town newspaper, the *Spencerport Star*, which I discovered a few years ago, I protested the shootings at Jackson State and Kent State with equal fervor.

Toxic Torts
Historians in the Courtroom

DAVID ROSNER

During the past number of years, historians have been brought into legal cases in unprecedented numbers. As the courts have tried to adjudicate responsibility for environmental and occupational diseases, history has played a more and more central role in decisions that affect the cases themselves and social policy regarding risk.

In suits over tobacco-related diseases, asbestosis, radiation experiments, and other toxic tort situations, more and more historians of technology and sciences, social history and public health are being brought to provide testimony aimed at assessing responsibility for risk for a variety of nasty diseases and conditions that have arisen years, sometimes decades, after exposure. The basic questions asked are those we became familiar with during the Watergate hearings: who knew what about specific toxins and when did they know it? Did industry understand that specific substances could cause disease? If so, when did they learn of the dangers and when did they begin to warn their workers or consumers of their products that they were at risk?

This chapter will look at the recent recruitment of historians into the world of toxic tort law and examine the ways that the craft of history is used and abused in the legal system, and will identify the important ways that historians' skills can be used on behalf of people victimized by a variety of industries as well as the ways that these same skills can be abused in order to defend the activities of huge corporations. I do not intend to provide a dispassionate analysis of the moral, ethical and legal dilemmas that confront the historian when she or he enters the courtroom. Nor do I mean to enter into a discussion of the problem of historical ambiguity and objectivity. Rather, I will provide a personal perspective on the growing gulf that will undoubtedly deepen among historians as the public agues over culpability for a variety of problems associated with the development of an industrial and post industrial economy. I will describe a personal experience where skills as an historian help in making important societal decisions. In the past, historians have been brought in to provide evidence in *Brown v. Board of Education*, the *Sears* case and other important issues. But, as Americans become more aware of industrial pollution and its impact on population health, I predict that the historians' role will become more and more pronounced.

The courts are both an important and troubling arena into which historians are being thrust. On the one hand, it is clear that unlike any other arena in which the academic historian functions, the information that we can provide can help thousands upon thousands of sickened people. We can help workers whose health was destroyed on the job, children brain damaged by lead paint and other toxins, and ordinary citizens living in polluted communities from Love Canal, New York through Times Beach, Missouri, to recover damages for their suffering. Further, we can even help shape future decisions of large corporations who are currently deciding on whether or not to look closely at the potential dangers of their products and, if found toxic, whether or not to warn consumers or remove them from the market.

While the ability to help people is well within the grasp of the practicing historian, there is also the possibility of doing tremendous harm. Throughout the nation, toxic tort cases are forcing companies and their lawyers to seek out their own historians to argue that companies bear no responsibility for a host of conditions that appear associated with exposure to implants, asbestos, pharmaceuticals and the like. The tobacco, mining, paint, plastics, and chemical industries have begun efforts to hire historians to use their skills to obscure and to confuse the historical record about responsibility, knowledge, and risk. In some sense, the role of historians of medicine and science has been to create confusion rather than to illuminate history. Some historians have earned literally millions of dollars to defend the tobacco companies from litigation; others have earned equally as large amounts preparing defenses of industries ranging from lead paint manufacturing through plastics and environmental pollution.

Why Historians in the Courtroom?

The origins of historians' role in these cases are rooted in the fundamental transformation of Americans' health beliefs during the course of the past

half century. For much of the first fifty years of the twentieth century the dominant concerns of most Americans were a series of diseases that could be linked directly to specific bacteria or viruses, or, alternatively, for the industrial worker, to specific acute exposures to a toxin. Generally, the symptoms that affected the individual were acute and specific agents—whether bacteriological or chemical—which could be identified in the laboratory using increasingly sophisticated technologies. Tuberculosis, for example, could be understood to be *caused* by a bacterium while the palsies, tremors, or wrist-drop of an industrial worker could be identified as *caused* by exposure to lead in a battery plant or other industrial setting.

But, during the course of the twentieth century, basic public health measures like improved sanitation, pure water supply, street cleaning, and nutrition, among others, began to have a dramatic impact on the health of Americans. Lower rates of infant mortality, longer life spans, and a decline in the importance of infectious disease as a cause of death fundamentally altered the epidemiological experience. Further, with the development of first sulfa drugs, antibiotics, and effective vaccines against polio and other childhood diseases in the middle decades of the century, many Americans believed that the dangers from infectious diseases specifically was passing. Chronic conditions such as heart disease, cancer, and stroke replaced tuberculosis and other infectious diseases as the major killers of Americans. By the 1970s, many in the public health community were seeking a different model for understanding what caused chronic disease.

The advent of a vibrant environmental movement fed a new paradigm for understanding disease. Chronic conditions were increasingly seen as being rooted in the industrial world in which Americans now lived. The emergence of the country as the predominant world economic and military power in the years after World War II fed a growing uneasiness. For some in the public health community, disease was increasingly perceived as a signal of the inequalities and injustices brought about by rampant commercialization of medicine, the poor distribution of services, and the greed of what some deemed the medical-industrial complex.

In the late 1970s and 1980s, disastrous examples of the impact of industry on the quality of life and the health of populations brought to national attention the negative impacts of industrial society on American health. Homes in Love Canal, New York, a community just outside of Buffalo, was found to be polluted by the waste products of the Hooker Chemical Company. A whole community of lower middle class homeowners had to leave their homes as the contents of leaking barrels and waste pits upon which their houses were built slowly bubbled up into basements and the backyards of residents; at Three Mile Island, Pennsylvania, a nuclear plant nearly went into meltdown just at the time when a film called the "China Syndrome" made Americans all-too-aware of the pitfalls of nuclear energy. In Times

Beach, Missouri an entire community was evacuated and huge areas of the town were roped off after it was discovered that dioxins and PCBs, known human carcinogens, had been polluting the streets of the town. In Bhopal, India, as well, thousands of poor people were killed, blinded and maimed by an explosion of a Union Carbide plant. Unlike the infectious diseases of previous eras—or even AIDS, SARS, and anthrax of the more recent past—the chronic diseases that frightened most Americans could not easily be linked to a specific exposure to a specific biological agent. Rather, the existing models for disease causation could only inexactly explain the complex pathways and mechanisms that led to a cancer years and often decades after exposure.

The growing awareness of the dangers of industrial pollution and industrial products more generally, have fed a widespread sense that the killer diseases that are of greatest concern—cancers—were produced by a variety of consumer goods that were now a mainstay of American life. Cigarettes, plastic bottles, corporate promotion of fatty foods and sugar-laden soft drinks to name but a few were no longer seen as symbols of the good life, but were now increasingly seen as responsible for the epidemics of lung cancers, heart disease, diabetes, obesity, and other chronic conditions. Increasingly, more and more people argued that the ways we die and the diseases that afflict us are, in large measure, reflections of the world we build and the environments we create. Whether it be the slums and crowded housing of the nineteenth century that led to the massive outbreaks of infectious diseases and tuberculosis or the environmental assaults or industrial toxins that are now associated with the cancers and other chronic diseases that are major killers today, disease and the ways we deal with it can be understood as a reflection of social organization, values and ideals.

It is here that historians have become central to the on-going legal and political struggles. Given our skills tracking down specific historical events we have been placed in the unenviable position of judging decisions of corporate executives whose actions led to the death, illnesses and disfigurements of smokers, workers, women in the home, African Americans living near toxic waste sites and children poisoned by exposures to everyday materials such as lead-based paint in the home or chromates in schools.

Gerald Markowitz and I were pulled into the contentious world of tort law because of a book we wrote approximately twelve years ago, *Deadly Dust: Silicosis and the Politics of Occupational Disease in 20th Century America* (Princeton University Press, 1991). As historians of occupational disease, we had stumbled onto silicosis, a disabling lung condition caused by the inhalation of silica dust, and that had struck down thousands of workers in the decades before World War II, being labeled "the king of occupational diseases" by commentators at the time. We had written the book with no knowledge that the disease was still of great concern, seeing the book as an exercise that could illuminate the ways that discovery of disease was rooted in very special historical circumstances. Interestingly, we had traced the heated debates around silicosis that occurred among workers, organized labor, government and a series of industries such as foundries, steel mills, construction, and sandblasting in which silica sand was used and workers exposed. Shortly after the publication of the book we learned from our publisher that the hardcover version of the book was in short supply and that they were considering a paperback edition. How, we asked, could such a book with a seemingly select audience be out of stock so quickly?

After quick investigation, the press discovered that, contrary to our assumption, the book was not being bought by large numbers of labor or other historians but, rather, by law firms. Soon, we found ourselves being called by law firms all over the country asking for us to consult with them about their cases. It appeared that workers in a host of industries, primarily in Texas, Louisiana, and other Gulf states were still coming down with silicosis and were suing a variety of suppliers for negligence.

At first, we were hesitant to get involved. It seemed repellent to us to testify in court, appear at depositions, and subject ourselves to possible pressures to meet the demands of court cases. We were scholars, not interested parties, removed from the events of the day by training and inclination, and scholars were not in the business of testifying, at least in court. Memories of the contentiousness that affected the historical profession following the engagement of two of our friends on different sides of the Sears case in the 1980s made us especially wary of getting involved.

Yet, after one lawyer came to New York and presented the haunting story of one of her clients, we changed our minds. She told of her client, a thirty-four year old Mexican worker who had been told of a lucrative job in the oil fields of West Texas. A huge oil company had contracted to have sandblasters come clean out old oil storage tanks in the 1970s, following the OPEC oil crisis when West Texas crude was once again in demand. They had shipped hundreds of Mexican workers to the area around Odessa, Texas and given them paper 3-M masks, which are ineffective in stopping silica particles from getting to the lungs, and a sandblasting unit, and had them enter into small enclosed tanks and blast sand at the layers of tar and oil that had accumulated on the tanks over the previous years and decades. Not surprisingly workers began to die, suffocating.

The cases, it appeared, would never have come to light was it not for the decision of a local physician to find out why so many of the migrant workers he was seeing were dying from a lung condition whose symptoms mimicked tuberculosis. Workers were coming to him as perhaps the only physician in town willing to see them, complaining of an inability to take in a deep breath, spitting, weight loss, and extreme fatigue. Some of the workers told him of other friends of theirs who had gone back to Mexico to die slow, horrible deaths at home. Others simply succumbed in Odessa.

It was clear why our book could be so important in providing some of these workers and their families some financial relief. In court case after case industry had been arguing successfully that since *no one* had ever heard of silicosis, *no one* could be held accountable for a disease that was unexpectedly killing workers. Our book was a direct contradiction to the central tenet of these defense tactics: we documented in minute detail what was known about the disease and the industry's attempts to hide silicosis from public view. We documented knowledge as early as 1900 and the industry's malfeasance from the 1930s and 1940s as they attempted to avoid responsibility for workers who were dying from exposures to silica. We agreed to become expert witnesses in two cases.

I will never forget my first deposition when I entered a room of over twenty lawyers representing some of the largest corporations in the country. Held at the Plaza Hotel in New York, I walked into the depositions thinking that this would be something akin to a seminar where I provided information and serious people debated academic issues. I couldn't imagine this "seminar" lasting more than a few hours. Nor could I imagine the grilling that I would go through for nearly five solid days from nine in the morning to five at night. For five days each company lawyer went after virtually every aspect of the book, from its footnotes through its index and pagination. What were my sources for the statement on page 45? Can I provide the document that was the basis for the statement on page 125? Was one reference to a point enough to *prove* that this quote represented a fair cross-section of the population? What were my credentials? How did Jerry and I work together? Did we walk to work together? Where did I live? What languages were spoken in my neighborhood?

Virtually no aspect of my academic life or my personal life was off-bounds in the free-for-all that seemed to have no end. As the deposition went on I realized the enormous stakes that were involved. A score of companies faced by potentially thousands of lawsuits had hired lawyers to undermine my credibility, lest I ever get to the witness stand and be able to speak to a jury. I also began to understand the stakes involved for the families, many of whom had no source of income to replace the meager wages that their husbands had earned while working themselves to death.

About a year later I was finally called upon to testify in that case. In the courtroom sat the worker and his family—he attached to an air hose connected to a portable air tank and his wife and children surrounding him. I was on the stand for the entire morning. Numerous objections and challenges were made by the defense attorney as he sought to undermine my book and my statements on behalf of the client. Comments I had casually said during the deposition were read to the jury as if they were the whole truth, with no subtlety or context. Sentences were picked out of long monologues that I had given in my attempts to answer complex questions with answers longer than "yes" or "no." It was a strange experience.

It was gratifying that by lunchtime, my testimony seemed to have made a deep impression on some of the company lawyers. Most of the defendants came slowly to the plaintiff's table and sought to settle their responsibility for damages, opting to pay something to the client rather than risk a jury verdict that might cost them much, much more.

It was a victory of sorts, but for me, the most meaningful moment came during a recess when I had the chance to speak with the defendant and his family. He told me of his life, his family and his children. His wife invited me to dinner at their home. It was clear that my testimony on their behalf was extremely important to the children who kept thanking me for coming to Texas for their father. They had translated for him throughout my testimony and they conveyed to me his deep gratitude. I had affirmed his experience and let his own family know that his experience was meaningful. This alone, it seemed, was worth the extraordinary pain that the day in court had cost him. I can't convey how moving this experience was for me. It made me realize that history does matter.

That first experience was searing for me. But, in coming years I found that I became less and less fearful of the deposition and courtroom process and more and more convinced that Jerry's and my own particular skill in writing history was making a real difference for many people throughout the country. One manifestation of this was in the strange transformation of defense arguments in some of the court cases in coming years. Before our book appeared, and before we entered into the suits, a standard argument of defendants in such silicosis suits was that they bore no responsibility for the outbreaks of silicosis because *no one* had known about the dangers of silica dust. Following our book, the argument changed substantially. A new defense was that the companies bore no responsibility because *everyone*, including the workers, knew about the disease. Hence, there had been no need to warn workers about exposure and no responsibility was borne by the company for their failure to warn workers about the dangers of silica dust.

Another singularly interesting and rewarding turn of events was the public rediscovery of the disease by the United States Department of Labor's Occupational Safety and Health Administration, and Mine Safety and Health Administration and the National Institute of Occupational Safety and Health. In 1997 we were invited to a National Silicosis Conference organized by these three agencies and shortly afterward Robert Reich, the Secretary of Labor, announced that silicosis was a target disease for the Administration who sought to eliminate it by the turn of the new century. Finally, after decades of stalling, in-door sandblasting (a practice that we had identified in our book as having been of particular concern) has largely been abandoned. We began to realize that there was a world that appreciated history for the ways it could really help people.

While our book on silicosis preceded our experience with the legal system, our next book on industrial pollution grew out of another law case. In 1996 we were called by two lawyers from the City of New York Law Department. The City's lawyers asked if we would visit them at their offices in lower Manhattan. It appeared that the City had been sued by some families whose children had been damaged by lead contained in the paint of some of the city's public housing. The city, in turn, had begun a suit against the lead industry claiming that the industry bore some responsibility for damages to these children. In the process of seven years of the suit, the City had accumulated a moderate-sized roomful of documents that were largely drawn from the Lead Industries Association, the trade association for lead paint and other manufacturers of lead-bearing products, and now they wanted to know what was in these hundreds of thousands of pages that the City had accumulated.

They had contacted us because we had published an article on the controversies around lead poisoning in the *American Journal of Public Health* in 1986. In that article we traced the history of the controversies around lead poisoning due to automobile exhaust. Coming as it did as the Environmental Protection Administration was determining whether or not to demand that the industry remove lead from gasoline once and for all, the article caused a bit of a stir in the public health community, even provoking an editorial from the *Journal* apologizing for its role nearly fifty years before in creating such a public health tragedy.

We were asked to evaluate the material in the room and we went about, with the aid of two Columbia students, to organize the material. The result was a long affidavit that became part of the New York City case and quickly was integrated into numerous other legal actions that began around the country. By the end of 2002, the cities of Chicago, New York, Buffalo, San Francisco, St. Louis, Milwaukee, and others had begun cases around the country, some of which were quickly dismissed by judges, some of which have been allowed to go forward. In Rhode Island, the State Attorney General has brought the first state action against the lead industry for having knowingly created a public nuisance in the form of hundreds of tons of lead on the walls of the up to 80 percent of the state's housing, thereby putting thousands of children in the state at risk of developing lead poisoning. This particular case is gaining national attention, with articles quoting our work appearing in *Barron's*, *Newsweek*, the *New York Times* and elsewhere.

Throughout the country lawyers are waiting for its outcome in the coming months. Significantly, the historical analysis that we developed is being challenged by the lead industry's lawyers and historians of medicine are being recruited to testify against us.

From our work in the archives of the city's law department came our book, *Deceit and Denial: the Deadly Politics of Industrial Pollution* (California/Milbank, 2002). This book, an analysis of the role of industry in creating a public health tragedy, could not have been possible without the law cases which freed up literally hundreds of thousands of pages of company documents. In fact, without the cases historians would never have seen internal memos and minutes of meetings in which the company representatives from the Dutch Boy or Sherwin Williams companies discussed the dangers of leaded paint to children as early as the 1920s. Nor would we have been able to learn of marketing campaigns aimed at counteracting public concerns over the dangers of lead—ads that claimed that lead paint was safe and sanitary and useful on children's walls, furniture and the like. This trove of documents, revealed through the lawsuits, allowed us to write a history that was based upon internal documents never before seen and it certainly gave us a new perspective on company responsibility for damage to hundreds of thousands of poisoned children.

In a number of other toxic tort cases historians are being called upon to study the responsibility of industry in causing disease and death. Allan Brandt at Harvard is working for the federal government on a suit against a tobacco company. Robert Proctor has been working on the same suit and has, in the past, worked for women damaged by radiation experiments at Vanderbilt University. David Rothman has worked on the Vanderbilt case as well. Industrial hygienists David Ozonoff and Barry Castleman have weighed in on behalf of workers injured by exposure to asbestos, developing sensitive historical arguments about culpability of Johns Manville and other asbestos manufacturers. All have gone through their own internal decision making process in deciding whether or not to work for those injured by industries, institutions or products. All have determined in one way or another that using their skills for a social good was important and made their history more meaningful.

While many historians have decided to enter the fray on behalf of injured parties, others have been hired by the tobacco, lead, and other industries as experts to defend the actions of a variety of companies. Rather than using their skills to try to clarify the historical record, however, these historians have often sought to contextualize past unseemly activities in which tobacco, lead and other toxins were marketed directly to children or knowingly sold, despite industry knowledge about their dangers. Kenneth Ludmerer, the current president of the American Association for the History of Medicine, and Peter English, a professor of history and pediatrics from Duke University, and a number of others have used their expertise and prestige on behalf of lead and tobacco. Other less prominent historians have chosen to work for the industries in a host of other toxic tort suits.

The growing concerns about the price we pay in health and well being for our unrestrained industrial and post-industrial society has created new arenas in which history will play a growing and important role. Especially as the current administration undercuts the regulatory agencies of OSHA, MSHA, EPA and others that have since the 1970s ameliorated some of the worst conditions affecting workers and consumers alike, we can expect more and more toxic cases being brought to the courts rather than to the professionals in these agencies. In this context, it is important for us to recognize the growing demand for our skills. We may be dragged kicking and screaming into moral dilemmas where we are forced to confront what are the boundaries of our involvement in public disputes. In part, this will be an unwelcome circumstance for us. Yet, I would argue that we owe society a great deal and we owe those who are often without voice a great deal more. I believe that the demands from the legal system will force us to crystallize our sense of purpose and the humanistic traditions that lend legitimacy to our field. A greater relevance and involvement of historians will force us to define what is *good* history, both methodologically as well as morally.

CHAPTER 9

The Most Craven Abdication of Democratic Principles
On the U.S. Attack on Iraq

GLENDA GILMORE

Prior to the war in Iraq, United States historian, Glenda Gilmore pro-tested U.S. occupation of Iraq in a letter written in the Yale Daily News. *Though her column offered an incisive analysis of the events to come, it sparked a nationwide controversy in which she was criticized for her political position and was personally attacked for being an aca-demic engaging in a public debate. We have reprinted here her initial article in the* Yale Daily News *as well as her rebuttal to the controversy, which she gave in a talk to the Yale Peace Coalition meeting on April 9, 2003.*

Variations on Iraq: Glenda Gilmore
Published Friday, October 11, 2002, *Yale Daily News*

A U.S. attack on Iraq, which seems inevitable, will be the most craven abdi-cation of democratic principles in our country's history. As I write, the House has approved, and the Senate is debating, a resolution that gives President George W. Bush, in Sen. Robert Byrd's words, "virtually unchecked authority to commit the nation's military to an unprovoked attack on a sovereign nation." The Bush Administration recently articulated its foreign policy plans this way: "Our forces will be strong enough to dissuade potential adversaries from pursuing a military build-up in hopes of surpassing, or equaling, the power of the United States." This means that the United States of America may invade any country, anywhere, any time, before it becomes a threat.

Bush's National Security Strategy makes the United States an imperial power in the most sinister sense of the term, and Congress' resolution will finally and unabashedly give George W. Bush the job he seems so sure he deserves: emperor.

Invading Iraq without immediate provocation is the first step in Bush's plan to transform our country into an aggressor nation that cannot tolerate opposition. In fact, to Bush's thinking, our country should not tolerate the possibility that other nations might someday oppose us. This is contrary to every principle on which we structure our society, not to mention every value by which we live our lives. Hendrik Hertzberg calls it a scheme for "world domination," Anatol Lieven declares that the United States "has become a menace to itself and to mankind," and Sen. Byrd predicts that Americans "will pay for a war with lives of its sons and daughters." That's you, Yalies. The situation before you is grave.

If the United States invades Iraq without provocation on the grounds that Saddam Hussein might hurt us in the future, we will forever change our national character. Who are we? Aren't we the nation that deplored Japan's pre-emptive strike against Pearl Harbor and denounced Hitler's invasion of Poland? Even in wars that provoked much internal criticism, we responded to what we asserted were invasions of South Korea, South Vietnam and Kuwait. This time we are the invaders. No matter how much Bush tells us we are the good guys and Hussein is the bad guy, the president will not be able to change the historical fact that we attacked another sovereign nation without provocation. We are the good guys. But good guys don't invade other countries, unless they have exhausted every other option for self-preservation. If they do, they become the bad guys.

Bush has failed to make a case for an immediate need to act in our own self defense. So many alternatives to invasion exist that there is not space to list them. In fact, in the words of columnist Charley Reese, "Bush Won't Take Yes for an Answer." First, the president demanded UN weapons inspectors go back into Iraq. In the smartest move of his life, Hussein agreed. Any reasonable statesman would have then thrown his weight behind getting inspections under way, but Bush whined; now that he had what he asked for, that it wasn't good enough. Any other leader might have been embarrassed to lay bare his real motive: an unrelenting desire to start a war with Iraq. Not Bush. He simply undercut the United Nations by continuing to threaten Iraq, even as he dragged a gutless Congress behind him. Meanwhile, chief UN inspector Hans Blix has reminded Bush that he works for the UN, not the U.S., and Blix is proceeding to send inspectors to Iraq. "Will we kill the inspectors too?" Reese wonders.

Not simply a miserable venture into statecraft, Bush's strategy defies common sense. He is seeking to eliminate the threat of war by waging war. How many Americans and innocent Iraqi civilians will die? Notwithstanding that a preemptive strike without immediate provocation is the moral equivalent of murder, it is also just plain stupid. George F. Kennan, the statesman who best articulated the policy of containment that drove Cold War diplomacy, knows that. Speaking against a pre-emptive strike against Iraq, he said, "I could see justification only if the absence of it would involve a major and imminent danger to our own country, or, at worst, to our most intimate and traditional allies. Of this I have seen no evidence." It is not enough for Bush to be President of the United States, he must become the Emperor of the World. This unclothed emperor is, as they say in Texas, all hat and no brains.

In the years before us, I fear there will be causes worth dying for. There will be tyrants so unstoppable that we will have to fight them to preserve our own freedom. But that is not the case now. Instead of standing up against tyranny, we are bringing it to our own doorstep. We have met the enemy, and it is us.

What Glenda Gilmore Really Said[1]

The following is the text of my remarks to the Yale Peace Coalition meeting on April 9, 2003. I invite you to compare it to the story written by two Yale freshmen and published in *David Horowitz's on-line magazine*. The "critical questioning" to which they refer, occurred when James Kirchick, a student columnist at the *Yale Daily News*, asked if I didn't think that Daniel Pipes, director of the Middle East Forum, who sponsors Campus Watch and wrote a column including me among five "Professors Who Hate America," and Andrew Sullivan, a journalist and a blogger who disagreed with my *Yale Daily News* column opposing the invasion of Iraq, were simply trying to get my opinions to a larger audience. I said that I had thought about that, but that Pipes's call for "adult supervision" and "outsiders" to "establish standards for media statements by faculty" made me think otherwise. That was the only question Mr. Kircheck asked.

April 9, 2003

In case you are wondering what we are doing here tonight, while film of jubilant Iraqis greeting U.S. troops in Baghdad runs on CNN, I offer this: Around lunchtime today, I got this e-mail from an old high school friend who acts as an armed escort for CNN news teams:

> GG,
> From the streets of Baghdad
> Liberation and Freedom, nuff said.
> Semper Fi,
> Mac

I'm here tonight to tell Mac—and you—that 'nuff hasn't been said, that amid the fall of Baghdad, it is our duty as citizens to continue to question how we got there, what we will do there, and what lesson our policy makers will draw from our invasion of Iraq in the weeks and months to come.

I was in Memphis last weekend when I read the obituary of Edwin Starr. Starr is best remembered for his 1970 #1 hit, War, a song that questions the value of war. Does it actually ensure our freedoms—and at what costs? War shatters the dreams of the young men sent to fight it. I almost wept as I wondered what the reaction would be today to such a song. Number 1 hit? I doubt it. Starr, who served three years in the military, would be condemned on Fox News (an oxymoron if I ever heard one) as a traitor.

I know, because I have been branded a traitor. I wrote an op ed in the *Yale Daily News* and received death threats and rape wishes, was called a slut in the *YDN* comments section by a Princeton PhD (whom I don't know and who offered no evidence to back up that assertion), won blogger Andrew Sullivan's Susan Sontag award for fuzzy moral thinking, and was named by Daniel Pipes as one of five "professors who hate America." It's tough to be an anti-war patriot in the vicious climate that Bush has encouraged and that Rumsfeld embodies. Tonight, I want to talk about the relationship between anti-war activism and patriotism, about who has the right to speak for our country, and about the organized plot funded by right-wing foundations to shut down dissent.

First, let me recap the position I took on October 11 in an opinion piece that the *YDN* solicited from me. I argued then that a preemptive strike on Iraq, which I defined as invading Iraq without immediate provocation, would be the most craven abdication of democratic principles in our country's history. It would transform our country into an aggressor nation if the U.S. followed the Bush Administration's foreign policy as articulated in his National Security Strategy: "Our forces will be strong enough to dissuade potential adversaries from pursuing a military build up in hopes of surpassing or equaling, the power of the United States." I argued that Bush was trying to do an end run around the UN, and that he seemed to want to undermine weapons inspections so that he could invade Iraq. Instead of standing up against tyranny, we were bringing it to our own doorstep, I predicted.

I pointed out that I, too, believed that Saddam Hussein was a bad guy, and that we were the good guys, but that good guys don't invade other countries unless they have exhausted every other option. We had not. If our goal was to disarm Iraq, we had a workable plan that was proceeding to do so.

Did I argue as an expert on the Middle East? No. I argued first as an American citizen who thought the entire scheme fantastical and devoid of common sense and, second, as a professor of U.S. history who teaches about the quest to perfect democracy in the twentieth century. You don't have to be an expert to say what you believe. It is every citizen's right to speak out. Okay, perhaps, as my momma suggested, I was a bit rough on Bush when I said he wanted to become the "Emperor of the World," and "This unclothed emperor is, as they say in Texas, all hat and no brains," a riff on "all hat and no cattle" that brought me scorn from bellicose Texans. But let me quote the much ridiculed and much beloved Imperialist Teddy Roosevelt on the subject of criticizing the President:

> The President is merely the most important among a large number of public servants. He should be supported or opposed exactly to the degree which is warranted by his good conduct or bad conduct, his efficiency or inefficiency in rendering loyal, able, and disinterested service to the nation as a whole. Therefore it is absolutely necessary that there should be full liberty to tell the truth about his acts, and this means that it is exactly as necessary to blame him when he does wrong as to praise him when he does right. Any other attitude in an American citizen is both base and servile. To announce that there must be no criticism of the President, or that we are to stand by the President, right or wrong, is not only unpatriotic and servile, but is morally treasonable to the American public. Nothing but the truth should be spoken about him or any one else. But it is even more important to tell the truth, pleasant or unpleasant, about him than about any one else.
> (Theodore Roosevelt, 1918, "Lincoln and Free Speech")

What I did not know when I wrote that op ed is that I would walk straight into a preplanned campaign aimed at antiwar university professors in an attempt to cut them off from their students, to endanger their jobs, and to shut them up.

By the next morning, a *YDN* columnist had sent my piece to Andrew Sullivan, a hawkish blogger (I didn't even know what a blog was), and probably also to Daniel Pipes. My inbox filled up with nasty, nasty little messages, and the comments section of the *YDN* (I didn't even know what a comments section was) filled up with the same. The kind of criticism I received fell mainly into four categories, all four tropes intended to discredit me in different ways by composing for me fantastical past lives that had nothing to do with my real life. More importantly, 90 percent of these messages—and there were hundreds—had absolutely nothing to do with my argument to protect U.S. and Iraqi lives by letting the UN do its work.

First, there were the people who accused me of being a left-over 1960s liberal professor, reliving my anti-war days and imposing them on my students. In this scenario, I had acted treasonously as a young woman in opposing the war in Vietnam, corrupted the minds of Ivy Leaguers for thirty years, and now I was baaack. . . . I was disloyal then and had simply been waiting to commit other acts of disloyalty. The truth is that I was married to a Marine Corps Captain and spent the Vietnam War at Parris Island, where many of the Marines themselves had turned against the war by 1970.

Second, there were the misogynists, those who thought they could scare me by impugning my sexual reputation. Hence, the slut comments, along with those who wished I would be raped by Saddam's hired rape squads, and finally to a pathetic guy who said he bet I was fat, dubbed me elephant woman, and guessed that I hadn't had a date until I was 26. Sassy girl gets slapped down.

Then there were those who called me a communist, or the child of Communists. This was baffling, since Saddam isn't a Communist and my parents were virulent anti-Communists. I grew up reading John Birch society publications.

Finally, there was the Ivory Tower/Ivy League nitwit criticism. In this fable, I knew nothing of the real world and was an effete snob to boot, trying to impose my eastern intellectual ideas on real Americans. Since I went to grad school after a career in business, and came to Yale with a degree from a public university, and with all of the effete snobbishness that one can pick up at a North Carolina barbeque joint, this was particularly funny.

Andrew Sullivan put a direct link from his blog to the *YDN* comments section, and it was clear that the vast majority of comments came from nuts with time on their hands who were outside of Yale. Why would they bother? They bothered because there was an organized campaign to shut up anyone from the academy who spoke out against the war. Within a month, Daniel Pipes had reached millions of people around the world, starting with the *New York Post* and the *Jerusalem Post* and moving on to syndication, by profiling my op ed, with four others, in an article entitled *"Professors Who Hate America."*

Here is Pipes:

Visit an American University, . . . and you'll often enter a topsy-turvy world in which professors consider the United States (not Iraq) the problem. . . . Yet, the relentless opposition to their own government raises some questions:

Why do American academics so often despise their own country while finding excuses for repressive and dangerous regimes?

Why have university specialists proven so inept at understanding the great contemporary issues of war and peace, starting with Vietnam, then the Cold War, the Persian Gulf War, and now the war on terror?

Why do professors of linguistics, chemistry, American history, genetics, and business present themselves in public as authorities on the Middle East?

What is the long-term effect of an extremist, intolerant, and anti-American environment on university students?

And here are Pipes's recommendations to solve the problem he imagines above. I'll continue quoting him, with emphasis added to the original.

The time has come for *adult supervision* of the faculty and administrators on many American campuses. Especially as we are at war, the goal must be for universities to resume their civic responsibilities. This can be achieved if *outsiders* (alumni, state legislators, non-university specialists, parents of students and others) take steps to create a politically balanced atmosphere, critique failed scholarship, establish standards for media statements by the faculty, and broaden the range of campus discourse.

In Pipes's imagination, professors give up their civil rights when they take the job.

Another professor mentioned in the article, Eric Foner, and I answered Pipes in the *Los Angeles Times*. We began to hear from people who had long been Pipes watchers. We discovered that his organization, the Middle East Forum, runs *Campus Watch*, an group designed to listen to and report to the right wing media what professors are saying on campus. I bet we have some members in this audience.

Dave Johnson of the Commonweal Institute, in a story on *History News Network* revealed how these organizations work. Pipes is funded by the Bradley Foundation, which funds the Heritage Foundation, as well as the American Council of Trustees and Alumni. The latter organization, set up to monitor speech on campus, was founded by Lynne Cheney, wife of the vice president. She is now a fellow at the American Enterprise Institute, funded by the Bradley Foundation. Moreover, these organizations meet weekly and generate "talking points" for the media. The talking point that they generated in early October last year was apparently "professors who hate America." The National Committee on Responsive Philanthropy found that these organizations had formulated an assault on academia, "to attack the patriotism of liberals and to convince trustees of colleges and universities to remove them, replacing them with ideological conservatives." Surprise, surprise, they maintain a "Collegiate Network" with links to seventy college newspapers. The campaign I ran into was a preplanned, carefully orchestrated attempt to ask, "Why do they hate America?" and to imply that antiwar professors are like terrorists, who also hate America." Johnson informs us that if you google the phrase, "they hate America," you will get over a million hits. He summed up what happened this way, "Foner and Gilmore encountered a well-funded campaign to pursue an ideological agenda."

Why does this matter to you? Because you should know that there is a campaign out there to shut me up and to shut you up. There is a concerted attempt to question the patriotism of anyone who criticizes Bush and, now that we have invaded Iraq, anyone who criticizes what we do there. That campaign will not die; indeed, its planners have perfected it on rubes like me. Next, it will be directed against anyone who speaks out against our country's policies.

On Sunday, Richard Perle (Pentagon policy advisor)[2] said, "There's got to be a change in Syria as well." James Woolsey, a friend of the administration, predicted last week that "the U.S. [will] have to spend years and maybe decades waging World War IV . . . in Iran, against the Hezbollah, in Syria. . . . " If this is the case, what of our country will be left? If our children—if you—must temper your disgust at war and take up the responsibility of invading other countries to "solve" their problems, we won't have lives worth protecting anymore. They can't do these things if we speak; they must silence us.

This censorship campaign drives the cost of deposing Saddam Hussein even higher, because it signals the extinction of our civil liberties. And I believe that is exactly what the cabal who attacked me wants. They want to extinguish civil liberties so that they can move, unfettered by criticism, to world domination. Why? Because they believe that they alone know what is right. What can you do? You can refuse to allow anyone to question your patriotism. As Paul Krugman wrote this week in the *New York Times*: "After all, democracy—including the right to criticize—was what we were fighting for" in World War II. Yet, today, he warns, "self-styled patriots are trying to impose constraints on political speech never contemplated during World War II, accusing anyone who criticizes the president of undermining the war effort." You can be strong, be loud, be patriotic, and be anti-war.

Do I still believe what I said on October 11? Yes. I regret risking and losing U.S. and Iraqi lives, and I believe—if our aim was to disarm Iraq—

that the UN was accomplishing that. If our aim was to silence dissent in this country, position the U.S. as an imperial power, and breed terrorism in the Middle East, then Bush may have accomplished his goals. Yesterday, a wounded and bleeding Iraqi civilian told the *New York Times*:

> Is this Bush's promised 'liberation?' no, this is a red liberation, a liberation written in blood. Bush said he would disarm Saddam, and look how he's doing it now—killing us, one by one. Please ask him, how do you liberate people by killing them?

And in case you think I exaggerate the enormity of the conspiracy against free speech, guess who President Bush nominated this week to the U.S. Institute of Peace, a federal think tank established by Congress to promote "the prevention, management and resolution of international conflicts?" George Bush nominated Daniel Pipes.

Note

1. Reproduced from the History News Network, April 14, 2003.
2. He resigned in February 2004, which is after I gave the speech.

Bridging the Gap Between
Academia and Activism

CHAPTER 10

Forging Activist Alliances
Identity, Identification, and Position

DRUCILLA CORNELL
KITTY KRUPAT

The discussion that follows was inspired by an exchange between Kitty Krupat and Drucilla Cornell during the session entitled, "Fatal Women, Feminist Futures and the Past that Would Have Been." Kitty spoke about a dilemma she has faced since publishing a book on the subject of lesbian/gay rights and the labor movement. Though she identifies as a heterosexual woman, most people assume she is a lesbian: Why else would she care about a gay/lesbian labor alliance? Until very recently, she refused to challenge this assumption out of a sense of solidarity with gay people. But at some point, she began to think that it was better politics to claim the privilege and assert the obligation of straight people to join the struggle for lesbian, gay, bisexual, transgender, and queer peoples' rights. Kitty also talked about the personal side of her dilemma. Maintaining silence sometimes made her feel dishonest or like a person with no identity to call her own. Drucilla responded by proposing a broader approach to defining identity by considering not only one's identity, but also one's identification and position. This, she argued, serves as a usable way to both complicate and clarify the way we understand ourselves and others in political movements. When we sat down to continue this conversation a year later, on March 30, 2003, the U.S. led invasion of Iraq had just begun. While the issues raised by the war are the subject of much of this dialogue, the themes addressed are central to many progressive political movements in the United States today:

- How can the university campus serve as a site of social justice activism?
- What is the relationship between feminism and U.S. exceptionalism?
- How can the left build successful coalitions?
- What is the role of the media and political rhetoric in a democracy?

1. Campus as Site of Social Justice Activism

We began the interview by discussing the recently commenced war, the responses of those around us in academia, and the strategies and actions of the anti-war movement. How should we as leftist educators respond within the university community? What is the potential role of the university in a time of crisis? Should we try to bring the system to a standstill and protest in the streets? Or, in times of chaos and uncertainty, are we better to maintain stability, to show up for our students, our commitments, and our work? What is our work anyway—and what is the work of the university? In this first section, Kitty and Drucilla speak of some of the ways that universities can function to unite social justice activism with academia. For Kitty, this occurs through the presence of organized labor on campus and building coalitions. For Drucilla, this is also the case, but using philosophy as a tool for political aims is critical.

—Jennifer Manion

Kitty Krupat: I'm at the Queens College-CUNY (City University of New York) Labor Resource Center, which is a model of academic activism at work. The Center provides research and other resources for the labor movement, forums for discussion and college education for working adults, most of whom are sponsored by their unions. Recently, we had a breakfast forum on the subject of "Labor in a Time of War." The audience was almost equally composed of academics, trade unionists, and activists in related fields. That combination made for an extraordinary and very provocative discussion. I'm also a doctoral candidate at New York University (NYU), where 500 or so students walked out of classes in protest of the war in Iraq. Interestingly, I heard about it, not from students, but from faculty members who identify themselves as activists. From where I sit in the academy, there's a small but visible movement toward political engagement among intellectuals. In times like these, we face the dilemma of going on with daily routines. I'm never sure when it's okay—or under what circumstances it's right—to go on with business as usual.

Drucilla Cornell: I agree with you. I want to connect philosophy to activism. One aspect of my work entails the defense of the importance of ideals, of the left defending ideals. So that the idea of freedom, particularly freedom, but also equality, aren't discarded empty shells or mere historical residues.

I decided to cancel my participation in a conference that was planned on my work. I felt if there was going to be a conference on my work I would have to turn it into an anti-war teach-in. In other words, it's not that I think we don't need to address Jacques Lacan, Levinas, Kant and Hegel, or any of the other philosophers that I've struggled to understand. Particularly now, they are more and more relevant to what I do as an activist at teach-ins, for example in defending the ideal of perpetual peace against just war theory. I think we do need to engage with philosophy. I decided against the conference, because I believe that what we are doing in "shock and awe" is a crime against humanity.[1] It was a way for me to say to some of my friends in the academy that we cannot go on anymore as if this is not happening, as if we were not in a serious political and moral crisis.

K.K.: I think it's probably normal to want routine in our lives and to keep routine going as a protection against chaos or loss of control. Or because we need relief from a sense of doom many of us have been carrying around since 9/11. But there are other, more compelling reasons for continuing with business as usual, especially if the work we do helps people to understand or interpret the world around them. Would you abandon the classroom if you were an educator? Whose interest would that serve? I say we go back to the classroom, but with a heightened sense of responsibility. Whatever you teach, whether it's music, mathematics, theater arts, nursing or computer programming, you're potentially preparing people to make their contribution toward a better world. But, in going back to business as usual, we need to bring a degree of self-reflexivity about what we teach and how we teach it. We need to re-think our assumptions. In that mood, maybe we could consider opening up the classroom and allowing students to shape and change the discussion. If we are able to make some productive changes, then of course we aren't really returning to business as usual.

D.C.: Indeed, we have to think hard about what business *as usual* is. Certainly, we don't want to desert the classroom. This semester I'm teaching a political theory pro-seminar for graduate students. We began with Hobbes, whom I read in a whole different light, because Hobbes' biggest concern is peace and security, arguing as he does that civilized behavior cannot emerge in an environment where people are so frightened and paranoid all the time (as in our current political climate!). Each of the thinkers I have taught in this pro-seminar, such as Hobbes, Hume, Rousseau, Kant, Hegel and Marx, has relevance in helping us come to terms with our current situation even though they're, of course, classical thinkers of the canon.

K.K.: To come back to business as usual: The academy is not just an intellectual sphere; it's also an activist and political one, where workers engage in struggles for rights and benefits. When we return to business as usual we have the opportunity to participate in these struggles, not only through direct political action but also through teaching and learning. One of the most important things for us and our students to understand is how the class interests of clerical workers, graduate students, maintenance workers, and faculty intersect. And because there is a visible academic peace movement, we have the opportunity to forge solidarity with other workers on campus through our mutual participation in the peace and justice movement. This possibility helps us to envision the academy as a larger site of political action in which all of the actors begin to discover their interdependence and interrelationship.

D.C.: I started out my life in the academy working as a phone operator at Columbia University and was fired for union organizing in 1973. So I'm very conscious of the class element of the university. I may, in canceling my conference, have been rebelling against part of the university that I'm not very comfortable with. We have huge discrepancies between adjuncts and professors, professors and secretaries, secretaries and janitors. The university really has to face the underside of the star system. Some people make $250,000 and some people make $23,000 and there's a connection between them. Some people are considered stars, some aren't. How did we get into this? It's an illusion. No academic is really famous. It's a terrible illusion, a fantasy. But we perpetuate it in our own circles, in the class hierarchies that have become so embedded in the university.

K.K.: The academic star system seems to reflect the society's appetite for celebrity, wealth and fame—in entertainment, in sports, so why not in education. The academy's mini star system is just another manifestation of the way our values have been shaped by a culture of commodification.

D.C.: I think, ironically, it's against thinking and intellectual creativity. It's certainly against the democratic project that you're describing, where you become very aware of how hierarchies in the university get played out to block the most productive, imaginative, and creative discussions we need to have as part of a movement for social justice.

K.K.: The war in Iraq seems to have motivated many academics to try to incorporate global political realities into theoretical discussions that might otherwise be abstract. This kind of pedagogy is typical in a hybrid academic world like mine, where trade union ideals and political principles underwrite the workplace culture. Here's a telling example. Two days after bombs began dropping on Iraq, Elizabeth Bunn, Secretary-Treasurer of the United Automobile Workers, spoke at a forum at the Cornell School of Industrial Labor Relations. The forum had originally been planned as a celebration of International Women's Day. Under the circumstances, it's not surprising that Elizabeth began her remarks with a reference to the war. What's interesting is what she said: The war, she said, is a wake up call to labor, reminding us of our mission to be a social movement. While there's a range of opinion on the war among union leaders, members and activists, we've been forced to enter a very necessary discussion that is drawing more and more unions and union members to the debate. As Elizabeth pointed out, that's very healthy. It may even be an opportunity to re-imagine ourselves as a social movement. Elizabeth's observations made me think that academics and activists should also think about what opportunities this awful war might present. What could we do to influence the debate or the terms of discussion? Could we change people's thinking in productive ways? Could we do our academic work in new ways, adding new dimensions to the same old discussions?

2. Feminism and U.S. Exceptionalism

The bombing of Afghanistan created immense interest in the plight of Afghan women among Americans. U.S. feminists who believed Afghan women needed to be liberated from their culture and their men found themselves allied with the Bush administration. Other feminists, often women of color, critiqued the racism that was inherent in this approach. Drucilla begins this section criticizing the exceptionalism that informs many U.S. feminists. Kitty also found using the "liberation" of women to justify the war a troubling development. Together, they consider the complexity of developing universal theories of feminism and equality.

—J.M.

D.C.: I am very active in Take Back the Future and in United for Peace and Justice. We acknowledge the need to take theoretical positions on multilateralism, the question of the relationship of social and economic justice, etc. I don't think that all philosophy has to be directly related to activism at all times. But right now I have felt very much the call to think about what practical philosophy is. What is its role in activism? What is the role of feminist theory in activism? Not that I ever didn't feel that call. Does that mean I'm against philosophy for philosophy's sake? Of course not. There is always a place for such work. But right now I have felt the need to be engaged with the burning issues raised by 9/11 and its aftermath. However, I have always seen my work as grappling with transformation, with how we change the world, not just with how we understand it. When we are citizens in a country that is engaging in an illegal and unjust war, indeed in a crime against humanity, I feel called to take a stand and explicitly condemn the militarism of the current administration. My recent Gilbert Ryle lectures grappled with competing ideas of development, contested the notion of the clash of civilizations, and tried to understand what is progress, war, terrorism. These questions all have a philosophical dimension, particularly given the failure of certain U.S. feminists after 9/11 to understand the ramifications of their support of the so-called humanitarian invasions.

J.M.: Would you elaborate on that?

D.C.: U.S. exceptionalism is deep both in the labor movement, and certainly very deep in feminism. Perhaps it is more theoretically deep in feminism. I think that some feminists have actually bought into the idea that there is a clash of civilizations and that western civilizations represent freedom and democracy, therefore failing to see that, for many feminists, it is perfectly consistent to be both a Muslim and a feminist. The challenge after 9/11 was to listen very carefully to organizations such as the Revolutionary Association of Women in Afghanistan, to hear how and why they condemn Muslim fundamentalism and indeed all fundamentalisms, and yet respect that religious women may find in their religion, including the Muslim religion, the inspiration for their feminism and their commitment to equality. It actually turns into a philosophical issue: what is secularism? What is its relation to the establishment of one religion as the basis of a state? Are they the same thing? I would say no. But there are political theorists, feminist theorists, who claim that multiculturalism itself, let alone the Muslim religion, is antithetical to feminism, and therefore what the United States did in Afghanistan was legitimately framed as a humanitarian intervention. Humanitarian interventions always have to go through the UN. Yes, when Europe and the U.S. bombed Kosovo, the UN gave it over to NATO, but this was done through negotiation with the UN. I was not for that bombing, although I was very much against what Serbia was doing. But I knew many Serbian feminists who were very active in Women in Black and other Belgrade feminists were out in the streets constantly fighting Milosevic during his regime. And again, the answer would have been to listen to them, because they were of course the ones who would have to endure the bombing of Belgrade. I was also against bombing of Afghanistan and remain against it today.

K.K.: I was puzzled by the feminist argument that suggested war in Afghanistan might be justified if it resulted in the liberation of Afghan women. I found that as hard to take as the argument that war in Iraq will be justified if it liberates Iraqis from Saddam Hussein. Of course, the liberation of women—as of all oppressed people everywhere—is hugely important. But who is to do the liberating and by what means? That said, I'm not clear how American exceptionalism figures in the discussion.

D.C.: What I mean by it is this idea that we really are the most *morally advanced* nation of the world. It then follows that U.S. feminists are *exceptionally* situated to teach other women about feminism, liberation, freedom and democracy. Hopefully that has now been shattered, as we see the recent attack on women's rights in the United States.

J.M.: When discussing the situation and rights of Muslim women in Afghanistan, I've heard students quickly swing from American exceptionalism to cultural relativism in defense of the oppression of women. How do you negotiate this jump from one extreme to the other?

D.C.: I would want to introduce a more complex notion of universality. If we actually had conditions of transparency, which I consider necessary for democracy in this country, we would be hearing the Iraqi point of view constantly. But the information that could help us consider their perspective is actually being kept from us. If we were involved in that dialogue, if we were listening to the Iraqi news station, if we weren't in a situation of having a major media manipulation, we would have to hear their voices. And I think we would find that those voices are voices that resonate with us in many ways. The way I think about universality is that it's always being translated. We're always seeking to take ideals like equality, freedom, dignity, and humanity itself and give them a certain reach. But as we do that, we understand that how we each grasp these ideals philosophically may be very different. A Buddhist may say, "I completely agree with you that torture is always wrong and I defend it as a human right. I do it from within my Buddhism, you do it from your Kantianism, but we get to the same universal. And we may even say that this is connected to something like humanity in its ideal form."

K.K.: All my life, I have been attracted to universalist ideas—universal peace, universal justice, universal equality. It turns out that universality is problematic, if you stop to think about where and how the idea is produced—out of what set of cultural values; in what historical moment; and by whom. I'm assuming the doctrine of universal freedom, as preached by American chauvinists at this moment in our history, is not what you have in mind when you imagine a universality, mediated by different cultures and different ways of knowing, seeing and being

D.C.: Like you, I'm very afraid when the United States sets the terms. We reach agreement over universal norms only by challenging the predominance of one road to them especially when these universals are imposed through military force. Otherwise, in spite of ourselves, we end up affirming a particular perspective as universal and right only because of the *might* that forces them down the throats of others.

K.K.: But I would probably also be afraid if representatives of other cultures imposed a notion of universality that was not attentive to the nuances and localisms of American life—whatever in all its diversity that is. I was raised to value as universal European ideas of right and wrong. Somewhere along the line, however, I adopted cultural and moral relativism in a big way. Who am I to say what's right for peoples of other cultures and different circumstances? Then I started to rethink relativism. Female circumcision was an important issue in the evolution of my ideas. The universalists say female circumcision is an atrocity, pure and simple, and intervention is required to eradicate it. The relativists say that it's part of a culture which is embraced by families and women in some parts of Africa. But the fact is, no one in either camp is actually listening to feminists in countries where female circumcision is practiced; or to the young women who have run away in order to escape circumcision; or to organizations in those countries that campaign against it. Those are the people and institutions who have taken the responsibility for social change. Their actions and ideas should inform our own political position on the issue. They are taking charge of their own lives. What we have to do is support them in their struggle.

D.C.: For me, relativism is a vague and indeed contradictory term because you're always saying relative to what? How do we reach the judgment that some norms should be universal, accepted say by all the world peoples. We for example argue that torture is wrong, circumcision is wrong, and this moral judgment should be sharable by everyone. How do we reach that judgment? Do we reach it just by U.S. feminisms saying to others that their understandings of female equality and freedom are simply more advanced than those of other women throughout the world? I often say, "We're a culture of hysterectomy" and people say, "Well, losing your uterus is nothing." But it is significant, and it forces us to recognize that our femininity is also defined by certain forms of invasive surgery. We are also a culture of breast implants. When it comes to how we view our own bodies, we find that we are caught up in all sorts of fantasies about the norms of female beauty necessary to achieve happiness our place in society, acceptance by men, etc. To reach a certain universality, we have to recognize how distorted our own femininity is. Why do we have breast surgery? Why do we have this heterosexual normativity that so many of us have lived in and been shaped by?

The idea that we represent female freedom in our bodies is a fantasy that we have to examine. We judge that a particular invasion of the female body is wrong. To universalize this judgment we have to undergo serious engagement with others, as well as critical engagement with ourselves. Can we take something like circumcision and say this is wrong for everybody? Can we take torture and say this is wrong for everybody? We are called to make such judgments all the time. An important aspect of universality is to be open to a constant process of translation that involves us as individuals and as members of groups reviving our own understanding of a norm we believe is universal. If we want to use western words, we might use dignity and respect for the other human beings in the course of struggle over these norms. Other peoples and individuals may use other words for how they approach the process of universalizability.

J.M.: This brings us back to the issue of academic activism. I assigned your short piece from *Signs* about RAWA (the Revolutionary Association of the Women of Afghanistan) and 9/11 to my women's studies class. Even though many had accepted the rhetoric about liberating Afghan women from the burqua, after they read your article and I had them read sections of the RAWA Web site, they quickly shifted their criticisms away from the removal of the burqua to the need for jobs, education, and healthcare.

D.C.: And RAWA said that so clearly. Of course no one should be killed for not wearing the burqua. But the act of wearing the burqua was not the primary issue for them at all. They were saying it very openly, as you put it. You see Gloria Steinem and others wearing the burqua pin, saying, "free women from the burqua." They were participating in what I'm going to call bad universalism, the assumption that somehow U.S. feminists represent the ultimate last word on what freedom is and that this freedom must involve a certain dress code, one not accepted for religious reasons. Again, think of how constrained many secular women remain by the images of fashion. Are we ever free of cultural dictates when we get dressed in the morning? Certainly I am not. There can't be any ultimate last word on how women should dress including according to their religious beliefs or it wouldn't be freedom anymore. If we say, this is your freedom, then it's not freedom because we have already denied your agency. There is the danger of assuming an integral connection between certain ideals and secularism. A certain fever-ish commitment to secularism implies that you know god is dead. I've said to so many people: "Did god tell you that he was dead? It's a famous argument of Immanuel Kant—How can you know that god is dead? If someone believes deeply in god, why would that have to mean that they are not a feminist?"

K.K.: I'm not a philosopher in any formal sense of that word, so my response to you has to be pretty simple. Which is to say only this: Feminism as a de facto form of secular modernism is certainly accepted as conventional wisdom in many quarters. But, I don't believe the idea is universal, in any profound sense of the word. Feminist scholarship hasn't coalesced around any one, encompassing or universalizing definition of feminism. Feminist studies cut across lines of class, race and ethnicity—and in fact intersect with those categories of analysis. Certainly in practice we see feminists doing activist work through faith-based organizations as well as through secular groups—especially in immigrant communities where the church or synagogue may be the one place women can come together to talk freely and openly about their concerns. So, I assume that—for the most part—feminist movements are not saying it's secularism or nothing all.

D.C.: Let's hope not. It doesn't characterize you and me. It does not characterize feminists in the peace movement more generally. Still, I was surprised by how many feminists supported the war in Afghanistan for these reasons.

K.K.: It's not so much that these radical feminists were for the war but that they saw complexities in the issues brought to light by the war. They were challenging us to consider the possibility that war in the service of women's liberation might be justified. It's something like World War II exceptionalism, when pacifists participated in the war effort because the fight against fascism was a special case.

D.C.: But of course the war against Afghanistan was not justified on the basis of the liberation of women. For years RAWA had been pleading with the UN and individual governments to take some action against the Taliban. Little or nothing was done. The United States turned a deaf ear. It seems both cynical and hypocritical to bolster support for the war through a last minute appeal to the liberation of women. I think the majority of feminists should have been able to see that they were being manipulated.

3. Coalition-Building on the Left

Both Kitty and Drucilla are committed to broad based coalition-building on the left. Kitty has done this through the labor movement for many years and has been a leader in getting unions to reach out to gay and lesbian workers. Drucilla has led the anti-war movement in New York as a cofounder of Take Back the Future. Both are active in United for Peace and Justice. Here they consider the success and limits of coalition building in the anti-war movement inspired by the U.S. bombing of Afghanistan and fueled by the war on Iraq.

—J.M.

D.C.: The anti-war movement is neither simply about the war in Iraq, nor is it just a negative condemnation of everything associated with the United States. We need to take positions and espouse ideals. Take Back the Future, a peace organization based in New York City, has argued for multilateralism, and for a real reconsideration of our domestic as well as foreign policy. We're against militarism, we're certainly against nuclear pro-liferation and ultimately we support the destruction of all nuclear weapons. The war in Iraq has brought this country into a serious crisis. The sense of crisis, indeed of emergency, seems at times to force us to say that we cannot go on as usual. And yet at the same time we have to balance the sense of crisis with a long-term movement that cannot survive if it is only directed by a kind of crisis sensibility.

K.K.: And that's not all. While we're not looking—because we're focused on the war—the Bush administration is systematically chipping away at our rights, not just women's rights or the rights of immigrants, but workers' rights. Behind our backs, Bush is trying to lower the forty hour week, take away overtime pay and attack the minimum wage. These attacks on entitlements cut across lines of gender and class. They're all connected by the administration's plan to turn our economy into a permanent war economy and to sacrifice the poor and working classes in order to reward giant corporations and the tiny percentage of America's wealthiest men.

D.C.: This is why Ann Snitow and I started Take Back the Future. Like you, we felt the need to connect the undermining of the infrastructure of democracy, including workers rights, medical care, schools, and the basic attack on constitutional rights through the U.S.A. Patriot Act and the Homeland Security Act. The economic and social policy of the administration needs to be understood as intimately linked to its foreign policy. This is why we so strongly believed that the movement against the war has to be a movement for social and economic justice.

K.K.: Absolutely. I'd like to come back to the Labor against War forum I mentioned earlier: The moderator of that forum was Leslie Cagan, coordinator of United for Peace and Justice. She opened the discussion by saying that organized labor can play a pivotal role in the anti-war coalition because it is in a unique position to help us connect the dots between the war in Iraq, the administration's goals for the Middle East and its attack on the poor, people of color, and women—not to mention its efforts to concentrate more and more wealth and power in a tiny minority of already obscenely rich people.

D.C.: I completely agree with you and that is why the organization of the labor movement within United for Peace and Justice is so important. We need mainstream unions to get involved now more than ever. Grassroots organizations such as the Workplace Project have played such a significant role in organizing immigrant workers and establishing workers' cooperatives that have often spoken out loud and often against U.S. foreign policy. These organizations have always tended to be anti-war. Many are refugees from other wars with the United States. But in the past twenty years or more, many unions have been reluctant at best to protest against U.S. foreign policy. It took most unions a long time and, even then, not all joined in the protests against the war in Vietnam. So I am with Leslie Cagan that this is an important opportunity to rebuild a labor movement that also represents significant opposition to the current foreign policy of this administration. Hopefully, a more wide spread opposition will develop in the academy. But we cannot wait for it. In my field, political science, many of my colleagues regretably supported the bombing of Afghanistan as the necessary response to 9/11. I was an isolated voice at that time in the academy. Actually, I should qualify that statement: many academics of color were actively opposed to the bombing. I was the only white person on panel after panel of academics that were explicitly against the bombing of Afghanistan.

K.K.: That's so interesting to me because my experience—at NYU—was quite different. Immediately after bombs started dropping in Afghanistan, there was a rash of teach-ins, hastily put together by different academic departments and campus organizations, clearly intended as critique of the war. I and many, many others found lots of support for our anti-war positions and our ideas about the domestic fallout of the war.

I'm optimistic, but then I'm a Pollyanna. I've been very encouraged by the development of U.S. Labor against War (USLAW), a national group with quite an impressive array of union leaders and local unions among its endorsers. It's actually history-making. Since the days of Samuel Gompers, the labor movement has been either silent on questions of war or outspoken in support of U.S. military policies. This time around, the AFL-CIO itself came close to taking an anti-war stance. True, it fell back the moment bombs began dropping, but what's significant is that the federation said at *some* point that war was a last resort; that Iraq should be disarmed through diplomatic means; and that the UN should be a partner of the U.S. in working toward this goal. Many of us took that to be an anti-war statement, however equivocal. Unfortunately—in my opinion—the AFL-CIO later issued another statement, supporting the invasion once troops had been committed. That was a disappointment. But there was an opening there. It's up to us to continue the discussion. I'm not sure how well we'll do. But I like to believe that Elizabeth Bunn was right when she said this moment—however awful—presents us with an opportunity to re-think ourselves as a social movement.

D.C.: Unlike Kitty, I have a tendency to be a pessimist, but I'm always struggling in the other direction as well. There is a danger that we all know we must confront in a nuclear world, a third world war where nuclear weapons will be used, which would be, as the philosopher Theodore W. Adorno said, a true catastrophe. Ironically, this is where Kant's optimism came in. He said at some point, what he called the unsociability of humanity would click in and we would recognize that we had brought ourselves to the point where we either embrace the idea of perpetual peace as an ideal or end up in the long and silent graveyard, a human species that killed itself through its own technological advances. You know Albert Einstein said nuclear weapons changed everything except our thinking. That's why I think just war theory is no longer appropriate. There aren't any meaningful non-combatant immunities in a nuclear war. As we've seen, there aren't any meaningful, non-combatant immunities for the people of Baghdad. What does it mean to survive "shock and awe" even if you're not one of the people actually bombed? I think of it in terms of how bad 9/11 was. It was, however, quickly over. We didn't expect it the next night, and the next night, and the next night. That in itself is imposing a horrible trauma on people. There is the dread that there is no end in sight. That the bombing will go on and on and with the horrifying intensity, which members of the Bush administration actually bragged about. Most of the countries who have spoken out have said that they consider the war to be illegal in terms of the UN charter and immoral under just war theory. Many countries have considered the strategy of "shock and awe" a crime against humanity, which is a perfectly legitimate claim. And I join these voices. I consider "shock and awe" a crime against humanity.

This anti-war movement has, however, not limited itself to the actual war in Iraq and the horrible effects of that war on the Iraqi people. It has also taken an enormous toll at home, including the loss of young people in the military. It was against the whole Bush agenda, which includes its foreign policy and its corresponding toll on our day-to-day lives in the U.S., that the huge mobilizations of the people in this nation directed their resistance. As we both have already said, the infrastructure of democracy is in danger through an attack on constitutional rights, workers rights, and women's rights. Interestingly enough—I never thought I'd hear myself say this—I would include the attack on the basic ideal of the rule of law as being better than the rule of men. The vice president said he's not insulted when he's called a "gun-slinging cowboy" because he thinks that's what we need.[2] This is throwing out the idea that there's anything to lawfulness!

K.K.: Well, if you think you're a "gun-slinging cowboy" who's above the law, it doesn't take you very long to abandon all pretence of civility and self-censorship. Your message gets out pretty fast. Before you know it, the cowboy press has a license to run a banner headline—as it did in the *New York Post* not long ago—calling Iraqi soldiers "savages." And the average reader hardly noticed. We start using new words and slogans that are meant to make atrocities seem attractive—like the famous "shock and awe." Labeling and selling war by these methods is the ultimate form of moral and political manipulation. It makes us all complicit.

D.C.: I want to really stick with the ideal of civility. I like the word. Civility implies that moment of self-reflection where I say that my behavior regarding you must be informed by my respect for your dignity, my respect for your humanity. That goes way beyond the simple idea that I never thought I'd find myself defending, namely the rule of law!

K.K.: Well, I guess the rule of law looks pretty good when it's under attack by the likes of Bush, Cheney and Ashcroft. These characters are masquerading as the standard bearers of law. In the meantime, they have been working over-time to curtail our rights and take away entitlements that have been won through painful political and social struggle. Some of us are afraid the loss of our civil and human rights may be permanent. That has made the anti-war movement a peace and justice movement, acutely conscious of its responsibility to draw parallels between war abroad and war at home. In that respect, these Bush guys have done us a favor, if only because they've raised our consciousness.

D.C.: I think you're right. I long for those days when Nixon felt like he actually had to get up and say I've done horrible wrong things and therefore I resign. He had to act at least like conscience was important to him. These guys aren't going to resign and worse yet they portray conscience as a faint-hearted response of the weak.

K.K.: Isn't it a joke. We wanted to impeach a president for fooling around with his intern but it's okay for a president to transgress international law and flout world opinion.

D.C.: Breaking international law! And undermining the UN! So now North Korea says "you're a gun-slinging cowboy, so am I and I got my nukes right here!" Except it's not guns we're playing with—it's nuclear weapons.

I think part of what you are getting at Kitty is that very early on in this movement people who would never have been in the anti-Vietnam movement or the civil rights movement, started to feel like they were about ready to lose everything they identified this country as standing for. So you have people in this movement who believe that this country actually has ideals including those embodied in the constitution and the Bill of Rights. If you look at United for Peace and Justice, there are some Republicans in it.

K.K.: What's unique about the current situation is that we had a full-blown anti-war movement before the first bomb dropped! That didn't happen during the Vietnam War for years, not until we began bombing Cambodia. I don't recall how many years into the war that was, but in any case it took time to develop a sizable, powerful anti-war movement. In the end, though, I think that anti-war movement played a very important role in ending the war.

D.C.: No other regime has so blatantly sought world hegemony with no apologies for it being about the advancement of the rich. No nods to international law or the constitution of the United States, which Ashcroft seems to think is an outdated document. The call to impeach Bush is beginning to get off the ground and hopefully will continue to grow strong. We are seeing the labor movement getting involved in it. I think that is going to be an important movement. It is going to take us a while to make it serious and real, but I think we need to invest in it as if we really believe it can happen. We protested for months and months and we really did push back the start of the war in Iraq. Every time it was pushed back that was a victory even though it did not keep the bombs from falling. We have to follow up with both a short term and long term program. I think this is the basis for our optimism: now that the Bush administration has taken it all away so graphically—the minimum of women's rights, workers rights, decency, civility—let's really rethink these issues and the political program they comprise. I don't think the left ever completely disappeared from public life. When my comrade Ann Snitow was asked what kind of peace movement she would be part of she began her response by stating that she had never left the peace movement. I didn't either. The left never truly disappeared.

K.K.: We've had only a few moments in our history when the American left appeared as a coherent and discernible movement. The 1930s and early forties was one of them. That period was largely defined by the Popular Front, the New Deal and the rise of the CIO. We haven't had another confluence of events quite like it since then. Nevertheless, the left has survived, in different configurations, of course. There was an anti-nuclear movement in the fifties; there was opposition to anti-communist witch hunts; leftists campaigned to free the Rosenbergs. Then, of course, there were the New Left social movements of the 1960s and seventies. I don't know if we will ever have a united-front left-wing movement, but there is a demonstrable continuity of left-wing activity in this country. The rise of a new student movement—one that is as deeply concerned about issues of class as it is about social identity—is a great example in the here and now.

D.C.: Let us hope we can build a United Front Left. If there's ever been an opening for it since the thirties it is now, precisely because of the unapologetic attack on just about everything that the left has fought for over many decades . . . I must say that I have been shocked at the way the Constitution itself and the Bill of Rights have been impugned by Ashcroft. It seems the constitution no longer has the symbolic hold it once did. We obviously have major problems with our first amendment. Journalism is controlled by a small handful of media moguls who prevent us from having the kind of transparency guarantees that democracy needs. We need to be able to watch on television what the French are watching—the debates happening at the United Nations, for example; especially since the UN building is in our city!

4. Justifiable Violence, Political Rhetoric, and the Media

While some in the anti-war movement advocated pacifism in all circumstances, others would not accept the idea that violence could or should never be used to end oppression. Memories of Nazi Germany and South African Apartheid inspired the need for a framework that was against militarism and excessive use of force, but still allowed for military involvement in limited circumstances. Just war theory, Drucilla argues, is an outdated model for the nuclear age. Kitty pushes for recognition of "ethics" in any future framework of justifiable violence. Media coverage following the bombing of Iraq also inspired an exchange on the meaning of violence and the power of rhetoric. How did the Bush administration manage to neutralize the violence they enacted on Iraqi people while portraying Iraqis as savages? What are the limits to what can be done in the name of freedom and what freedoms have Americans actually lost by the hands acting in the name of their defense?

—J.M.

D.C.: In certain cases I would support preventive counter violence, but I would not want violence defended as such. I want to move away from Michael Walzer's just war theory, to the ideal of perpetual peace. That is why I would want to defend armed struggle including that of the ANC in South Africa as preventive counter violence. Wrongs were committed in the armed struggle in South Africa and the Truth and Reconciliation Commission insisted that the ANC faced those wrongs in public. It was not enough simply to say that the armed struggle was itself righteous and explain away the deaths of innocent people on the occasions when they occurred. Perhaps most importantly the ANC never at any time justified offensive terrorism against civilians. Their efforts were mainly directed toward sabotage of electrical plants, factories, etc. Mandela saw the death of human beings as a tragic result of flaws in the best-laid plans, plans that were meant to succeed without killing. Some just war theory concedes too much to realism. Pacifists have to be against all wars and all forms of violence. I think as a matter of politics and ethics, we have to accept the need for preventive counter-violence and yet I want pacifists to be respected in the place the give to the ideal.

K.K.: The phrase preventive counter violence doesn't roll off my tongue very easily. Where does the word "ethical" fit in?

D.C.: Let us name it "ethical preventive counter-violence."

K.K.: If we don't get the idea of ethics in there, the phrase "preventive counter-violence" is just the thing for reactionaries and police states. Which, of course, gets us right back to the debate between universalism and relativism. How do we define ethical without either essentializing the term or *denuding* it of meaning? And how does it resonate with someone like me, whose grandfather was killed in Auschwitz. Frankly, I find it hard to think of the war against Hitler as an act of preventive counter violence. It's a struggle to take an experience like mine—which is not mine alone or unique to me—and try to transform it, to give it some larger ethical meaning. My outrage—and my fear—is too personal. In defining our terms, we have to account for political and moral contradictions, based on emotional and subjective realities.

D.C.: Preventive counter-violence has to be fought within my commitment to the ideal of perpetual peace and my insistence that we need to move beyond just war thinking. One of the projects I am working on now is to examine how black South Africans through words like ubuntu were able to express that kind of rage and yet temper it through forgiveness and reconciliation. Ubuntu is an interesting ethical word that was used in the 1993 post amble of the constitution that spoke to the need for reconciliation and justified the provision of amnesty under certain conditions to those who confessed their wrong doing. It resonates with dignity, but it is irreducible to dignity, it is a stronger word. If you are harmed in some way and you suffer a wrong, I am diminished in my humanity. So if we watch bombs fall on Baghdad, whether we are being bombed or not, our humanity is being diminished. It implies a very strong commitment to the singularity and preciousness of every human life.

K.K.: The hypocrisy of the Administration's pro-war rhetoric is incredible. Here are these bible-quoting Christians, for whom—presumably—the most important body of law is the Ten Commandments. And President Bush violates one of the most famous ones every day, without blushing. Thou shalt not kill, but Bush doesn't flinch when he says, "We will kill Saddam Hussein." He says it on TV, in press conferences—any public setting at all—as though there is no moral problem contained in such a statement. It's not, after all, about the rules of military engagement; it's about murder; and hardly anyone bats an eyelash. The administration has heroicized war by giving it a grandiose name—Operation Iraqi Freedom. That helps them popularize or neutralize violent crimes and unlawful acts—like murder.

D.C.: Not only is it neutralized, but we are associating it with freedom. Two scary headlines stand out in the news. The first one is "Smoking Baghdad," smoking is a street word for killing, so we are killing a whole city. The other one is "Blood in the Sand, Theirs not Ours" which gloats over "their" spilt blood.

K.K.: The most horrible headline I have seen was one I mentioned earlier. It was in the *New York Post*. There was a full-page cover photo of two Iraqi soldiers, pointing a gun at someone lying on the ground. The screaming headline in bold-faced type was one word: "SAVAGES." Not a line to explain the circumstances of the photo or to suggest that in war soldiers do what they have to do to defend themselves—or what they think they have to do. What responsible human being thinks this scummy brand of journalism is defensible under any circumstances?

D.C.: I participated in a discussion on the same headline at a book party in an Irish bar. The general consensus was that this headline tells us why Iraqis are monstrous and why we had to kill them all. I jumped in and said, "Did you see any contradiction in what you just said? These people are at war defending their country and they killed some of our soldiers. We killed how many of theirs? If we're proud of that killing, does that make us savages too? Or does it make all of us human beings?" I got hit with a tirade, of well, let's just say impolite descriptions of my sexual difference. I said "are you saying that I'm out of humanity now because I've asked you to reflect if killing takes you out of humanity? Because if it does, we've taken ourselves out. Are "cunts" human beings to you?" I have found many people in the United States have accepted that we represent civilization and that the Arab world has remained savage. Bernard Lewis has written the same book twenty times defending this hypothesis. What I was trying to get these gentlemen to see is that they were doing exactly what they were criticizing.

K.K.: The news reports about Iraqi plans to subvert an invasion by burning oil fields and blowing up bridges were very telling. Instead of reporting these plans as defensive tactics, in response to bellicose threats coming out of the White House, reporters cited them as examples of Saddam's brutality and lawlessness. They pretty much followed the administration line, saying these things proved that war was necessary in order to rein in Saddam and bring Iraq under our control. It's incredible how we are being manipulated. That *Post* headline, for example, is creating and circulating knowledge—or what passes for knowledge. It's one thing to argue about who is in or out of the human circle. It's quite another to ask who gives us the authority to decide that question.

D.C.: The anti-war protests did not even make it to the news for months. At the same time the news bolsters the fantasy of the savages, the ghouls on the other side. This is a dangerous combination. Our violence becomes violence against monsters. Self-reflection becomes more difficult because at the same time we are shut out from the necessary information we need to get a sense of our actual situation. How can such a big percentage of the population of the U.S. actually believe that Saddam Hussein had a part in the attacks of 9/11?

We need to listen to what other countries are saying when they say not only that the war is illegal; but that it's immoral, and a crime against humanity. We need to hear it! We've lost the ability to get the anti-war movement on meaningful talk shows, except in tiny little snippets. According to the U.S.A. Patriot Act, it is possible to be seen as someone who is violating the so-called security of this country by speaking out against some of the Bush administration's activities and policies. It hasn't reached the point where we've seen peace activists prosecuted, but it will.

K.K.: What about that guy at the mall who got arrested for wearing a shirt that said, "Peace Now"?

D.C.: Forgive me, you're right, we are starting to see it. The fourth amendment says that you cannot have your house searched, your car, your personhood without probable cause established. And yet many members of the Muslim community are being forced to endure such searches.

K.K.: I had occasion to go to New York Hospital several times after 9/11. Security guards would stop me and search my car. They would ask me—and presumably other patients—"What are you here for?" Then you have to say you're going to the proctologist or the gynecologist or you're going for chemotherapy—talk about invasion of privacy!

D.C.: We know that habeas corpus has simply been suspended for many members of the Muslim community. We know there are disappeared people. Bush has no moral standing to call upon the international community to condemn crimes against humanity when he refuses to take international law seriously. We have not treated prisoners from the Taliban, let alone from Al Qaeda, in accordance with the protocols of the Geneva Convention. The Fifth Amendment says you can't be forced to testify against yourself and now it is okay for torture to be used, but maybe it's not torture? For instance, if you're shot four times and you don't get medical aid, is that forcing someone to testify against themselves? I think it is a form of unacceptable coercion, and, yes, torture which can be committed by omission. So the fifth, fourth, and first amendments, these very basic rights, are being whittled away. We gave Bush unheard of war-making powers. If there is one thing the founding fathers were terrified of, it was the executive branch running politically and legally amuck. Congress alone was to declare wars. But the Congress conferred on Bush the right to go to war without a national congressional declaration of war. That's unheard of in two hundred years of constitutional history! The basic infrastructure of the United States is in serious danger.

Notes

1. "Shock and awe" is a military strategy that aims to destroy the enemy's will to fight by overwhelming them with force rather than physically destroying its military forces.
2. For reference to Bush as "gun-slinging cowboy," see Richard Bernstein, "Two Years Later; World Opinion, Foreign Views of U.S. Darken after Sept. 11," *New York Times*, September 11, 2003, A1.

CHAPTER 11

Calling All Liberals: Connecting Feminist Theory, Activism, and History

JENNIFER MANION

What happens when politically conscious historians do not take gender or sexuality seriously as intellectual inquiries? Does it matter if historians of women and gender are not cognizant of the ways gender or sexuality function in their lives? Why have the fields of women's history and queer theory grown so far apart when some of the earliest works on sexuality and gay and lesbian lives came from historians? What follows is both a critique of and an impassioned plea to liberal faculty and graduate students to be aware of the political and personal impact of homophobia and heterosexism in the classroom on *all* students. This chapter aims to identify an experience that many gay and lesbian students share but few have the opportunity to articulate within the academy.

This erasure of gay experience and the perpetuation of heterosexism occurs on multiple levels, including individual, disciplinary, and institutional; in the production of scholarship, the selection of course material, and the classroom dynamic itself. Along with all of their credentials and experiences, scholars bring their personal biases to work. Homophobia is still pervasive in the United States. A study by the Gay, Lesbian, and Straight Education Network (GLSEN) states that 84 percent of gay and lesbian teens reported verbal harassment at school because of their sexual orientation and 82.9 percent report that faculty "never or rarely intervene when present" for such harassment.[1] Conservative politicians and religious leaders challenge the very humanity of gays and lesbians on a daily basis, promoting fear and hatred for their own political and economic gain.

Jerry Falwell used his appearance on *The 700 Club* with Pat Robertson to blame gays and feminists for the attacks of September 11, 2001. Even conservatives thought Falwell went too far—and he apologized within days. Yet the attacks persist—most notably when Pennsylvania Republican Senator Rick Santorum equated homosexuality with polygamy and incest.[2]

In the United States, there is no federal hate crimes bill that includes sexual orientation, sexual orientation is not a class protected from employment discrimination under the 1964 Civil Rights Act, gays and lesbians are denied adoption and second-parent adoption rights in many states, and cannot openly serve in the military. Our relationships are not deemed legally significant enough to ensure the transfer of pensions, social security, and property to each other in the event of death, nor to guarantee hospital access, health benefits, or recognition in life. It is no surprise in this context that a fair amount of homophobia—defined broadly as an aversion to gay or lesbian people or their lifestyle or culture—resides in the hearts and minds of academics.

Within the field of history, gay and lesbian history is marginal, to say the least. Despite twenty years of highly original articles and numerous books—some of which significantly challenge historical convention and knowledge—a history major could easily graduate without reading any of this literature.[3] Scholars with gay-themed doctoral dissertations are often deemed inadequate to teach the U.S. history survey by hiring committees. While many schools do have sexual orientation in their nondiscrimination policies, it remains an empty promise on many campuses. Without employment protection laws on the books, gays and lesbians can legally be fired for their sexual orientation. This fact alone keeps even gay and lesbian scholars from incorporating sexuality into their syllabi or challenging heterosexism in their pedagogy. Without institutional or departmental support, individual faculty who take on this important political and intellectual task also take risks.

Heterosexism is commonplace in the scholarship of most historians, even those who study women and gender. Though more historians put women in their work than ever before and analyses of gender are increasingly common, many still fail to understand the relationship between sex roles, gender presentation, and homophobia. Historians can work their way out of these traps by reading feminist theory. Without a critique of the current sexual order of society, it is difficult to offer an intelligent assessment of historical meanings that doesn't simply reproduce our own values.

I have taken courses in feminist theory three times, twice at the graduate level. I suffered in these courses, for good reasons and less pleasant ones, but they were all integral to the development of my thinking as a historian of gender and sexuality. It is the best tool we have to deconstruct the relationships between sex, gender, sexuality, and power. Understanding why people behaved the way they did and how individual and collective actions shaped the experiences of people on large and small scales—this is the work of a historian. Feminist theory offers a multifaceted framework for the analysis of power—what forms it takes, why certain people have it, how they keep it, what they do with it, and the struggle of others to get it. Feminist theories of deconstruction also challenge the universality of the liberal subject and some historians have raised these questions to very productive and insightful ends. Several scholars have demonstrated the exclusion of women in the formation of the liberal subject and definition of democratic citizenship.[4] Others show how whiteness is created though the bodies of African Americans.[5] Feminist theorist Judith Butler contends that heterosexuals come into being and acquire a meaningful identity similarly—through the abjection of the homosexual.[6] This framework alone opens up the possibility for historians to interpret the meaning and function of heterosexuality regardless of available sources on homosexuals.

Still, many historians are averse to theory for legitimate reasons. It forces us to re-think our assumptions and challenge our ways of knowing; it undermines our ability to speak with certainty about the categories we deploy in our work; it is often written in a language that is difficult to comprehend and requires re-reading and collective consideration. Theories that contest the boundaries of categories often make choices less clear-cut, and political action more complex. At its best, theory challenges us to critically examine aspects of our own lives that we don't necessarily want to think consciously about. Who wants to acknowledge privilege? Who wants to dissect the inconsistencies between our political values and lived lives?

What follows is a reflection on my experiences in various feminist theory classes. I have struggled *against* theory as much as anyone, for many of the same reasons listed above. But I have also been challenged by it in the most productive ways. When things become too abstract and destabilized, I can return to the methods of history and consider theoretical concepts in relation to a historical *subject*. There is a reason I am a historian and not a cultural theorist or literary critic. I enjoy working with historical evidence, events that really happened, and people who actually lived.

As a junior in college, I enrolled in English Professor Lynda Hart's course titled "Sexuality on Stage." I tried to enroll in feminist theory in another department, but the professor would not allow me in without prior theoretical training, despite my interest in the subject and demonstrated commitment to feminist activism. Lynda, however, took in everyone who wanted to learn—especially activists, especially queers. Like me, she came from a working-class family and was a first generation college student. She did not know what the Ivy League was until she was hired to teach there—and she never privileged the students from elite prep schools and the upper class.

We read work by Foucault, Judith Butler, Peggy Phelan, and Eve Sedgwick. We viewed performances by cutting edge feminist artists in the aftermath of the politically motivated culture wars that led to the de-funding of artists who challenged heterosexism, sexism, and other hegemonic values. We talked about the culture wars, sexual violence, class privilege, and bodily fluids. Class was always about the theories and always about our lives: our desires, our experiences, and our struggles. There was never a separation. There was never a separation for me, either. The course pushed me to think more critically, more consciously about the goals of my activism. What did it mean for me to be a lesbian-feminist activist after Lynda blew open the categories of "lesbian" and "feminist"—exposing the racism, elitism, and Puritanism which they often contained? Were our actions true to our ultimate aims? Did our categories enable or interfere with our activities? Did they contradict our mission? Academia was the site of much of my activism. There was a logical connection, a natural flow between the two.

Years later, upon entering graduate school in the Midwest, I enrolled in feminist theory again. In this particular course, there was no connection between the theory and real lives. It was always abstract, never contextualized, and never meaningful. This pedagogy of abstraction led to a classroom of disengagement. I learned the hard way that when the professor raised a theoretical dilemma, I wasn't supposed to answer her, but was to wait for her to answer herself. My classmates somehow knew this. After I accepted the politics of disengagement, class went more smoothly. It also, however, drained my belief in the power and importance of doing feminist scholarship. I wondered whether I should aspire to be a feminist scholar, because whatever the political positions of my colleagues and the professor for the course, they were not at all like anything I had ever defined as feminist. The class spoke primarily of lesbianism in relation to sadomasochism—as if the two were synonymous. I struggled to understand why I was so put off by the class and how it could possibly not relate to my life at all when my life revolved around being a lesbian feminist activist. Was I more invested in contemporary politics than my classmates? Was I more connected to the goals of the gay rights movement? Or was I just stupid? On cold, snowy, lonely days in the middle of nowhere, isolated from the movement and my friends, I concluded the latter. Rather than inform my scholarship, my activism, and my life, this theoretical training threatened to pull me away from graduate school entirely, to drain what I saw as the power of doing feminist history.

One doesn't need to study theory, however, to be a successful historian. I still wanted graduate training in history, especially when I recalled why I ever thought history was worthwhile or interesting in the first place. In history, before graduate school, I found heroes, answers, and possibilities; heroes who blazed trails I can't imagine having the courage to walk down, answers to my deepest and most frivolous questions, and possibilities for new ways of living, dreaming, fighting, and understanding. So I switched to a program with an established commitment to the study of women's history, along with the largest concentration of feminist historians in the world.

In history departments nationally, it is not uncommon for there to be an anti-theory contingent. It can be a bizarre source of pride for some to resist critical theories of deconstruction, representation, and power. Some speak of theory as some big *other* thing that they would read if they had more time, if it was obviously more integral or critical for their work as a historian. In this context, I began to value theory again. Theoretical critiques of historical methods and content have gotten to me, gotten under my skin and into my brain. Theories of sexuality, deconstruction, power, and even psychoanalysis have fundamentally, irrevocably changed my orientation as a historian and my view of the world. History, I concluded, had no inherent value or uncontested meaning, and the process of history making should always be questioned. My relationship to history—the process, product, and discipline—needed to be redefined, again. I needed space to do this, so the time I previously would have spent at university functions, I put into my activist community in Philadelphia—mentoring and educating gay, lesbian, bisexual, and transgender youth at the Attic Youth Center, doing political advocacy on the statewide level with the Center for Lesbian and Gay Civil Rights, raising money for local AIDS organizations through the AIDS Fund.

And I enrolled in a feminist theory course, again. I also enrolled in a course on the history of women's activism. And the spring semester began. The reading list for this latest version of feminist theory was different from what I was used to. I wondered what political theory, freedom, and development had to do with feminism—or feminist theory. But I was relieved to have a syllabus without historical monographs and I was looking forward to the change. I didn't expect how significant the change would be, however.

There were no longer separations. Feminist theory with Professor Drucilla Cornell, as it had been with Lynda Hart, was always about the theories and always about our lives. We talked about the terrorism wars, sexual violence, racial privilege, and bodily integrity. It pushed me to think more critically, more consciously about the goals of my teaching, my research, and my life. What did it mean for me to do United States women's history when Drucilla had just blown open the categories of "United States" and "women"—exposing the racism, elitism, and imperialism central to the how the U.S. government treats other governments, how western women view other women? What is my responsibility as an American citizen to the people of the nations that my government exploits, oppresses, and destroys? How do I challenge white, middle-class heterosexual women's claim to the label "woman" in my work? Theory became the unexpected bridge between my politics and my intellectual work.

Back in the history department, the situation was more complicated. In the Women and Gender Colloquium, we dealt with feminism, activism, and social justice on a weekly basis. We read monographs and articles on women's activism and a wide range of aspects of women's lives by feminist scholars who were redefining the subject of legitimate history. We were studying activists, learning to teach about activism, and arguing over the success and skill with which various activists approached their work. We even talked about sexuality and homosexuality intelligently, though the instructors were obviously more comfortable and well versed in the material than some of my classmates. In fact, more often than not it was one of the instructors, Professor Nancy Hewitt, who raised the question of sexuality for discussion.

At the end of four years of graduate school, however, the extent to which ideas about sexuality in general and histories of homosexuality more specifically are not taught or engaged has been astonishing. The problem is two-fold. The first issue is the exclusion of gay and lesbian history from history courses. Why does it not make it onto many syllabi, undergraduate or graduate? Gay and lesbian themed books which also speak to political activism, reform movements, cultural studies, medicine, and racial identity, for starters, have been published by respected historians.[7] And yet even liberal faculty often deem such works as special interest subjects, those with narrow appeal that can't speak to greater issues in the historical narrative. One way of understanding this is through the pervasive presence of the liberal subject. As feminist theorist Judith Butler has argued, straight people come into being as heterosexuals through their rejection of homosexuality; resistance to gay experience as a worthwhile subject of social and political history is the reenactment of a centuries old battle over the definition of the liberal subject.

The second problem is the absence of an analytical framework that problematizes the categories of sex and sexuality. This is precisely why inclusion of gay and lesbian social history is only a partial solution to the heterosexism of history. Feminist theories offer historians ways to situate evidence and anecdotes within larger frameworks of meaning. Theories of sexuality provide a critique of social structures that have *produced* sexuality as an identity maintained through a homo/hetero binary rather than a practice. For historians of women and gender, Carole Patemen's, *The Sexual Contract*, Judith Butler's *Gender Trouble* and Monique Wittig's *The Straight Mind and Other Essays* are useful reading.[8] Women of color and third world feminists have demonstrated the particularly racialized nature of sex, sexuality, and gender, most poignantly engaged in the following collections: *This*

Bridge Called My Back: Writings by Radical Women of Color, Cherrie L. Moraga and Gloria E. Anzaldua, eds., *Home Girls: A Black Feminist Anthology,* Barbara Smith, ed., *Third World Women and the Politics of Feminism,* Chandra Talpade Mohanty, Ann Russo, and Lourdes Torres, eds., and *Feminist Genealogies, Colonial Legacies, Democratic Futures,* M. Jacqui and Alexander and Chandra Talpade Mohanty, eds.[9] Such works are widely cited and valuable entry points for the historian new to feminist theory.

At this time—30 years after gay liberation—gay and lesbian history and the history of sexuality is still marginalized. My experience is not unique; the problem spans higher education. There is no built in expectation that a historian—even one whose work has a heavy gender component—can at all speak intelligently about histories of sexuality or sexual minorities. If gay and lesbian history is not important enough to be taught in graduate school, then gay and lesbian history must not be important; if gay and lesbian history is not important, then gay and lesbian people must not matter.[10] Historical invisibility intact, the heterosexist narrative of history continues.

Sexuality is currently categorized as a subfield, even of women and gender history. Sexuality has been a marginal category of analysis because many still believe that only gay and lesbian people have sexuality. Historical evidence supporting gay and lesbian identity—particularly before the twentieth century is hard to come by. The invisibility of gays and lesbians in historical records has led to their invisibility in historical writing. Without proof to the contrary, the interpretive default has always been heterosexual. What kind of intervention is needed for sexuality to be understood as a significant analytical concept in history? Even a reading of the feminist classics, "Compulsory Heterosexuality and Lesbian Existence," by Adrienne Rich or Carroll Smith-Rosenberg's, "Female World of Love and Ritual," offer possibilities.[11] Failure to incorporate analysis of sexuality and its relation to gender and race and class perpetuates heterosexism and leaves the structures of compulsory heterosexuality unnamed and unchallenged.

But lack of evidence is only one reason for the erasure of lesbians in history. In his provocative account about the political nature of writing history, Michel-Rolph Trouillot lays out four crucial moments when silences enter the process of historical production: the making of sources, the making of archives, the making of narratives, and the making of history.[12] The creation and perpetuation of silences are central to the project of making history—even those histories which explicitly claim to give voice to the silenced. The consequences of the production and reproduction of invisibilities are difficult to measure. Trouillot writes, "Any historical narrative is a particular bundle of silences, the result of a unique process, and the operation required to deconstruct these silences will vary accordingly."[13] Few people's histories in the United States have been as affected by the process of historical silencing as that of lesbians. Women who enjoyed intimate sexual and romantic relationships with other women often destroyed evidence of such.[14] Surviving family members and archivists erase, destroy, or exclude sources that prove or infer a lesbian inclination.[15] Scholars knowingly deny this information by not writing about the personal and/or sexual relationships of lesbians who were otherwise noteworthy women for their professional or political accomplishments.[16] The construction of the archives already makes researching the lives of women a challenge.[17] Finding lesbians in the archives is, to use Trouillot's word, an "operation" only those most committed to challenging the heterosexist narrative of American history have undertaken.[18]

To illustrate this multi-pronged process of the production of silence, consider the circumstances surrounding the life and death of Lynda Hart, former professor of English and Theatre Arts at the University of Pennsylvania. Lynda, as I mentioned previously, introduced me to feminist theory. She was a prolific scholar, writing and editing many volumes on feminism, theatre, pop-culture, and queer theory.[19] The following story provides insight into the process of destruction of records of lesbian lives—even to this day. It highlights the ways that both heterosexism and homophobia ensured her marginal status in the department and on campus, despite her promotion to full professor shortly before her death. It is also a tribute to Lynda, who first taught me the value of feminist theory and modeled a challenge to heterosexist normativity in her teaching, scholarship, and life, at a time when I needed it most.

It had been five months since Lynda died. My friend Jim and I were back at Penn for a conference. We wondered what had been done with her things—her books, her files, her history—the life that she kept in her office. It didn't seem like five months. It didn't yet sink into me—into my heart or even my mind—that she was no longer around. I was acutely aware of what she meant to me—who she was in life. It was the death part that I didn't get—I didn't think her death really affected me. I didn't yet know what she meant to me—who she was in death. But Jim did. At least that weekend. To him, Lynda was the late night phone call for a turkey sandwich, Diet Coke, and help with her footnotes. He told that story over and over—in her southern accent: "Now Jim I need you to come ov'r here right away, Jim. I lost everything. I need you to re-do the footnotes, Jim. I've been here all night. Oh—and bring me a turkey sandwich and a diet coke. Get here quick, Jim—I need you." In death, it seemed, Lynda didn't need Jim—at least at that moment.

We went up to the third floor of Bennett Hall, where her office had been for fifteen years. Jim had been her research assistant and still had keys to her office. Only later would we learn the extent to which the office was really her home. That day we had our own memories—mine of us smoking cigarettes one day after class, sitting on the worn brown corduroy love seat, complaining about how elitist and homophobic Penn students were. That was back when I smoked, when she was still alive, when I thought she was crazy. Ten years later, I still think she was crazy—but now I see that the craziness started as courage, passion and determination. Refusal to sell out, sell her soul or compromise her truth in a world which rewards denials, secrets, and numbness—that is what makes people eccentric, what made Lynda so outrageous, what led me to believe she was crazy.

Jim got to her door first. The office had been partly cleared out—with only boxes of books remaining for shipment over to the Women's Center. Jim became visibly upset. I didn't understand. As it happened, he was in the office two days prior and everything had been intact. Eyes scanning the mess, he hurled a string of curses into the air. In the trash, on the floor, strewn in boxes in the hallway for any passersby to see were Lynda's personal papers: her high school yearbook with markings over her face, an unpublished manuscript, a note her sister had written to her dad, and several unfinished articles. The scene indicated a complete disregard for her life's work—and legacy. We—two of the many students Lynda adopted over the years—are historians. She was a prolific scholar, respected in her fields of performance studies and feminist theory. The primary sources of a late twentieth century out-lesbian academic's life were in the trash and thrown across the floor. No wonder lesbian history is so impossible to find—we couldn't even save Lynda's.

The notion of the subject in social history is often categorized, knowable, and stagnant. Feminist theories of subjectivity challenge this stability and cohesion—so did Lynda, in her work and in her death. In *Fatal Women*, she writes on the instability of the sexual subject, "For on the one hand, heterosexuality secures its ontology by constructing the homosexual as external and foreign, and hence implicitly hostile. On the other hand, the homosexual is intrinsic to the constitution of the heterosexual—the "other" within—the "perversion" always only comprehended as a deviation from "normality."[20] Three months prior to her death, on the instability of life, as her own precarious subject she wrote, "I am beginning to really understand the connection between life and death, the deepest connection, that one cannot really live until one has fully faced death. Wouldn't it be something if death were actually a release into the fullness of life?"[21]

In the beginning of this chapter, I raised three questions about the relationships between identity, politics, feminism, and history. First, what happens when politically conscious historians don't take gender or sexuality seriously as intellectual inquiries? Politically conscious historians of the 1960s exploded the field of social history, focusing on everyday life, common people, and history from the bottom up. Not averse to theory conceptually, many of the most influential works employed a Marxist framework. Feminist theories which challenge a cohesive subjectivity, the liberal individual, and Marxist theories of power, however, were not well received.[22] The marginality of sexuality studies within the field is in part a consequence of the resistance to contemporary feminist theory. But nothing has expanded our conceptual frameworks of gender, sex, sexuality, and power the way feminist theory has.

Second, does it matter if historians of women and gender are not cognizant of the way gender or sexuality function in their lives? The project of the historian is one of recovery, documentation, and analysis. Most women's lives have not been considered important enough to merit the preservation of their records. The surprise success and institutionalization of women's history reflects an increased consciousness of the importance of women's experiences on the part of both men and women (though largely women—students and teachers of women's history are disproportionately female). While some women have had experiences that enable them to conceptualize questions that are difficult for most men to understand or accept, being a female does not ensure that one is an especially skilled or gifted women's historian. Certainly some men have done excellent work in the field and other women remain politically and conceptually opposed to it. Generally, however, those who exist outside of socially sanctified gender roles are more likely to see the social construction of gender. Heterosexuals have the privilege of not thinking very consciously about their heterosexuality because it is the social default and legal standard. Gay people have the privilege (or burden) of thinking about sexuality all the time, because ours is contested and has to be named to exist. Identity politics do not legitimate or authenticate intellectual pursuits. People who occupy positions of social privilege via class, race, sex, and sexuality, however, must go out of their way to understand the function of their power. In other words, historians who have not had to think extensively or consciously about the role of gender or sexuality in their lives need other tools to instigate this kind of critical thinking. We all do—being gay is not a ticket to theoretical superiority; it just makes it more likely that you've thought about the power of heterosexism to threaten your very existence.

Finally, why have the fields of women's history and queer theory grown so far apart when some of the earliest works on sexuality and gay and lesbian lives came from historians? From its inception, women's history has always also been gender history and sexuality history, though what gender meant in the early seventies was different from what it meant after 1986 with the publication of Joan Scott's influential essay.[23] Sexuality as a line of study has developed its own methods and questions and has not been integrated into women's history. While some women's historians have always considered sexuality integral to the project, others allow it to rest within the category of gender and lie largely uninterrogated. Historians who don't specialize in women's or gender history rarely consider sexuality at all. This is unfortunate, as the structural relations of enforced heterosexuality shape women's experiences as much as the sexual division of labor does.[24]

The translation of Foucault from French to English and the increased use of poststructuralist theories were both crucial moments that divided historians of sexuality from women's historians. Foucault's *History of Sexuality* reframed the central assumptions of the field and opened up many new areas of investigation and interpretation. The history of sexuality exploded in the early 1990s, and was marked by somewhat of a separation from women's history, which can be accounted for in several ways. First, many questions of the history of sexuality were related to or sprang from the debates of gay identity politics by gay scholars. Heterosexual historians were less quickly to consider their own sexuality a vital topic of inquiry and reflected society's tendency to marginalize and ghettoize gay people and their work. Second, sexuality studies deploy—and indeed produce—queer and feminist theories that are marginalized by historians but have become central in literary studies, women's studies, and American studies. Sexuality studies have gone far in exploding the hetero/homo binary. Historians of sexuality consider far more provocative questions than whether or not one is gay or straight. New scholarship demonstrates moments when sex isn't really considered sex, when the participants' class, status, age, or race are far more integral to the framing of the interaction than their sex.[25]

It is no secret that cutting edge feminist scholarship is more likely found in literature and American studies than history, though this certainly hasn't always been the case. Perhaps the disciplinary emphasis on empiricism over theory has created this. But no discipline's tools and boundaries are permanent; history has shown great expansive ability in the past 30 years. In the November 2003 issue of the newsletter for the Organization of American Historians (OAH), executive director Lee W. Formwalt addressed a concern which would have been unforeseeable in the field even twenty years ago. He writes, "Another complaint that we hear is that the OAH annual meeting focuses too much on race, class, and gender and not enough on the more traditional fields of military, diplomatic, and economic history."[26] The questions asked by historians have actually changed quite dramatically over the years.

Finally, a personal plea. In the introduction to her collection of writings entitled, *A Fragile Union*, teacher, writer, activist, and cofounder of the New York based Lesbian Herstory Archives Joan Nestle writes, "I have experienced three sublimely beautiful things in my life, and each has been judged unacceptable by large parts of this society: the taste and touch of women lovers, the wondrous feeling of being part of a people working to free themselves, and for almost thirty years, the trust and attention of students many others did not want to teach. In my bed, in the streets of political protests, and in the classroom, I felt the possibilities of life most keenly, I saw the wonder of human hope and creativity most clearly."[27] This statement captures multiple aspects of my own experience.

My radical politics, gender identity, and sexual orientation have earned me the disapproval of large parts of American society. This deeply informs the way I read and write history, supplying me with a suspicion and mistrust of the mainstream narratives. Nestle's statement brings to the fore a somewhat unconscious decision I have made—to want to effectively teach the students "many others did not want to teach." This desire was born of my own experiences—both of being rejected and dismissed by teachers who were uncomfortable with my androgynous appearance, lesbian identity, and research that highlighted my feminist and queer politics—but also of being supported, engaged, and mentored. I'd never explicitly thought of myself as a student others did not want to teach. I knew I was difficult and made some people uncomfortable—but this apt description reminds me of how frustrated I was with school before my life was touched by teachers who valued the opportunity to teach me, someone who was so passionate, engaged with ideas and hungry for a challenge but marginalized by the intellectual community and classroom dynamics of my peers.

It is because of this possibility that I am in graduate school. Had such teachers never entered my life, I would not have seen the college classroom as a possible site for empowerment, truth seeking, and radical challenges to hegemonic values, including heterosexism and homophobia. When I left college after my junior year, burnt out on campus politics, I would have never returned at all—even to finish my BA—if my only memories were of an English professor telling me that a homoerotic interpretation of Ishmael and Quequeg's relationship in *Moby Dick* was not legitimate or any of the countless other hostilities aimed at me by teachers, administrators, and students for refusing to be silent.

Social, political, legal, and economic power is delegated not only along lines of sexuality, but also by sex, race, and class. As teachers and scholars, we are also human beings who live in the world and are shaped by society's greater prejudices. Efforts to create a body of knowledge or classroom pedagogy that is inclusive of difference, both historical and contemporary, are valuable. This will only ever be a partial solution, however, in the absence of a critique of how the categories which give meaning to historical subjects, such as women, African Americans, heterosexuals, and others, came into being. And this is one of the most powerful insights of contemporary feminist theory.

Notes

My thanks to Barbara Balliet, Jodi Bromberg, Kathy Brown, Brian Connolly, Jim Downs, Nancy Hewitt, and Michal Shapira for reading earlier drafts of this essay and especially Barbara Balliet for her extensive comments.

1. See 2003 National School Climate Survey conducted by the Gay, Lesbian and Straight Education Network (GLSEN). Report is available at www.glsen.org/cgi-bin/iowa/all/library/index.html
2. Viewers of the program noted Pat Robertson nodding in agreement with Falwell. Falwell's apology was widely covered. See www.cnn.com/2001/US/09/14/Falwell.apology/. Santorum's comments also stirred controversy. See Sheryl Gay Stolberg, "Persistent Conflict for Gays and G.O.P.," *New York Times,* Wednesday, April 23, 2003, sec. A, late edition-final.
3. Groundbreaking studies include Carroll Smith-Rosenberg, "The Female World of Love and Ritual: Relations between Women in Nineteenth-Century America." *Signs: Journal of Women in Culture and Society* 1 (1975): 1–30; John D'Emilio, *Sexual Politics, Sexual Communities: The Making of a Homosexual Minority in the United States, 1940–1970* (Chicago: Chicago University Press, 1983); Estelle Freedman, ed., *The Lesbian Issue: Essays from Signs* (Chicago: University of Chicago Press, 1985); John D'Emilio and Estelle B. Freedman, eds., *Intimate Matters: A History of Sexuality in America* (New York: Harper and Row, 1988); Martin Duberman, Martha Vicinus, and George Chauncey, Jr., eds., *Hidden From History: Reclaiming the Gay and Lesbian Past* (New York: New American Books, 1989); Elizabeth Lapovsky Kennedy and Madeline D. Davis, *Boots of Leather, Slippers of Gold: The History of a Lesbian Community* (New York: Routledge, 1993); George Chauncey, *Gay New York: Gender, Urban Culture, and the Making of the Gay Male World 1890–1940* (New York: Basic Books, 1994).
4. For example, see Joan Landes, *Women and the Public Sphere in the Age of the French Revolution* (Ithaca: Cornell University Press, 1988); Carroll Smith-Rosenberg, "Dis-Covering the Subject of the "Great Constitutional Discussions," 1786–89." *The Journal of American History* 79, no. 3 (1992): 841–73; Genevieve Fraisse, *Reason's Muse: Sexual Difference and the Birth of Democracy* (Chicago; London: University of Chicago Press, 1994); Linda Kerber, *No Constitutional Right to be Ladies: Women and the Obligations of Citizenship* (New York: Hill and Wang, 1998); Nancy Isenberg, *Sex and Citizenship in Antebellum America* (Chapel Hill: University of North Carolina Press, 1998).
5. Kathleen M. Brown, *Good Wives, Nasty Wenches, and Anxious Patriarchs* (Chapel Hill: University of North Carolina Press, 1996); Jennifer L. Morgan, ""Some Could Suckle over Their Shoulder": Male Travelers, Female Bodies, and the Gendering of Racial Ideology, 1500–1770." *The William and Mary Quarterly* LIV, no. 1 (1997): 167–90; Walter Johnson, *Soul By Soul: Life Inside The Antebellum Slave Market* (Cambridge, MA: Harvard University Press, 1999).
6. See chapter 2 of Judith Butler, *Gender Trouble: Feminism and the Subversion of Identity* (New York: Routledge, 1990). Thanks to Brian Connolly for bringing this connection to my attention.
7. See second footnote of article as well as John D'Emilio, William B. Turner, and Urvashi Vaid. *Creating Change: Sexuality, Public Policy, and Civil Rights* (New York: St. Martin's Press, 2000); Lisa Duggan, *Sapphic Slashers: Sex, Violence, and American Modernity* (Durham: Duke University Press, 2000); Estelle Freedman, *Maternal Justice: Miriam Van Waters and the Female Reform Tradition* (Chicago: Chicago University Press, 1996); Farah Jasmine Griffin, ed., *Beloved Sisters and Loving Friends: Letters from Rebecca Primus of Royal Oak, Maryland, and Addie Brown of Hartford, Connecticuit, 1854–1868* (New York: Alfred A. Knopf, 1999); Leila Rupp, *Desired Past: A Short History of Same-Sex Love in America* (Chicago: University of Chicago Press, 1999); Marc Stein, *City of Sisterly and Brotherly Loves: Lesbian and Gay Philadelphia, 1945–1972* (Chicago: University of Chicago Press, 2000); Joanne Meyerowitz, *How Sex Changed: A History of Transexuality in the United States* (Cambridge: Harvard University Press, 2002); John D'Emilio, *Lost Prophet: The Life and Times of Bayard Rustin* (Free Press, 2003).
8. Carole Patemen *The Sexual Contract* (Stanford: Stanford University Press, 1988); Judith Butler, *Gender Trouble: Feminism and the Subversion of Identity* (New York: Routledge, 1990); Monique Wittig, *The Straight Mind and Other Essays* (Boston: Beacon, 1992).

158 · Jennifer Manion

9. M. Jacqui Alexander and Chandra Talpade Mohanty, eds., *Feminist Genealogies, Colonial Legacies, Democratic Futures* (New York: Routledge, 1997); Chandra Talpade Mohanty, Ann Russo, Lourdes Torres, eds., *Third World Women and the Politics of Feminism* (Bloomington: Indiana University Press, 1991); Cherríe Moraga, Gloria Anzaldúa, eds., *This Bridge Called My Back: Writings by Radical Women of Color* (Watertown, MA: Persephone Press, 1981). Barbara Smith, *Home Girls: A Black Feminist Anthology* (New York: Kitchen Table: Women of Color Press, 1983).
10. John D'Emilio makes this point about the impact of the absence of gay and lesbian content in graduate training in history in his essay, "Not a Simple Matter: Gay History and Gay Historians." *Journal of American History,* 76, no. 2 (1989): 435–42.
11. Adrienne Rich, "Compulsory Heterosexuality and Lesbian Existence." *Signs* 5, no. 4 (1980): 631–60. Carroll Smith-Rosenberg, "The Female World of Love and Ritual: Relations between Women in Nineteenth-Century America." *Signs: Journal of Women in Culture and Society* 1 (1975): 1–30.
12. Michel-Rolph Trouillot, *Silencing the Past: Power and the Production of History* (Boston: Beacon Press, 1995), 26.
13. Trouillot, 27.
14. Again, consider Estelle Freedman, "The Burning of Letters Continues: Elusive Identities and the Historical Construction of Sexuality." *Journal of Women's History* 9, no. 4 (1998): 181.
15. Leila J. Rupp, ""Imagine My Surprise": Women's Relationships in Mid-Twentieth Century America." In *Hidden From History: Reclaiming the Gay and Lesbian Past,* edited by Martin Duberman, Martha Vicinus, and George Chauncey, Jr., (New York: New American Books, 1989).
16. The above cited article by Rupp as well as recent work by Lillian Faderman challenge this phenomenon. See Lillian Faderman, *To Believe in Women: What Lesbians Have Done for America: A History.* (Boston: Houghton Mifflin, 1999); Also, watch the Ken Burns documentary, *Not for Ourselves Alone: The Story of Elizabeth Cady Stanton and Susan B. Anthony* to see the centering of Stanton's heterosexuality and the silence surrounding Anthony's sexuality.
17. Bonnie Smith, *The Gender of History: Men, Women and Historical Practice* (Boston: Harvard University Press, 1998).
18. The Lesbian Herstory Archives of NYC has done an extraordinary job of collecting and organizing sources of lesbian lives. Among their extensive holdlings is an index to lesbian and feminist organizational newsletters. See www.lesbianherstoryarchives.org
19. *Sam Shepard's Metaphorical Stages* (Westport, CT, Greenwood Press, 1987); *Making a Spectacle: Feminist Essays on Contemporary Women's Theatre* (Ann Arbor: University of Michigan Press, 1989); *Acting Out: Feminist Performances,* with Peggy Phelan (Ann Arbor: University of Michigan Press, 1993); *Fatal Women: Lesbian Sexuality and the Mark of Aggression* (Princeton: Princeton University Press, 1994); *Between the Body and the Flesh: Performing Sadomasochism* (New York: Columbia University Press, 1998) and *Of All the Nerve: Deb Margolin, solo,* with Deb Margolin (London, New York: Cassell, 1999).
20. Hart, *Fatal Women,* 16.
21. Lynda Myoun Hart, "Saving Grace," in *Women and Performance: a Journal of Feminist Theory* 13, no. 1 (2002): 184.
22. Two collections that productively engage the relationship between feminist theory and women's history are, *History and Theory: Feminist Research, Debates, Contestations,* Barbara Laslett, Ruth-Ellen B. Joeres, Mary Jo Maynes, Evelyn Brooks Higginbotham, and Jeanne Barker-Nunn, eds, (Chicago; London: University of Chicago Press, 1997) and *Feminism and History,* Joan W. Scott, ed., (Oxford; New York: Oxford University Press, 1996).
23. Joan Wallach Scott, "Gender: A Useful Category of Historical Analysis." In *American Historical Review* 91, no. 5 (1986).
24. Other theorists have engaged this idea extensively; Iris Marion Young cites the sexual division of labor and enforced heterosexuality as the two social structures that make women into women. See Iris Marion Young, "Gender as Seriality: Thinking about Women as a Social Collective," *Signs* 19, no. 3 (1994): 713.
25. Indrani Chatterjee, "Alienation, Intimacy and Gender: Problems for a History of Love in South Asia", in Ruth Vanita ed., *Queering India: Same-Sex Love and Eroticism in Indian*

Culture and Society (New York; London: Routledge, 2001), p.61–76; Matthew H. Sommer, "The penetrated male in late imperial China: judicial constructions and social stigma," *Modern China* 23, no. 2 (1997): 140.

26. See the OAH newsletter online at: http://www.oah.org/pubs/nl/2003nov/formwalt.html
27. Joan Nestle, *A Fragile Union: New and Selected Writings* (San Francisco: Cleis Press, 1998), 15.

CHAPTER 12

Producing for Use and Teaching the Whole Student
Can Pedagogy Be a Form of Activism?

KATHLEEN M. BROWN
TRACEY M. WEIS

Preface

Although this chapter focuses on pedagogy as a form of activism, the authors met in an archive in Richmond, Virginia in 1988. Research, scholarship, and the production of knowledge have all served as a backdrop for the friendship that subsequently blossomed. By coincidence, both of us moved to the same Pennsylvania town, just blocks away from each other, in 1993. Over the years, our friendship has included conversations about new books, teaching methods, research projects, and our efforts to balance these academic and political passions with our personal lives. For both of us, these lives revolve around families with children. Each of us makes her living as an academic at an institution for higher learning in Pennsylvania. Each of us has spent numerous research hours recovering the history of slavery and the experience of enslaved people in eastern North America. As important as these similarities are, they should not obscure our view of the differences in our situations. While both of us have experienced professional pressures to publish in conventional formats, Kathy's institution, University of Pennsylvania, requires a light teaching load and supports sabbatical leaves necessary for completing research projects destined for these conventional forms of publication. Tracey, in contrast, carries a heavy teaching load with little opportunity for a research leave. At Millersville University, publication is also a requirement for tenure but other forms of scholarly production are increasingly recognized as legitimate, in part because of Tracey's persistent efforts. This institutional context, as well as our collegiality and friendship, is important background for this essay, our first collaborative project to appear in print. In many ways we feel that it represents years of informal collaboration.

Introduction

Can pedagogy be a form of activism? This is the question we met to discuss in the autumn of 2002. Using an interview format, we interrogated each other for nearly four hours on tape and in several long meetings thereafter to try to make sense of our reasons for turning to the academy for training as historians and the combined effect of life experience and professional training on our practice in the classroom. This chapter highlights excerpts from these conversations and offers brief interpretations of their meaning.

We have organized the chapter around the three major themes that appeared in our analysis of this material: the impetus to enter the academy, the consequences of graduate training and subsequent professional experience for our intellectual development, and the efforts at pedagogical innovation—very different for each of us—that define our classroom practice today. In addition, several themes run throughout the interviews and subsequent analyses: The search for appropriate tools, fulfillment through personal connection, and an intellectual commitment to methods of historical inquiry. We will return to these themes at the conclusion of our essay to consider how they illuminate the issue of pedagogy as a form of activism.

Part One: Intention/Impetus

Tracey: I graduated from Duke in 1977 and I ended up at Rutgers' History Graduate program in 1985. I spent seven or eight years after I graduated doing a variety of community organizing projects. The one that was the most formative for me in terms of graduate school was working with the Highlander Center, specifically with their land ownership study . . . The land ownership study was the experience that really catapulted me to graduate school, although I think maybe I might have ended up there eventually.[1] I remember the experience of working with a large group of people—fifteen or twenty people in six different states—trying to figure out how to conduct community-based research. With one exception, most of the people were political scientists or sociologists. I remember feeling kind of frustrated and somewhat lonely in that crowd. As eager as I was to help develop contemporary profiles of land ownership, I was really much more interested in what the origins of those ownership patterns were. I felt that only knowledge of those origins would really help us to develop effective strategies to change those patterns. Simply knowing what they were in 1977 wouldn't take us very far. I think it was probably a frustration with my practice, my individual sense but also collective sense that deeper grounding in historical methods and historical investigation might help.

One of the insights that I gained from my experience working in the mountains at the Highlander Center around the use of technology is that technology could be a powerful tool for people in local communities to describe and analyze their local political and economic realities and that they could use the technology to communicate those understandings to other communities. And we could establish these processes of intercommunication that would result in local communities being able to draw on a wider range of strategies to solve everyday problems. When I think of the use of technology in community development work or in college classrooms, one of the things that strikes me immediately about it is its capacity to make what have essentially been private exchanges, to make those public and to give those exchanges a broader audience. In the past five years at the university, I have become much more engaged in that kind of work and those kinds of potentials but I realize that that [the use of technology] has a much longer history in my own life.

I think I approached going to graduate school with a great deal of trepidation. I didn't have a clear sense of what I thought I would do with it. I was quite worried that I would see what I hoped would be an opportunity to test theory against practical experience and observation, that is what I think I imagined graduate school would let me do would be to test theories— take if you will, the case study, the land ownership study, and try to understand it in a much broader context. I think I was afraid that in the interplay between practice and theory, that theory would kind of trump practice; I would get caught up in a situation where the practice became unimportant; and the goal of social change would become subordinated to what might become endless rounds of theorizing. I remember talking with a colleague at the land ownership study who had just finished his PhD at Oxford; he was very encouraging about the back and forth between community-based research and academic training and academic work. That there could be some useful exchange was very encouraging. I think I thought I could deepen my own practice, and I think I sought an alternative to education as a round of hierarchically imposed solutions to the problems that people faced. And I think I thought with education, people could be equipped to resolve their own problems and not necessarily be reliant on so-called experts.

Kathy: I definitely thought about it [graduate studies in history] because I thought that I wanted to go back to school after college, but I wasn't quite sure what I would do . . . maybe go to law school or joint law/history programs . . . I didn't really know what life as an historian was like, but having attended a small liberal arts college I knew that the historians I came in contact with were primarily teachers in my life. So I thought I ought to spend some time teaching to see if I liked it before I got myself into graduate school. So I taught high school for a while just to see if I liked it day-to-day. I loved the teaching that I did . . . [because] it wasn't narrowly focused on an academic subject . . . You got to actually know the student in a much more well rounded way than you do in the college setting.

My frustration, actually, wasn't with the teaching so much as it was with the curricular reform. I was teaching at a private girls' school where the history program was called "Ages of Man." Girls took "ages of man"—ninth-, tenth-, eleventh-, and twelth-grades. I taught ninth and I kept pointing out to them the irony of being at a girls' school and having a curriculum named "Ages of Man." This was 1981. And their response to me was, "Well, if you aren't happy with the curriculum, why don't you make some suggestions about how to change it?". . . I knew I was interested in women's history. I just couldn't even get off the ground with any kind of curricular suggestions that had any usefulness because I didn't even know where to go. I was living in Washington, DC, and I would go to bookstores and try to find books in women's history . . . it was very isolating and there weren't a lot of other people that I knew who were interested in this.

A friend of mine from high school who had gone to Bowdoin . . . knew about the Berkshire Conference for Women Historians and she told me she was working there. She let me sleep on a sleeping bag on the floor, which technically violated all the rules, but I did it anyway. I saw Gerda Lerner doing a presentation from her then forthcoming book on the creation of patriarchy . . . I went to as many panels as I could. I took tons and tons of notes. I just knew that that was what I had been hungering for and that's what I wanted to do . . . everyday life as a high school teacher in the DC area, however was not the Berkshire conference. It was living off the memories of that and wondering how to take the energy from that and actually make something happen at the school where I taught . . . I also brought stunning naiveté to the process of applying [to graduate school]. Any institution that I had ever heard Gerda Lerner affiliated with, I applied to because I wasn't sure where she was exactly . . . I applied to a few other places and I'm not even sure anymore how I picked them out . . . It was a shot in the dark. I really had no idea what I was doing or what I was in for.

Part One: Synopsis and Analysis

Tracey describes her experience with community organizing as both the formative moment for her intellectual and political development and as the impetus to go to graduate school. Researching with a group of scholars and community members, Tracey experienced a heady sense of the possibilities of collective scholarship destined for a public and practical application. This resonated with her previous experiences applying audio-visual technology to connect communities separated by geographic and linguistic barriers but facing similar problems. Such uses of slide shows and videos also promised to democratize knowledge by bringing it to a wider audience and possibly expanding its impact, an issue that came to the fore during her days at the Highlander Center. It also spoke to her sense of the importance of community. In addition to this concern, she brought some dissatisfaction with the historical shallowness of the Highlander study and imagined that graduate study in history would enable her to learn more about the origins of political and economic inequalities that studies like that of the Highlander group could only reconstruct cross-sectionally. Despite this optimism, she entered graduate school with some trepidation as to whether concerns about theory would trump the concern with practical applications for research.

Kathy's journey to graduate school began with an interest in scholarship on the history of women that was piqued by her fortuitous attendance at an early Berkshire Conference for Women's Historians in 1981. Filled with a sense of the possibility of women's history, but lacking the practical knowledge about existing literature or how one might remain connected to such an inspiring community of scholars, she began her first post-college job as a high school teacher in a history curriculum titled "Ages of Man." When she found she was ill equipped to do more than complain about the problems with such a curriculum at a private school for girls, she began to think seriously about acquiring the training necessary to do such transformative work. The practical goal of learning enough to create an alternative feminist curriculum, rather than the pursuit of scholarship, motivated her application to graduate school. Like Tracey, she felt trepidation at committing to such a lengthy program of study when she knew next to nothing about what she was getting into. She kept open the possibility that a few years of graduate school might prepare her to achieve another one of her goals: to write a historical novel that would evoke the experience of her great-grandmother, an Irish immigrant who worked as a maid until a nervous breakdown required that she be institutionalized.

Part Two: Institutional Constraints

Tracey: One of the things that the academy did enable me to do was to get some more thorough and specific grounding in methods of historical investigation. Research and interpretation are two general skills I think I was able to refine. I think the one question that I felt throughout most of my graduate education was this issue of producing for use, even though I wasn't using that vocabulary then. I felt that I wanted to continue with this community-based research or continue to have the community be a sounding board for the utility of academic research. [It] seems as if the trajectory that was expected at graduate school was that one would perform more conventional historical interpretation—[conventional] in format, not necessarily in content—and then at the midpoint or endpoint of one's career, one would turn to public history. That one would do academic history first and then public history. I felt a little confused because I thought I was coming in with what I might now call some experience in public history that I had to almost discard in order to be socialized into this other particular form of academic research and interpretation. It is only after maybe a decade of teaching that I feel I have been able to make a full circle and go back to that period of my life before I was in graduate studies and bring the experience of graduate studies, the experience of teaching in the academy to that.

I think what enabled me to continue to pursue and develop my teaching practice was, initially, the companionship of Women's Studies faculty in my institution, people who were open to interdisciplinary thinking, people who were willing to go beyond their disciplines, and also people who were very clearly committed to investigating the transformative role of pedagogy. . . . But I do think the real turning point for me came in my involvement in the New Media Classroom Project in finding a cadre of disciplinary colleagues who were interested in exploring the uses of technology in the classroom. They were also interested in public history and interested in changing the world. . . . One crystallizing experience was serving as a local scholar for a Pennsylvania Humanities Council project. At one of the workshops, each of the local scholars was to stand up and explain what he or she had done with the local institution. For some reason I was about the last person to report, and I remember feeling a little anxious as I heard the other local scholars because they were giving accounts of their work in the archives and the interesting and exciting things they had found. They didn't all seem to have a close connection with the institution or even a sense of how that research that they had done could be used in public programming. In contrast, I hadn't really spent that much time in the archives. I had really spent more time trying to figure out how some existing resources could be deployed, perhaps more effectively, in local communities. That moment of waiting until it was my turn helped me to remember that kind of anxiety around what it means to be a scholar and the feeling when I was at Rutgers that the definitions of scholarship were more narrow and that I might not fit into them. Even though I was happy with my work, it might not necessarily be work deemed by others in the profession to be, as my advisor said, scholarly with a capital S, it might be scholarly with a small s.

Kathy: I guess I felt that initially through graduate school, through my dissertation, and through first few years, that my personal resources, my engagement with my scholarship were not, in any way, at odds with the way the profession worked. I really didn't experience a lot of conflict. Actually, I was very fortunate in the funding that I received at the time I was writing my dissertation. I was very fortunate in the years immediately after finishing the dissertation with postdocs that allowed me to quite quickly get around to what you were conventionally expected to do: revise the dissertation and get a book published. I was more than amply supplied with the resources to do what the profession at large expected you to do along the most conventional of career paths: Scholarship with a capital S.

I think for me the sort of bumping, the sense that this isn't fitting my life as well any more, came with children because they were pitted against the sort of primal feeling that you have when you are engaged with your scholarship which is a very consuming feeling. It works best when you can shut out the rest of the world and it consumes you in a way that doesn't leave much room for the rest of the world. I worked very well in that model as a scholar, but it was very clear to me once children came into my life that that kind of life wasn't going to be available to me and that I actually no longer wanted that kind of model because the other kind of primal urge with children is to want to spend the time with the children. That is very consuming. It is consuming in a way that doesn't leave much of you left to go into that very seductive zone where it is you and your thoughts and you are wrestling with the material and you can forget what time it is and you can forget to eat and you can forget to clean your study and you can forget to email—a lot of things. I think the incompatibility is really upon me right now. It's really hitting me. I feel that I am as efficient as anyone about using small bits of time so I am taking it as a challenge to see if I can manage to quilt a book together in small blocks as opposed to weaving it or knitting it or something that implies a much more seamless process.

I think I am an example of somebody who has been socialized into the profession the way the profession likes to socialize people into it, but right now my identity is much more connected to my scholarship than it is to my teaching, though my teaching remains very important to me. When I started, among my motives, teaching ranked very high. In a certain way I feel as if the profession put an imprint on me in its own image and, unfortunately, that image is not always so compatible with my goals as a mother.

Part Two: Synopsis and Analysis

Graduate training in history honed Tracey's research and analytical skills, but also made her aware of the difference between her own assumptions about the importance of community-based research and the ruling model of academic history, scholarship with a capital S. She occasionally felt that her experience doing public history impeded her socialization into the academic mainstream. This sense of dissonance continued after she completed her dissertation and began teaching at Millersville. She recalls one incident, in particular, that captured her sense of being at odds with academic historians. Waiting to deliver a report to the Pennsylvania Humanities Council Project, she realized how much her approach differed from that of her fellow scholars, who had devoted all their attention to archival research but spent almost no time thinking about its usefulness or reception by a wider audience. She credits her Women's Studies colleagues with providing support and a model of interdisciplinary and innovative pedagogy that encouraged her to continue to experiment with new teaching practices in the classroom. Tracey identifies her involvement with the New Media Classroom as an important turning point and one that brought her full circle to many of the concerns that had motivated her entry into graduate school. Participating in this project enabled her to bring together her interest in technology with her desire to continue developing her pedagogical practice.

Kathy describes her own graduate training as less ridden by conflict with the demands of the academic mainstream of the profession. She was well funded and less skeptical than Tracey about what she was being socialized to do. Indeed, she believes that her identity as a historian shifted from being mainly grounded in her teaching to being more grounded in her scholarship during this period. Her main conflict with the ideals for academic scholarship developed with the arrival of children in her life. She describes scholarly production, as she experienced it before becoming a mother, as an all-consuming process at odds with the priority of taking care of young children. Lacking the large blocks of concentrated time to think and write, she imagines her current process of scholarly production as akin to quilting small pieces of work together. She implies that this sense of conflict might not have been so deep had her primary identity remained rooted in teaching rather than in scholarship.

Part Three: Pedagogical Strategies

Tracey: I was very influenced when I was working in central Appalachia, working at the Highlander Center, by a number of other community educators, many of whom had experience in Latin America and had come to work in the coal fields [after] five, ten, fifteen years of experience in Latin America doing community development work. In particular, their insistence on what they would call "reading" reality. Myles Horton . . . and his methods of education were very influential. Horton, founder of the Center, drew inspiration from the folk school movement in Denmark. An internationally known popular educator, he lived by the conviction that "Nothing will change until we change—until we throw off our dependence and act for ourselves."[2] So when I was thinking about the notion of activist pedagogy, pedagogy as a conceptual bridge between my experience as a community educator and my work in the academy, I went back and I thought, "What is an activist?" I looked in the dictionary "activist: practitioner of activism," which took me back to activism, and the definition I found there I thought was very provocative, which was "the use of direct action." The examples given were "demonstration or strike in opposition to or support of a cause; the policy of taking direct and militant action to achieve a political or social goal." The part of it that sounds perhaps familiar in the context of African American Studies or Women's Studies or Latino Studies, is purposeful action, although I am not sure it is *always* relevant. It just drew me back to the cause: self-determination as an antidote to having decisions made for people by other people who presume to know more than the people who are mostly going to be affected by those decisions. So I think it was that principle of people who are affected by decisions should be equipped as best as they could be to participate in making those decisions. . . . The approach of Highlander was to bring together people who are affected by a social, economic, or political problem and to get them to talk about that problem and begin to share with other people in similarly affected communities what some of their efforts at solving that problem had been. And that that kind of exchange would generate more sophisticated solutions to common problems that people face. And I think of the classroom in a somewhat similar fashion.

. . . There came a moment at the land study near the end, when we were trying to figure out, we've done the research, what do we do now? One of the participants raised a question to Myles Horton about how can we be sure people won't take the research that we've done and turn it to other ends? And his response was very direct, which was, you can't be sure of that. Almost the only way you can assure that is to use the research yourself. He cautioned us against thinking that we could somehow just produce research and leave it for other people to figure out the implications and to implement a course of action, that the point of research was to be useful. He argued that the same people who were involved in collecting the research should be involved in figuring out the implications and implementing the solutions that might come out of the research . . . His life, his experience, the whole approach to the Highlander study really influenced my understanding of education, which is that education was purposeful. I've developed a little slogan from that in my own teaching with university students, which is to "produce for use." The work that students do in the classroom should have a purpose for them and it should have a purpose beyond the classroom as well. They should, for example, produce knowledge that is socially useful. What "socially useful" means is a subject of lifelong discussion and student direction.

One of the ways that I can do that is through this culture of teaching and learning, in particular, the Visible Knowledge Project that I am engaged in right now. One of the questions about that project that I am trying to adapt for my students, to get back to your question about process, is how to share experiences and evidence in ways that make [for] reflective practice. There are four criteria: visible, shareable, portable, and expandable. If those are the goals I have for my own scholarship, that my practice of teaching be visible, shareable, portable and expandable, doesn't it make sense that I have the same goals for my students? That their work should be visible, shareable, portable in some fashion, and expandable beyond the confines of that one semester course. One of the big challenges is visibility, moving from having the classroom as private space to the classroom as a public space in which others are invited into that space to see both the process and the product of education. Sometimes that is a novel, and for some people, a scary thought, that other people could see your classroom, that they could see what you do as a teacher, they could see what your students do. I find it an invigorating experience, but I can see how there is a certain wariness that people bring to that. This notion of going public for both teachers and students . . . raises the ante for everybody. It makes me think about class-rooms as rehearsal halls for that moment of going public. Not everything that students produce in the classroom is ready to go public in the sense of being published on a website for the world to see. If students produce work that is useful for their public, their public might be their family [or] their high school.

Kathy: . . . I have moved from a model of fanatical effort to cover mate-rial in class to a looser structure in my classroom. Now my classrooms are still, by anybody's definitions I think, fairly conventional places of learning and that has something to do with where I teach and what the general model of learning is where I teach. I feel like in almost every class there are oppor-tunities where I try to do something with the assignments within a more conventional framework to make the knowledge . . . I don't think of it as much as trying to give them . . . let's see, how do I say this . . . when I place them in the position of doing their own production of knowledge they are doing it in a very personal way . . . I have geared the assignments for stu-dents to really think about the past and to think about their relationship to the past in a personal way. For example, in the class that I am doing right now, I have them try to think about the appropriateness or the boundaries of their assumptions that people in the past were like them, versus the dan-gers of assuming that any human being any time any place is not like them.

How do we figure out where those boundaries are and how do we avoid the kind of risks of the position of assuming that human beings are exactly the same and the opposite risks of deciding that some human beings, for whatever reasons, because they lived in the past or of a different race or ethnicity, are fundamentally not like you? . . . By giving them an assignment where they actually have to ask themselves, "So, if I were an Englishwoman going to the colonies, where do I think I would have flourished better? Where would I have wanted to take my chances?" Asking them that question raises all kind of difficult issues for them. Well, are they trying to think like an Englishwoman? Are they trying to think like themselves? By the time I ask them that question they know enough about how an Englishwoman of the period might have made her decision, on what basis she may have made her decision. They also know that their own values are very different and they have to wrestle with that. So, I guess within fairly conventional bounds, I try to seize my moments.

I hedge my bets maybe a little bit more than you do about what I think has, or potentially has, practical value through application. In part because it seems to me that whatever judgments I am going to make right now about what has practical value might give me a small pool of things that most immediately have practical value, but might foreclose certain lines of inquiry that actually might be tremendously valuable. Even though we might see their value ten or fifteen years from now. An example—this actually comes up sometimes in our women's studies class at Penn—there are post-colonial theorists, among other scholars, whose work has been and continues to be difficult for people to comprehend. This is a debate within programs that want to bring in speakers or scholars who will enrich their intellectual community for a semester or whatever to be affiliated. My feeling has always been that although I have no special ability to make their work comprehensible, I guess that I'm not so sure that I will always feel that way. So, my feeling is if a women's studies program or someplace like that should rightfully always lean toward practical applications, should always have those goals in mind, if women's studies doesn't embrace people whose practical value perhaps we can't fully assess yet, if we don't embrace them, who will? Especially if they are coming to us under the rubric of some kind of feminist project. So, in that sense I think I may be willing to put up with some people who are very frustrating in the academy simply because what we see them producing we don't know what to do with exactly. In places with scarce resources you think, "What are we doing?" But I guess I hold out that possibility that they'll look different to us at some point and so we might want to sustain them in some way in their projects. We might even want to influence those projects by being in dialogue with them. But in a more general way, in a very basic way, I think, through teaching and through my scholarship, my bigger message is to have people question, skeptically, this very weighty argument about what they are told is natural for them to do. I feel like that connects almost everything for me. It's not that I don't believe there is such a thing as the natural, but I am kind of skeptical about our ability ever to get at that except in ways that serve pretty self-interested purposes of the people who do the identifying of what is natural. So, I feel like that really unites a lot of my teaching. It really propels a lot of the work that I have done trying to understand relationships between gender and race particularly. I think when I teach courses that don't even come close to the present day in their chronological sweep that is very much the message of those courses—that we can look to the past and see that it was really very different from the present and that people then also had an argument about what was natural for women. Might that not lead you to question what you've been told in the present about what's supposed to be natural? So, in a sense, I think that's aimed at trying to free people up to think critically, also about their own lives and about their place in the world and how the world works and what they can look at and have to accept and what they can look at and say it doesn't have to be this way.

One of the reasons that Jen Manion had wanted me to get involved in this is that she felt that when she took the second half of the women's history course that I taught that it was the first time she had had a course where anybody, first of all, taught about lesbians, but also taught about them in a way that seemed completely integrated into the main body of the course. They weren't just, "Oh yeah, and then there were some lesbians doing their thing and really nobody thought about them, lesbians, before, but starting around 1920 . . ." It wasn't just a tag on, but it was actually integrally part of how I thought about the material. That actually means a lot to me because what that tells me is that even within very conventional bounds it's possible to do unconventional things and reach students who really are served by that, students who really need much more. They need a curriculum that finds a way not to make them always feel like the exceptional case. We can say this about African American students. We can say this generally about female students. We can say this about gay and lesbian students where they can tell by the way the narrative is presented to them in a conventional lecture course or in a textbook that the generalizations about Americans are not about them. I think within that fairly conventional lecture framework and even the conventional framework of scholarship one thing that I feel that I'm pretty good at is questioning and adjusting the use of that term American, so that I am always thinking as I am about to make a generalization "who fell out of that generalization?" and I'm able to make an adjustment. I feel like that allows me even in a lecture situation to be able to lecture in a way that still gives them some kind of coherent story to hang on to, but it is not a story where the coherence is based on marginalizing difference. It's actually a story where I try to do my best to kind of embrace difference and rethink what mainstream means or what the big narrative thread is, based on all the different stories that don't seem to fit. So, that's still very important to me that I don't lose sight of that. If I were to think that students came to my class and didn't feel that anymore then I think I wouldn't be serving the purpose that I originally got into this to serve.

Part Three: Synopsis and Analysis

Tracey's vision of her classroom evokes the philosophy of the Highlander Center, where director Myles Horton pursued a philosophy of self-determination and interactive exchange for people in communities afflicted by social, economic, and political problems. When she consulted the dictionary to come up with a working definition of the term *activist* to help her determine whether her own pedagogical practice qualified, she discovered that the notion of *purposeful action* resonated with what Horton had tried to do at Highlander. It also echoes the philosophy of women's studies and African American studies programs and her goals for her own students. Tracey sees Horton's wisdom about the need to follow research with action as formative of her own view of education as purposeful. She reminds students that they need to "produce for use," in their own lives and in the world beyond the classroom. Her involvement in the Visible Knowledge Project, which is based on the tenet that knowledge production should be visible, shareable, portable and expandable, has reaffirmed her commitment to opening her classroom, her teaching practice, and the products of her students' labors to public scrutiny. Intimidating as this might seem for some teachers, Weis finds it exhilarating and believes that it makes for fundamentally different teaching, learning, and knowledge production processes when one knows one's work will eventually reach a public larger than the classroom.

Kathy describes her pedagogical practice as an effort within fairly conventional bounds to enable students to think about their relationship to the past in a personal way. She is particularly concerned to elicit in students a struggle over how to think about connections to other human beings across time, space, ethnic, racial, and religious difference. Should a belief in common humanity guide our investigations of the past? How do we acknowledge differences produced by the contingencies of historical time, race, and culture without risking an effacement of that assumption of common humanity? Part of the challenge of hewing to the conventions of the lecture format is that such a format works best for the presentation of a tightly bundled, linear narrative rather than for questions about narrative

devices—for example, about the exclusions implicit in the term "American."
Kathy feels that the goal of making history personal for her students helps
her to question the assumptions behind any mainstream history narrative.
This is part of a larger intellectual project she describes as questioning the
meaning of "natural," however it might be defined in a given historical time
or culture. Steeped in this skeptical framework, Kathy has doubts about
measuring all feminist scholarship against the yardstick of practical value.
Scholarship that seems not to have a practical application right now or that
is difficult to comprehend might be exactly what we are looking for twenty
years from now. Kathy feels more comfortable supporting some of this scholarship and trying to enter into dialogue with it, just on the chance that its
practical value will become apparent at some later date.

As we wrote this chapter, we noticed several similarities in our otherwise
quite different stories:

- The search for appropriate tools. Both of us searched for tools/methods
  to enable us to satisfy a larger vision for our lives, our intellectual development, and our political commitments. For both of us, this search
  took us to graduate programs in history, although our experience of
  graduate school was different in each case and ultimately had a different long-term impact on each of us.
- Fulfillment through personal connection. Both of us have struggled in
  the past and do struggle in the present with a sense of personal alienation from the profession we chose to join, and both of us currently
  encourage our students to forge personal connections to the past even
  as we insist that they acquire sound methods of historical inquiry.
- Intellectual commitment to methods of historical inquiry. Both of us
  have found historical methods crucial to our efforts to understand the
  past, to analyze the present, and to imagine the possibilities for social
  change.

As we worked to turn this transcript into a chapter, we were fortunate to
be able to try it out on Tracey's colleague, Dr. Barbara Stengel, and Tracey's
Women in U.S. History class at Millersville. In the course of that discussion, Kathy realized that many of the same goals she identified as part of
her teaching practice have motivated her published scholarship. She concluded that her published work was also part of her effort to teach students
to think critically about history and what is defined as natural. Students
responded enthusiastically to learning more about Tracey's biography and
teaching philosophy, which they felt resonated with the goals they had discussed for their course. Kathy also noted that in characteristic fashion, Tracey
had managed to produce for use by incorporating the article into an introductory unit in the class designed to help students re-think the trajectory

from interview to transcript to article. Students will next apply these insights to revising their own educational autobiographies and to preparing to conduct oral history interviews with women associated with Millersville's past as part of that institution's celebration of its 150th anniversary.

Despite the similarities we have identified and in part because of the differences in our backgrounds before entering graduate school and our current professional situations, our classroom practices are very different. We have enjoyed exploring these differences in our conversations and hope that they will resonate with the diverse teaching experiences of our readers. For both of us, this chance to reflect on the sense of purpose we bring to our teaching and scholarship has invigorated our pedagogical practice and sparked new efforts at outreach with colleagues with similar motives.

Notes

1. The Highlander Center, founded in 1932, sponsors research and educational programs addressing issues of social, economic, and environmental justice in the South.
2. Horton, Myles, *The Long Haul: An Autobiography* (New York: Doubleday, 1990).

CHAPTER 13

Teaching Across the Color Line
A Warning About Identity Politics in the Classroom

JIM DOWNS

I didn't teach African American studies because I was part of the civil rights movement or a disciple of black power. I didn't teach African American literature and history because I thought it made me progressive or radical, or, even worse, because it was politically correct; nor, did I teach African American studies because I had to.

I taught African American studies because it was fundamental to the American experience, because by ignoring African American literature and the history would not only undercut the major achievements that black people contributed to this nation, but it would also undermine any definition of freedom that I would attempt to explain to my students. As any historical accounting of black people in the United States would uncover, when the question of freedom was placed under political scrutiny, it was black people who put the question on the table. From the Emancipation Proclamation to the Fourteenth Amendment to the U.S. Consitution to the civil rights movement, black people's fight for freedom has set the stage for the feminist and labor movements and provided the vocabulary for countless other political discussions.

In many colleges and universities, the fight to incorporate African American history and literature topics into the curriculum as either part of the larger survey courses or even as individual departments—for the most part—has been won. Certainly, college teachers continually struggle to teach these courses, but, at least, they can find the support of the outside scholarly and professional communities to support their work. In high schools, however, across the country, the story is markedly different. Courses are not taught, historical events including African Americans are not mentioned, and representations of black people in literature remain distorted and marginal. The emphasis on preparing students for standardized tests, and focusing on math and science courses has only worsened the problem. Many of these students are not even getting social studies, let alone a history course that includes the African American experience. And, in many places where African American history or literature is taught, the rationale for teaching it often derives from issues relating to identity politics, not historical accuracy.

What follows is not an examination of the problems of secondary education or even an objective review of curriculum agendas. Instead, it is a personal meditation on my experience teaching African American literature in secondary schools. The motivation for this chapter stems largely from my own need as a former secondary teacher—who often fought against administrations, colleagues, and even parents—for a pedagogical strategy and context to situate my experience. This is not intended as an academic analysis to be locked off in academic journals and relegated to scholarly meetings, but as an accessible narrative, a guide through the tumultuous and controversial confrontations that I faced in the classroom and out of it.

My interest in becoming a secondary school teacher resulted largely from the ways in which my college professors had inspired me. As a college student in the 1990s, discussions on racism raged from topics as salacious as Anita Hill's allegation that Clarence Thomas, the then Supreme Court nominee, sexually harassed her to the pernicious publication of the *Bell Curve*, which attempted to link race with IQ, to the never-ending debates on multiculturalism. As an undergraduate at The University of Pennsylvania, these discussions more closely hit home: Lani Guinner, of the Penn Law School, entered the national spotlight when President Clinton nominated her for Assistant Attorney General for Civil Rights. Misunderstood by her critics, she unfairly became touted as the "Quota Queen" due to her ideas on voting rights,[1] meanwhile a group of black sorority girls, who were pledging outside my dorm room, received national publicity for being called "Water buffalo" by an outraged and allegedly self-identified nonracist white student. Add a few tenure battles, a campus lecture by the polemical author Camille Paglia, who denouced multiculturalism, and debates on whether the historically black dorm on campus should remain open, and no matter where you looked or to whom you spoke, questions about racism seemed to be everywhere. My professors, however, did not shy away from all that was happening around us. They used the examples of the "Quota Queen" and the *Bell Curve* to talk about the historical construction of race. And besides providing an often useful historical analogue to the many political debates that were seething on campus, they found ways to use these moments to illuminate themes in American literature and history. I quickly learned, that being an academic was not about measuring the beats in a poem or allowing cobwebs to grow on my sweater in the basement library; instead it meant being right in the center of the action, at the rallies and in the protests, and, most importantly, using the classroom as a laboratory to test ideas and to experiment with various arguments and intellectual positions.

For me, questions about the history of racism were my intellectual passion. My classmates, then and still now, were intrigued by questions relating to gender, class, and sexuality, and have in their own ways continued to be part of important intellectual and activist discussions of these topics. When it was time to graduate, instead of joining a non-profit organization or going to graduate school, I wanted to go back to where I was from. To return to the place that most needed a teacher committed to using the classroom as not only a place of learning and intellectual stimulation but also of social change. I knew that where I was from few people read books by black authors or knew about the history of slavery. To define my hometown as having suffered from historical amnesia would only be to imply that they once knew that former slaves fought in the Civil War or created the Harlem Renaissance. But, to them, the Civil War was something that happened more than a hundred years ago, and had no relevance to these proud descendents of mostly Irish, German, Polish, and Italian immigrants—who, through hard work and "no free hand-outs," managed to successfully send their children to school and make a decent a living.

For better or worse, I was hired by the first school that I applied to: an all boy's Catholic preparatory school. The headmaster, after first meeting me, was nervous and a bit uncomfortable. During the interview, he would glance down at my transcript and then read off a course title, like "Venus Rising: Black Women's Nonfiction, Theory, and Criticism," and without trying to stumble, he adjusted his glance, and said, "So what did you actually read?"

I confidently responded with a list names that ran the gamut from the nineteenth century slave writer Harriet Jacobs to the contemporary poet Ntozake Shange. Still uncomfortable, he hired me. His second in command later confessed to me that the school was evaluated the prior year by Middle States, an accrediting agency, and was criticized for not having any multicultural courses. He then told me that hiring me was the solution, and at twenty-two, with sand still in my shoes from a summer on Cape Cod, the vice-principal appointed me as the chair of the diversity committee. In high school and college, I had served on a number of committees, and thought this was similar. At the first meeting, I soon recognized that the room was full of people my parents' ages. I then found myself telling them their curriculum, which they had taught for the past twenty years, was outdated and useless.

While I was certainly naïve and cocky, my curriculum suggestions were not entirely off base. In the classroom, I met the products of their courses: students who after looking at the syllabus, complained that it was all about black people simply because it listed readings by Phillis Wheatley, the first known African American writer, and Frederick Douglass, the former slave, abolitionist, and author, in the course of twelve weeks. Two black authors in a syllabus that previously included none was clearly too many. When it came time to discuss Frederick Douglass, the students refused to read his auto-biography. When I tried to redirect the conversation to something historical and less interpretive—since they didn't do the reading—they abruptly responded with comments about black people taking their place in the race for college admissions or black people buying homes in their neighborhoods. Granted, I wanted to provide a context to discuss social issues, and in retrospect, as a first year teacher, I could have done more to control the direction of the discussion; but the truth was these students were mad, culturally and ideologically bound to the idea that black people had in someway destroyed their lives. I was then called in by the head of the school and scolded for teaching too much about racism—although that was what he hired me to do.

After a few more discussions like this, and faculty meetings in which I confronted hostile colleagues, who thought I was trying to justify crimes committed by black people, multicultural consultants came to the school to essentially mediate a discussion among the faculty about the politics of racism. In the midst of some ridiculous exercise, one of the other younger teachers made a comment that it was fine if our students wanted to feel *better* than the public school students down the street because public school students were "bad students" who listened to loud music and wore baggy jeans. And, while the multicultural consultants forced him to really think about what he meant by "bad students," in a fury, he jumped up, grabbed his chair, and broke it in half. "See," he said, "now this chair is a bad chair, you can't sit on it anymore."

Interrupting him, I said, "No, it's a broken chair."

By this point, the room was silent. I was later coached by senior, more sympathetic faculty members to keep my mouth shut at faculty meetings. So I did. By December, things had cooled down significantly, the students had relaxed a great deal and they finally began to become more interested and engaged in the material I presented. In one exercise in which we discussed the question of censorship in the early twentieth century, I decided to organize a debate in class that placed the question of censorship in a contemporary context. At the time, the National Endowment for the Humanities (NEH) and the National Endowment for the Arts (NEA) were under major scrutiny, and their funds were being dramatically cut. Among the controversies surrounding the NEA funding were questions about the artistic integrity of Robert Mapplethorpe's artwork, and the Piss Christ, a controversial depiction of a crucifix submerged in urine.

In order to structure these debates, I first gave the students some background on these organizations, which they were unfamiliar with, and then I asked them to take sides. They evenly divided. I then had a book on performance theory in my room that included some photographs that depicted these artists' work. As part of the debate, I wanted to use this as evidence, and while they were drafting their arguments, they would each have the opportunity individually to come up to the center desk and flip through the book. Although most were seniors and the photographs in my estimation were not pornographic, I, nevertheless, said that it was optional to look at the material and asked those interested to write up a permission slip first in order to look at the photographs. Ideally, in a perfect world, their parents would have signed the slips, but I thought that having them think about it for a few minutes, would have been enough, and it was. They were fine. They looked at the book; they debated the material, and they began to understand that the definition of art was subjective.

A few days later, word got to Mr. Bad Chair, the teacher down the hall, that I showed the students the Piss Christ. He then ran to the headmaster and told him that I was corrupting the students. I was called in to the headmaster's office and asked if I showed the students the Piss Christ, I admitted I did. I then held the intellectual ground for a few minutes that only Catholics would get such a photograph, that it was lost on non-Catholics, who would have no reaction to seeing a cross submerged in urine. I was then told that since I got there, I did nothing but start trouble. All I talked about was racism and black people, and that I had maddened the parents and frustrated the faculty. He then went on to say that I was "angry," that I had something to prove, that I didn't understand the "real world," and that my crusade to teach African American literature was overblown. And, now this alleged debate, he said, about the crucifix had been the last straw. The debate gave them, in their mind, legitimate ground to indict me. They could not fire me for simply teaching African American authors, so they instead used this debacle as the scandal. And so, on December 15, a few days before the winter break, I was fired, just in time for them to truly enjoy a *white* Christmas.

Experiences like this are not unfamiliar to many teachers who tried to pioneer new curriculum changes. Certainly, my experience was wrought with some poor decisions on my part, my own inexperience, and the school's need to simply have someone fulfill a state mandate, but the polemics surrounding the teaching of African American literature or history are not necessarily limited to only those who protest its place in high school curriculum. Sometimes, the problems lie with those who believe they are doing the most important work.

Fast forward five years. I now have a substantial amount of teaching experience under my belt—still a novice, but no longer a fire starter. I get a job at a seemingly progressive independent school in a Northeastern state. The white liberal dean of faculty once again peers down at my transcript and then awkwardly looks at me. By this point, I have earned an MA degree in American Studies, and courses on the Civil War and African American history line my transcript. And, then, in between glances of reading my resume and skimming my recommendations, she blurts out, "I just love it here, because it is diverse, and I get to live in a town with black people."

Ok, I think, I will get you a subscription to *Ebony* for Christmas. "Yeah, she says, I need to live around black people."

Looking at her, she does not appear to be Carl Van Vechtens'[2] lost love child but she looks at me, waiting for a response, like I should say something, like, "Finally, a progressive white person." Despite her eccentricities, she was right. The school was diverse and the surrounding towns were not as highly segregated as most. The year, overall, was fine until the twelfth grade English teachers needed to decide on which novel to teach in the spring. In years past, the department head, told me, they taught Toni Morrison's *The Bluest Eye*. "Wow," I responded, "what a great choice."

But, the department head whispered, "Barbara doesn't teach it." Barbara was the soft-spoken twelfth grade teacher, who like the three other black women on faculty had graduated from Yale. That's odd, I thought, why wouldn't she like it? After the meeting, I approached her and asked her why. I noticed a few other faculty members stayed to listen. She told me that when she was growing up she never knew people like the characters in the novel that it didn't ring true to her experience. I wanted to engage her, debate her on the point, that its not about her or her experience but it's a novel with a theme that stretches well beyond the personal, but by this point, she had noticed that the others were listening. And so I dropped it. She then quickly said that she would teach Dorothy West's *The Wedding* instead.

Leave *The Wedding* to Oprah's book club, I thought, I am going for *The Bluest Eye*. Like any author who challenges her readers, Toni Morrison's debut novel was no exception; my students got it, but it took a lot of discussion and a lot of work. The problem of the book's meaning, however, arose when a senior faculty member asked me to substitute for her and to discuss the book with her class. Walking into the class, I heard the students complaining about the book. When I asked them a question about the characters, they responded not with statements about how Claudia, the protagonist, teaches a lesson about beauty and self-worth that sharply cuts across racial, class, and gender lines, but instead they responded with statements, like "This was the way black people lived" or "this is what happened to blacks after slavery" in response to the poverty, abuse, and lack of family structure in the novel.

"Well," the girl in the front row stated, emphatically, "that is what Ms. Multiculturalism [their teacher] told us." "This is what happened," a boy in the back chirped in, "after slavery but before Civil Rights." He acted as if he knew something that I didn't.

The book takes place in a small town in Ohio in the 1940s; it is not a book by any stretch of the imagination that attempts to unravel a historical narrative. Yet, this teacher, however, had thought it did. I responded to their questions by drawing a timeline on the board, highlighting the major moments after the Civil War: Reconstruction, The Great Migration, and the Harlem Renaissance. I took a breath and quickly told a story about Madame C. J. Walker, the inventor of black hair products and first black millionaire, to illustrate the point that not all black people at this time were poor or unsuccessful, as they had assumed from their reading of the novel. And, in the midst of this, I remember Barbara's comment that she didn't teach this book, because it was not like her family and that she couldn't relate to it. It made sense now why she made that decision. These teachers had set up the parameters for reading the novel that in some brought it back to identity politics.

When Ms. Multiculturalism found out that I spent the majority of the class period drawing a timeline on the board, she questioned my assertion that *The Bluest Eye* was not representative of black life in the 1940s. She responded by arguing that using fiction to teach historical fact is appropriate—which it is, when it is done correctly, I told her. She then laughed at me when I suggested using a scene from Fitzgerald's or Joyce's novel as examples of their respected periods, but thought nothing of using an African American text in the same way. In fact, she almost felt that they should have been congratulated and praised for abandoning the all white, particularly male, canon of Western literature for a few weeks and teaching a novel written by a black woman about alienation and abuse.

What was most disconcerting about my discussion was her insistence that the poverty and despair that Morrison described in the novel was a fair representation of African American society. Perhaps, in her world, where black people are crowded into ghettos and are the recipients of their Christmas donations, it made sense that the characters in *The Bluest Eye* have real flesh and blood parallels in society. And it makes even more sense that teaching the novel allows them to continue their community service. Yet, as teachers of African American literature, it is critical that we distill good intentions from historical fact.

While I would like to close with an important and useful anecdote, one experience that does not neatly fit alongside the others continues to press forward in my mind. Early in my teaching career, I taught at an Afrocentric, independent school. Founded by two civil rights activists, the school was an alternative to the public school system for members of the surrounding black community. I was hired to teach African American literature in the middle school. The opportunity to teach in such an environment where curriculum battles and questions about identity politics seemed inapplicable was particularly appealing to me.

Yet, even in this environment, where Harriet Tubman or Martin Luther King Jr. were not just names whose accomplishments were mentioned every February, but were part of the everyday curriculum, identity politics pervaded. I was required to teach nineteenth-century literature, but could not spend too much time on slavery. I could mention the Harlem Renaissance, but had to ignore author Nella Larsen, whose characters' sexual orientation was questionable; and instead focus on Jessie Fauset, whose characters, according to the administration, better reflected black society. If I played classical music during Arts and Crafts, I had to pick black composers. And, if the students wanted to believe that Beethoven was black, because the music teacher told them, I couldn't disagree. If I wanted to show them a movie that dealt with triumph over adversity, I could not bring in a movie that had Italian or Chinese characters, but instead—and I am not lying—I had to show them *Mahogany*. And, last but not least, when the administrator and founder of the school, called me "European" in front of my class, I was speechless. When my students—who were more astute than he gave them credit for—asked me what part of Europe I was from, and I said Philadelphia. He went on explain to them that he meant my ancestors—which, for the record, he had no inside information about my mixed ancestry. What he meant was that since I appear white, I am presumably of European descent.

By bringing back the discussion to my identity, he unwittingly undermined the whole point of his institution and my being there. I was there because I believed that his school could be an alternative to the public school system; that in his school, the American experience from the colonial period to the present could truly be explored. By evoking my identity, he empowered the whole idea that there is something truly empirical and pedagogically valuable in drawing lines between black and white people. If the whole point of his school is to offer an opportunity, a chance, an alternative to students, who otherwise do not have one, he only confused the students more by bringing the discussion back to identity politics and away from history.

Furthermore, if we study and teach African American history and literature based on a teacher's identity, we have already lost the battle. The point of teaching African American studies is to fully understand U.S. culture and history. The politics of identity, as sexy, and, as titillating, as they may seem, offer little in the way of support for one's academic agendas after being in the trenches. Truth—or at least some poststructuralist derivative of it—offers a more productive and comforting path to change.

Note

1. For a detailed discussion, see Lani Guinier, *The Tyranny of the Majority: Fundamental Fairness in Representative Democracy* (Free Press, 1994).
2. Carl Van Vechten was an early twentieth-century white patron and enthusiast of black artists.

CHAPTER 14

2.5 Cheers for Bridging the Gap Between Activism and the Academy; or, Stay and Fight

To Which Is Added an Account of Radical Scholar-Activists in the Wake of the Iraq War

JESSE LEMISCH

The conference on "History of Activism, History as Activism" in April, 2002 was not sponsored by or officially connected with the Columbia University teaching assistants (TAs) and research assistants (RAs) union, Graduate Student Employees United (GSEU), and the program included some antiunion students. Ironically, union activists were at a crucial stage of organizing and were too busy to give the conference much attention, although some participated. However, the conference took place in a context that I think had been largely produced by union activism at Columbia, which is part of a larger movement at many universities across the country, including Yale, Brown, the University of Minnesota, Michigan State, Cornell, New York University (NYU), Tufts, and elsewhere. (On March 29, 2002, one week before the Columbia conference, a radical history conference at the University of Minnesota surprised its organizers—and university administrators—by drawing two hundred people.) Many history graduate students are active in GSEU.

Less than three weeks before the conference at Columbia, research and teaching assistants had voted on whether to be represented by GSEU, which seeks higher stipends, better health care, a grievance procedure, and workload guidelines.[1] Although union poll watchers believed that they won, the bal-

lots were impounded. Columbia, using the prestigious union-busting law firm Proskauer Rose, which NYU had used earlier and unsuccessfully, had appealed an earlier National Labor Relations Board (NLRB) decision classifying TAs and RAs at private universities as employees. Columbia stakes its hopes on the possibility that the January 2002 addition of two management-friendly Bush appointees to the NLRB will reverse the earlier decision. (As of May 2004, the ballots are still impounded!)

This is the context in which the conference took place: activism in academia was a concrete reality. On April 29, three weeks after the conference, GSEU staged a one-day strike. Unionized clerical workers joined the picket line, where the cry was, "Count the Votes!" A large inflated rat sat upright at the 116th Street main entrance to Columbia University, as it often does in union pickets elsewhere in New York City. As of this writing, the outcome is unresolved. If, to its shame, Columbia holds out, I hope the rat will take up long-term residence there.

✶✶✶✶✶

We're all here *because* we're in favor of bridging the gap between activism and the academy, and we're hearing lots of good ideas here about how to do it. But far less frequently considered among leftists and other dissenters are the 0.5 reasons *not* to build that bridge, or at least not to make this our primary goal. I'll get to those. But first, a few words in favor of gap bridging, at a time when this campus, among others, is the site of some of the most important union organizing going on in this country, which I fully support.

Being an activist is a necessary prerequisite for historians who want to see through the reigning lies, and I take it as a given that we *must* be activists. Writing history is about challenging received authority. Activist experience gives the historian experiential understanding of the power of the state, repression, social change, agency, surprise in history, the distortions peddled by authority, and the depth of commitment of those with power to maintaining the standing order through their journalists, historians, police, and law firms. Activism shows us how it is that people told that there is no alternative to the way things are, can, in fact, invent new alternatives, particularly in the streets and on the picket lines.[2] You can't *begin* to understand how history happens unless you have this basic training as a historian/activist. A good dose of tear gas makes us think more clearly as historians.

✶✶✶✶✶

Let me (after the conference) develop a little further some of the points made in the preceding paragraph:

- *Surprise in history:* I can't be the first to note the role of surprise, and I am sure that others have seen this. Historians (Marxists in particular!) can always establish a persuasive causality *after the fact.* This misses the reality of surprise in history as it is actually lived. Radicals who are living history should take heart (or, often the reverse) from the fact that things do not necessarily have to turn out as they appear to be headed, and that history is marked by sudden turns.

- *Journalists and the standing order.* Speaking in the shadow of Low Library (as I was at the conference), where soon-to-be-no-longer Columbia President Grayson Kirk's office was located in 1968, it is hard not to recall the *New York Times*' placing on the front page Abe Rosenthal's despicable classic article, written after the police attack on protesting students at Columbia in April of that year. Rosenthal exaggerates the damage wrought by students and all but ignores the bloody police assault. The article begins with Kirk returning to his office at 4:30 a.m. after the police bust that removed the student occupiers, passing a hand over his face, and saying, as he observed the condition of his office, "My God, how could human beings do a thing like this?" The first passing mention of the bloodied heads of students appears in paragraph fifty.[3]
- *Law firms and the standing order.* Columbia's law firm, Proskauer Rose LLP, boasts that it has, in its "Labor & Employment" practice area, "160–plus . . . lawyers [who] provide unmatched breadth of expertise capable of addressing the most complex and challenging labor and employment issues faced by employers."[4]
- *Tear gas and the historian's education.* One friendly but critical hearer of this phrase at the conference thought that I was presenting an idea left over from the bad side of the sixties, implying that consciousness will rise if enough of us are beaten by police. I can understand this misreading, but I retain my phrasing, since it is literally true: my capacity as a U.S. colonial historian, to understand the terror and flight involved in eighteenth-century crowd behavior was enhanced by the experience of being in a crowd that was tear-gassed and nearly blinded by Chicago Mayor Daley's police on Michigan Avenue in August 1968 during the Democratic Convention.

So much of my generation once knew experientially the necessity of activism for the historian, but it has been deradicalized and demobilized. I remember the 1988 John Jay College building occupation by students, when I tried to get our faculty group, heavy with one-time radicals, to organize in support. (The issues involved racial composition of the faculty—as compared to the student body—and CUNY-wide (City University of New York) issues having to do with tuition and cuts in funding.) One member of our faculty group, a well-known American historian, told me, no, we should not picket because such action might fail, and, anyway, it was our job as faculty to lay the theoretical groundwork for resistance by composing *position papers*. Another famous left historian told me, "We must get the kids out of the building before they get hurt," failing to understand that "the kids" knew very well what risks they were taking and that holding the building was their only leverage.

Another big Upper West Side left intellectual and sixties veteran spoke to Columbia Architecture students three or four years ago. Some of the students seemed to wonder how they, in a profession that depends so much on the rich, might still be able to be radicals. This person, who looks so sixties, with an admirable collection of multicolored T-shirts, in no way addressed the students' yearning. He could only say to them that the Disneyfication of Times Square wasn't really so bad, and that we should just wait and see how it all works out. But the sixties were not about our being passive spectators, waiting to see how things worked out, but rather about being active makers and participants, and it saddens me that so many of my cohort have put themselves into voluntary retirement from activism. (In 2000, I described this widespread predisposition as "a kind of I-wonder-what-will-happen-next attitude, a spectatorial stance that waits for others to make a movement.")[5]

In talking about the deradicalization of former radicals, I haven't begun to mention the increasing inability of many of them to distinguish radicalism from liberalism. It's bad times when *The Nation* adorns its cover with an adoring piece by Kennedy fan and journalist Jack Newfield on Teddy Kennedy,[6] at that time Bush's new friend—with Teddy pictorially represented as a knight on a white donkey—and boasts that "Mario Cuomo is a longstanding *Nation* reader."[7] Why in the world would we want to read a left magazine that boasts of its appeal to Mario Cuomo, the Clinton-before-Clinton, whose cutbacks as governor of New York, especially in public higher education, had such devastating effects?

A decline on another front: Cindy Cisler, an unsung hero and pioneer of the pro-abortion movement (I said pro-abortion, not pro-choice), told me that in speeches she was invited to give to young academic feminists in the late 1980s she had taken to saying, in confiding stage whispers, "you know, feminism was a *movement* before it became an academic discipline." The program for the 2002 Berkshire Conference on Women's History,[8] though full of wonderful things, in some ways reflects this academicization, depoliticization, and specialization. The program looks a lot like that of the American Historical Association. Leafing through it, people my age recognize a tier of older veterans of feminism balanced precariously on top of the younger scholars' more academic sessions, with the older women speaking on general topics and trying to relate scholarship in women's history to feminism. Nonetheless, the accumulating scholarship in the field is immensely valuable.

But it's no big news to you that there's a lot around that calls itself radical but has lost touch with what radicalism means. I'll now turn to the 0.5 part beyond my 2.5 cheers for bridging the gap between activism and the academy. Why do I carp in the midst of this fine conference, with all this fine work about the history of activism? I'm here to speak for the importance to the left of doing history, *regardless* of its relevance or irrelevance to current movements of resistance. I see doing history as deeply connected to building a democratic and self-critical left, and as preparing the way for utopia, as well as for the joyful and playful intellectual life that will be part of utopia. Let me explain by looking back for a moment.

In 1968 some of us founded the New University Conference (NUC), an attempt to organize academic-based activists and to build on and promote the organization of radical caucuses that was then in process across the academic map, from the Modern Language Association to the American Historical Association and beyond.[9] The opening session at NUC featured a talk by my friend and sometime coworker, the great blacklisted radical historian Staughton Lynd,[10] who is now a creative radical labor lawyer in Youngstown, Ohio.[11] At the 1968 NUC, Staughton issued a call for us radicals to get out of the university: "Not Marx," said Staughton, "not Engels, not Plekhanov, not Lenin, not Trotsky, not Bukharin, not Rosa Luxembourg, . . . not Antonio Gramsci, not Mao Tse-Tung—put bread on his table by university teaching."[12]

Although Staughton argued well, his idea fit nicely with the *tsunami* of guilt then passing through movement people in academe ("We're not where it's at"; "We're irrelevant to The Struggle"; "We're being paid [$8000]"). Since I believed, and do believe, that the challenge is not to get out of the university—God knows, the universities *wanted* us out; they were making little brown-bag lunches for us, saying, here, take this peanut-butter sandwich with you, have a happy trip—but rather to stay and fight, to be radical wherever you are—in dance, in arts, at your workplace, in history, in science, in architecture, in academics—I wrote a leaflet that was circulated at the conference, and later by the New England Free Press, and reprinted in the *Journal of American History*, with perhaps the oddest title that journal has ever published.[13] I called my leaflet (which ridiculed the sexist terminology popular in the movement in 1968), "Who Will Write a Left History of Art while We Are All Putting Our Balls on the Line?"

I asked then, and I ask you again today, "What is going to be your attitude toward intellectuals who call themselves left but whose work has no immediate or even apparent long-term usefulness to the movement?" Then I turned to a question that I think is also relevant for this conference, a question that arises from a perspective that sees intellectuals not as better than anybody else, but as necessary, independent critics within the movement.

"I wonder who is going to write a Marxist history of art in America?" I asked, and went on, "What if the movement is wrong?" as it was at the time in sharing the larger society's sexism. "If the movement is wrong on this and on other matters, will its intellectuals have served it well by responding to its 'needs?'" "And what kind of an enduring left will we have in this country if left intellectuals feel that they have to apologize for leaving the picket line to go back to the ivory tower to write a Marxist history of art?" Today, I would add that the attitudes I was criticizing echo the old notion that "those who can, do; those who can't, teach." For reasons that should be clear, this is an ultimately sexist notion widespread in the mainstream (it was certainly common when I was a Yale undergraduate in the 1950s), which the left often adopts unquestioningly.

After its founding and early peak, NUC died a fairly rapid death as, in its ardor to prove its activist credentials, it lost its academic identity and became indistinguishable from so much of the rest of the activist left in the grim years following the self-destruction of SDS (Students for a Democratic Society) in 1969. NUC failed largely because, as those of you who are now organizing academic unions know, you can't organize academics around their guilt and shame at being academics, reducing them to self-hating and self-sacrificing cheering squads for other people's movements, no matter how worthy those movements are. Columbia's John McMillian has described NUC's "peculiar ethic of self-flagellation."[14] (Something of the same sort happened in the student movement of the sixties, which started to die later in the decade after such glorious earlier high points as Berkeley's Free Speech Movement,[15] as students began to grow ashamed of seeking student power, which many New Left leaders saw more and more contemptuously as merely parochial and privileged.) You went into history presumably with some element of passion for figuring out how things really were, and some excitement over ways of reconstructing the past, even about arcane questions of methodology. There will even be times when you feel joy in this work. Don't bury those passions in shame, under some idea that your political mission must directly determine your research agenda. The quest for a better society only loses when you define your purpose so narrowly.

Not discussed here is another frequently heard argument: we live in such dire times that we cannot afford the luxury of a non-relevant history. But, terrible as these times are, history is in fact a perpetual state of emergency, with atrocities committed on an hourly basis, and we will never develop a left that is proactive, and more than a response to emergency, unless we manage to keep working on this vital project even in the midst of the dire present.

So here I am at this great conference, railing against relevance and arguing for constructing a broadly ranging left culture not all of which is necessarily immediately useful. The conference papers on activism are wonderful and fulfill the left intellectual's duty to write the history of and assess social movements. But letting a movement define your scholarly goals and the questions that you ask isn't good for the left. A vital source of debate and criticism will be cut off if the left's intellectuals become captives of a current left and reduce themselves to—as Staughton would have it— a merely "accompanying" role, or, in his words, "to live amongst [the poor and marginalized] for a time, and to assist, if possible, in articulating and transmitting their collective experience.[16] Staughton takes his term, *accompaniment*, from Archbishop Romero of El Salvador, and I think it may be a fine role for the Church, but for an intellectual, mere accompaniment is an abandonment of the historian's critical responsibility and apt to lead to the kind of distortion that we see in a spectrum that extends from, for instance, Helen Garvy's recent film on SDS[17] to the magnificent but highly ideological popular front mythologizing of Studs Terkel.[18] We don't serve the people very well by uncritical admiration.[19]

Concern for what may seem even the most abstract and nonactivist kinds of questions, such as form in art and music, can be part of building a better left. To understand the rebellions involved in the breaking of form, you have to understand what artistic form is. Who knows, until we have actually done it, what unanticipated fruit may come from studying such seemingly abstract questions? Sneaking into, er, sitting in on, an introductory history of art course at Barnard College four years ago, I found that notions such as form, beauty, and even art itself are not in fashion. I can't see much hope for an enduring left that lacks contact with art, science, truth, and beauty. Yes, I did say, truth.[20] We need people who know about everything, not only about movements. For instance, although it may sound like an oxymoron, we need left engineers. The collapse of the World Trade Center in 2001 was the result of a vile assault. But it appears to the layperson that a factor contributing to the resultant catastrophe was the weakening of the structures by market values: supports placed so as to maximize rentable space; cheap and inadequate fireproofing, etc. If the left discourages people from becoming engineers or building designers by denying the "relevance" of such fields, then we won't have people with the skills to make informed judgments about the complex causalities in the WTC's collapse. And, to look at a related larger issue, after the seventy-plus-year-long debacle of the Soviet Union, the left appears to have utterly lost touch with the notion of *planning* and the expertise necessary for it.

One major difference between 1968 and now is that you are making your own unions. Hallelujah and congratulations, and hurray for the movement that picks up where the movement for student power started to fail in the sixties when it gave up on this allegedly too privileged a goal. What will your unions be about? We know that they need to be about wages, hours, and benefits. But a union of academics should also be thinking about whether teaching assistants have academic freedom[21] and should provide a center of intellectual activity, offering to its members an alternative in intellectual life to the university's still medieval hierarchy, in which your fellowships, jobs, and lives depend on currying favor with one professor—who may be capricious, or utterly insane—and your fate depends on carrying on his or her ideas in your own research. If a union doesn't include in its agenda the creation of alternative arrangements that enable us to function as intellectuals, I fear that it will wilt and lose touch with its members' passions. So, in this sense, this conference is a fine step, connecting as it does history and activism.

To conclude: I hope you will be both activists and historians and will figure out how to put the two together, maybe not only in the kind of mechanical and unexamined way suggested by the session title, "Bridging the Gap between Activism and the Academy," but also by thinking deeply about alternative roles for intellectuals. You are here because you want to do history—don't let anybody embarrass you about this. Try to get beyond the repeated invocation of the word *community*, which seems always for left academics to be code for *someplace else*. Face the challenge of figuring out how to be radical where you live. I say, *stay and fight*.

Epilogue, August 2003. Radical Scholar-Activists in the Wake of the Iraq War: Can the New Activist/Intellectual Organizations Take Root and Survive? With a Reflection on What We Can Learn from Marc Bloch

The events leading to the U.S. war in Iraq in 2003, and the war itself, led to a rekindling of activism among left historians, and other scholars in opposition. Historians signed anti-war petitions, brought before professional associations resolutions on the war, repression and free expression, protested in the streets, refounded radical caucuses and participated in a nascent alliance of radical academic/intellectual organizations.

Two organizations that have emerged from the anti-war ferment are of particular relevance to this essay: Historians Against the War (HAW), and the Alliance of Radical Academic and Intellectual Organizations. I have been a member of the steering committees of both organizations during their founding periods, so what follows is in a sense a report from the trenches. First, I will sketch in the history of these organizations; then, I will assess their chances of survival.

Historians Against the War[22]

In November 2002, as war seemed to be approaching, the Campaign for Peace and Democracy (CPD) circulated a statement entitled, "We Oppose both

Saddam Hussein and the US War on Iraq: a call for a new, democratic US foreign policy." I signed and sent it on to History News Network, where it was published with a short introduction by me (December 17, 2002) under the title, "Why I am Opposed to War with Iraq."[23] Although not intended as a historians' petition, the CPD statement drew the signatures of many historians.[24]

Meantime, historians were organizing themselves. Historians Against the War was formed at a meeting at the annual convention of the American Historical Association (AHA) in Chicago in January 2003. This continued the sixties radical caucus pattern of radicals meeting in, around, and in spite of professional associations.[25] HAW drew up a statement:

"We historians call for a halt in the march towards war against Iraq. We are deeply concerned about the needless destruction of human life, the undermining of constitutional government in the US, the egregious curtailment of civil liberties and human rights at home and abroad, and the obstruction of world peace for the indefinite future."

Within less than three weeks, more than a thousand historians had signed the HAW statement, which was circulated widely on the Internet, and got 2,209 signatures (as of April 28, 2003). After the AHA, HAW members connected with each other, sometimes in actual gatherings, sometimes in conference calls, and most of all via the Internet. On February 15, about sixty members marched, under HAW's new banner (with a logo designed by the talented artist-historian Josh Brown), together with perhaps a million others in the New York City portion of a huge world-wide anti-war protest.[26]

The next major professional meeting of historians was that of the Organization of American Historians (OAH), which met in Memphis April 3–6. On the evening of April 4, while U.S. troops were advancing through Baghdad, in Memphis fifty to seventy people participated in a HAW meeting.[27] This was, among other things, the first activist gathering of historians that Staughton Lynd and I had participated in together in more than twenty-five years. (We found ourselves mostly in agreement at that point). Spirits revived in this collectivity, and some of the old comedy was also in the air. A steering committee was chosen (including Staughton and me). We presented the OAH Executive Board with a resolution (April 5; written mainly by Alan Dawley, Professor of History, The College of New Jersey), which the Board changed slightly and then endorsed. This was then adopted by the OAH business meeting (April 6):

In view of the threat to free speech in the current climate, the Organization of American Historians affirms the centrality of dissent in American history, the sanctity of the rights guaranteed by the First Amendment, and the necessity for open debate of public policy issues, including United States foreign policy, in order to maintain the health of this democracy.[28]

Another event that is relevant to the history of the interconnection between scholarship and activism among historians took place at the OAH. Immediately before the April 4 HAW meeting described above, I had participated, along with Staughton and others, in an OAH session called, "Remembering the Student Non-Violent Coordinating Committee (SNCC) and Students for a Democratic Society." This took place at the Lorraine Motel (now the Civil Rights Museum) thirty-five years to the day, and almost to the minute, after the assassination of Martin Luther King, Jr. there. Other participants included early SNCC activists Bob Moses and Judith Richardson, early SDS president Al Haber, and historians Marcus Rediker and Wesley Hogan (with Rev. Jesse Jackson joining the panel). Most of the panelists had been founders or early members of SNCC or SDS—the two organizations that had been so central to the anti-Vietnam War and Civil Rights movements in the 1960s. The room was packed, well beyond capacity, with people sitting on the floor and standing against the walls. With the country in the midst of war, Rediker began by reminding the audience of Dr. King's rejection of the Vietnam War in his April 4, 1967 Riverside Church speech, "Beyond Vietnam: A Time to Break Silence." Staughton, aided both by his experience (he was Director of the Freedom Schools in the 1964 Mississippi Freedom Summer Project) and by some SNCC documents uncovered by the young historian of SNCC, Wesley Hogan, gave a paper on the Mississippi Freedom Democratic Party's attempt (unfortunate, as he saw it) to be seated as the official Mississippi delegation at the 1964 Democratic Party convention. It was an excellent work of history, critical and enriched by Staughton's own activism and by his distinctive perspective. I gave a paper, "Was SDS Pushed, or Did it Jump?" This was an attempt by a historian/ participant to write a sympathetic yet strongly critical account of what went wrong in SDS, leading to its demise in 1969. At Memphis, the mood and the moment were such that vehement applause broke out in the largely antiwar audience when I said, of SDS, "we were making history from the bottom up, as we're doing again in today's anti-war movement—may we stop this grotesque war, and the others ahead!"; and again, when I held up the Campaign for Peace and Democracy's petition and read its title, "We Oppose both Saddam Hussein and the US War on Iraq."[29] All in all, this session at a professional meeting was an extraordinary moment of intersection between left activism and history.

Since April, and after the supposed U.S. victory in Iraq, HAW has continued its activities.[30] There have been internal debates and discussions about such issues as: immediate withdrawal of U.S. troops, and whether or not we should endorse a "provisional international administration" for Iraq;[31] about different approaches to publicizing our activities and stands; and about unilateralism and multilateralism.[32] HAW contemplates issuing pamphlets with conflicting arguments on such matters; circulating and publicizing a new sign-on statement on Iraq, U.S. foreign policy, and civil liberties; increasing our membership; HAW subcommittees are also working on teaching materials (curriculum and resource development), a speakers' bureau, academic freedom in the face of repression, government deception, bylaws, various forms of public outreach, research towards war crimes trials, and possibly towards impeachment of President Bush. And HAW was active and visible at the American Historical Association annual meeting in Washington in January 2004. [33]

Alliance of Radical Academic and Intellectual Organizations

A number of the radical caucuses and left intellectual organizations of the sixties and seventies did not vanish with the end of the Vietnam War. The Historians Radical Caucus, beginning in 1968, morphed, over the years, into the *Radical Historians Newsletter, Radical History Review,*[34] and now, Historians Against the War. The Modern Language Association's (MLA) Radical Caucus in English and Modern Languages saw some of its members (Louis Kampf and Florence Howe) elected to that organization's presidency in the early 1970s. The Union for Radical Political Economics (URPE),[35] organized in 1968, continues to be strong.

With primary initiative coming from the MLA Radical Caucus, in the winter of 2003 efforts to create an alliance of radical academic and intellectual organizations began. (As of this writing, the organization has not made a final decision as to what to call itself, so I will refer to it simply as "the Alliance.") On April 19, ten days after the prematurely vaunted fall of Baghdad to U.S. troops, the organization held its first meeting, at the City University of New York Graduate Center.[36] About thirty representatives were present from: Radical Caucus of the Modern Language Association, Radical Philosophy Association, *Radical History Review,* Historians Against the War, New Political Science, Brecht Forum, Research Group on Socialism and Democracy, Latin American Studies Association, North American Congress on Latin America, New Caucus of the CUNY Professional Staff Congress, Union for Radical Political Economics, Working Class Special Interest Group, Conference on College Composition and Communication, and Caucus on Class of the Society for Cinema and Media Studies. As the call for that meeting says, "The types of scholarly and intellectual groupings in the Alliance are diverse, including radical caucuses in academic disciplinary and professional organizations; organizations publishing radical scholarly academic journals; radical caucuses of faculty, professionals, and graduate students both organizing and already within unions."

Of themselves, the organizers say:

> We are radical scholars and intellectuals. Many of us are activist-scholars and activist-intellectuals who work in non-academic settings. Some of us are veterans of the sixties, and some of us are younger; all of us are active participants in today's new movements. In 2002–2003, we came together in the streets, the teach-ins, the academic associations and elsewhere in opposition to the 'war on terrorism' and to the war-related fiscal crisis in higher education and across the economy; we oppose the governmental lies that brought the US into war, and we oppose US imperialism and the emerging US empire. We are deeply concerned about growing repression and, in particular, its impact on critical thought and expression.

The Alliance's statement of purpose concludes:

> We are all activists, and we affirm the dignity and value of intellectual work. We seek to build a better society, free of . . . bigotries and in-equalities . . . , in which the passion for knowledge will flourish. We believe that activism, as well as teaching, research and writing have an important role to play in bringing about a just and humane society. We want to establish institutional and social conditions that will en-courage analytic and critical thought as well as [to] foster the full de-velopment of human potential and creativity. To these ends, we seek to build and be part of a re-born left."

The "Call for a Founding Meeting" is addressed to "all collectives, caucuses and organizations—. . . all groups working in, around, and in spite of insti-tutions of higher education." The Alliance seeks "to create an organizational structure to facilitate communication among member organizations for action around... The Empire, The Fiscal Crisis [and] Repression of Civil Liberties." It will engage in "action in the academic arena" and also seeks to support "research bodies and think tanks to present new alternatives for public debate."

Can These Organizations Survive?

I rejoice at the rebirth of activism among left academics and intellectuals: bliss it is in this new dawn to be alive. But my re-immersion in this kind of activism has forced me to consider anew the fragility of left intellectual or-ganizations, and to try to figure out what impedes their survival and what might give them extended life. Will the academic radicalism born in oppo-sition to the war put down roots and last?

It is an unfortunate truism that our left is reactive rather than proactive. We thrive and grow in times of conflict, like Vietnam, like Iraq. But what will happen to our organizations if conflict lessens, or at least slips back beneath everyday immediate visibility? Will this activism outlast the present crisis? How can our organizations be sustained?

As we remind ourselves of the old problems in left organizations, we must also deal with new ones. We have to figure out how to work with the Internet. It has been an extraordinary instrument for circulating information (particularly information from beyond the moronic and Tom-Tomorrowish U.S. press during the Iraq war), for calling demonstrations, distributing and signing statements and petitions, and building our organizations.

But there is a negative side of organizing via Internet that has not yet been faced. Let's call it the "Kitty Genovese Phenomenon," drawing the name (admittedly, with some hyperbole) from the notorious murder in New York City in 1964 in which it was widely believed that not one of thirty-eight witnesses who heard Genovese's cries in their homes helped her or called the police. Part of the psychology behind such nonresponse lies in the widespread assumption among witnesses to crime that surely, somebody else is doing something about this. And so it sometimes is on the Internet. While the Internet is a magnificent instrument for organizing, again and again something comes along in an organization—an idea or a task—that must be responded to and dealt with in some way, and nobody responds, always (in the privacy of their own homes) assuming that someone else will take care of it. We have to be aware of this problem and face it with a renewed sense of responsibility.[37] And, recalling the old debates about structure and structurelessness, we should note that the Internet has not done away with the need for leadership (even if only on a rotating basis for some matters),[38] people who will see the agendas that group discussion is expressing and will also initiate new ones, and will remind people of what needs to be done.

One of the reasons for the occurrence of the Kitty Genovese phenomenon is that we are in fact too busy: baited and maligned within the left (even sometimes by a guilt-ridden left professoriate itself) as no other workers are, and yet working as much as seventy-hour weeks, often unable to take off to celebrate whatever our personal sabbath might be.[39] Observing the Kitty Genovese phenomenon, one friend with whom I have argued about this has complained about professors limiting their anti-war activity due to what he denounces as mere "personal projects," "freelancing," and "doing their own thing," by which he means their teaching, research, writing, professional activity, travel, personal lives—and even other political activities. This exudes disdain for the lives, struggles, passions and contributions of academics. In addition, hadn't we learned from the sixties that we can't sustain movements which demand participants' total commitment? People will participate as well as they can, but if they are made to feel that what they are doing is never enough, then they will vote with their feet to get out: one day, they just won't be there anymore. (The Alliance's Steering Committee fell, in a short time, from nine members to five—and the missing four, including the chair, could not be located despite several APB's). So the Kitty Genovese problem has to be faced with a more fully developed sense of responsibility in organizing by Internet, and with more face-to-face contact, but also with recognition that the Alliance's constituency works among the longest hours in the United States.

Although we have not yet seen in these organizations what Jo Freeman brilliantly named, years ago, the "tyranny of structurelessness," there has been a slowness to think about issues of governance and procedure, and how conflicts will be resolved, and what processes we want to follow in defining our organizations' politics. So far, the Alliance has managed to weather internal political disagreements about: government repression of dissidents in Cuba; the minuses as well as the pluses of "collectives"; whether we believe in the notion that a person can be a radical without being a Marxist (believe in it? I've seen it with my own eyes, in the mirror); and the organization is attempting to work through its relation to demonstrations organized by other progressive groups, such as one for Immigrant Rights. After a seeming consensus that this wasn't the time to argue out the Alliance's politics on, say, repression in Cuba,[40] some continued to stoke the flames by posting inflammatory Fidelista statements which they apparently thought were as neutral as, "pass the biscuits, pappy." There was intense disagreement over my unsuccessful proposal that we dedicate our founding conference to the memory of Edward Said, a model scholar-activist. In HAW, as previously mentioned, there have been internal disagreements about advocating multilateralism in U.S. foreign policy, and about supporting the idea of a provisional international authority in Iraq; about whether stating our position in an ad in the *New York Times* is "elitist";[41] and about my unsuccessful proposal that we attempt to set up a debate between the brilliant linguist and left political analyst Noam Chomsky and U.S. Deputy Secretary of Defense Paul Wolfowitz. As yet, neither organization has defined its politics very amply, nor even decided to what degree it should aim to define its politics; and neither organization has made enough progress in the direction of having elected and accountable officers. If the experience of the sixties is relevant, there will be problems ahead unless these blind spots are faced.

The large solution to many of our problems brings us back to one of the central topics of this chapter: can left intellectuals escape the chains of relevance and their own supposed inauthenticity to affirm the dignity and value of what they do? Is it permissible for the scholar to do research out of a passion for it, and to derive joy from it? Or must intellectuals, as I have

suggested some feel pressure to do, bury their scholarly passions in shame? These were the rocks on which the most pertinent earlier effort, the New University Conference, foundered.

At one point during the process of drafting a statement of purpose for the Alliance, I criticized its "utter lack of vision or passion, especially [the lack of] any statement about the value of intellectual work, or any statement that we see this organization as part of building the left." Some of this had an impact. But then I ran into various kinds of opposition in advocating, as I have earlier in this essay, that critical scholarship is "deeply connected to building a democratic and self-critical left, and . . . [to] preparing the way for utopia, as well as for the joyful and playful intellectual work that will be part of utopia." In accord with this thinking, I attempted to build into the Alliance's statement a phrase about seeking a better society, "in which thought of all kinds will flourish, and intellectual values including playfulness and truth will enrich the lives of all." This phrasing did not make it through the drafting process—"too abstract" was the judgment. (But note that one other reasonable basis on which the Alliance rejected the notion of playfulness arises from the feeling that post-structuralists have run off with the term).

What do I mean by playfulness? I use the term to summarize the joy of history: discovering truth and new truth; figuring things out, imagining, testing and revising explanations; and doing work that is often non-instrumental and not directly relevant. It is this that keeps many of us in the libraries and at our computers. Earlier in this chapter, I wrote of the danger of intellectuals letting their scholarly agenda be defined by whatever it is that an existing left seeks to know for its present purposes, and of responding to a movement's sometimes limited perception of its "needs," an approach that impedes and devalues research that is not immediately relevant and refuses to allow intellectuals a role as I wrote earlier in this chapter, as necessary, independent critics within the movement. How will we get to utopia if we are not free to imagine it, beyond the seeming realities and needs of today? So, I want to reaffirm that we are going no place as a movement, and no place in building a better society, unless our intellectuals (and artists as well) have free rein. You can't organize academics and intellectuals—many of whom went into this line of work with a passion for research and truth—on the basis of a narrowly instrumental definition of what their work is about. And if we do not honor intellectuals and artists for doing what they love,[42] their continuing participation in activism will be uncertain and our attempts to combine activism with scholarship will fail. Let's not go there again. For us, our longevity as activists is connected to our joy as scholars.

The Joy of History in the Midst of War: Marc Bloch

The great French medieval historian Marc Bloch, was, in a deep sense, both a historian and an activist. He was cofounder in 1929 of the influential *Annales d'Histoire Economique et Sociale*. A French Jew, he fought the Germans in World War II, and, in 1942, went into the Resistance, where he was a member of the regional directorate and headed a group centered in Lyons. He refused to leave Vichy France for a job at the New School for Social Research in New York. In March 1944, he was arrested and tortured by the Gestapo—bones broken and crushed, thrown in cold water—and taken to prison unconscious. He was shot to death June 16, 1944. (On the way, he told a tearful teenager not to be scared, that it would be over quickly.) Under these grim circumstances, and without library or books, Bloch had written, beginning in 1941 and continuing into 1942 and beyond, and left unfinished at his death, the classic that was later to be published as *The Historian's Craft*.[43] And Bloch's experience confirms my belief that the writing of history, and the joy in such writing, may legitimately continue in what I have called above the "dire present," even, as in Bloch's case, in the gravest of circumstances.

Bloch was certainly a powerful example—indeed an astonishing one, given his circumstances—of a historian who refused, even in the midst of terrible crisis, to put aside his work as historian or to treat it as if it were a mere personal project. To his death, Bloch remained a historian and functioned as one. And if he speaks to us today as both activist and historian, the content of what he wrote is also relevant to our situation. "Tell, me, Daddy," Bloch begins, "What is the use of history?"[44] Bloch's answers in his introduction focus on some of our present concerns. He acknowledges that history's "role, both as germ and, later, as the spur to action, has been and remains paramount." Nonetheless, what comes through is his willingness, without any embarrassment, to see writing history as a source of joy:

> Certainly, even if history were judged incapable of other uses, its entertainment value would remain in its favor. Or, to be more exact, it is incontestable that it appears entertaining to a large number . . . As far back as I can remember, it has been for me a constant source of pleasure [—] as for all historians, I think. If not, why have they chosen this occupation? . . . each scholar finds but one [field] that absorbs him. Finding it, in order to devote himself to it, he terms it his 'vocation', his 'calling'.

Speaking of the "keener pleasure of true research," Bloch continues:

> Moreover, this charm will be far from diminished once methodical inquiry, with all its necessary austerities, has begun. On the contrary,

all true historians will bear witness that the fascination then gains in both scope and intensity... history has its peculiar aesthetic pleasures. The spectacle of human activity which forms its peculiar object is, more than any other, designed to seduce the imagination—above all when, thanks to its remoteness in time or space, it is adorned with the subtle enchantment of the unfamiliar . . . Let us beware of the inclination, which I have detected in some, to be ashamed of this poetic quality . . . the good husbandman takes as much pleasure in plowing and sowing as in the harvest.[45]

It seems to me that Bloch speaks directly to our concern for scholarship and activism. He would die for his political beliefs, but while struggling against the Nazis, he would without guilt or remorse speak of history's "charm," "aesthetic pleasures," "subtle enchantment," seduction of the imagination, "poetic quality," and as a "constant source of pleasure." His work outlived him, and our work will have lasting effect only if we can figure out how to respect the activist within us without crushing the scholar within us.

Notes

Copyright 2003, 2004 by Jesse Lemisch. My thanks to conference organizers Jim Downs and Jennifer Manion; also Joanne Landy, John McMillian, Gerald Markowitz, Bryan Palmer, Naomi Weisstein, Staughton Lynd and my colleagues in Historians Against the War and the Alliance of Radical Academic and Intellectual Organizations and our friends in Graduate Student Employees United at Columbia University. This chapter is a revised and significantly extended version, with an added epilogue, of an essay that first appeared in *Radical History Review*, 85 (Winter 2003), 239–48. This chapter builds in part on some themes presented in Jim O'Brien, "'Be Realistic, Demand the Impossible': Staughton Lynd, Jesse Lemisch, and a Committed History," *Radical History Review* 82 (2002): 65–90.

1. For this and the following, see "TA's to Vote on Union Issue This Wednesday," *Columbia Daily Spectator*, March 11, 2002; "Columbia Graduate Assistants Strike to Support Union Effort," *New York Times*, April 30, 2002; "GSEU Strikes, Classes Temporarily Disrupted," *Columbia Daily Spectator*, May 1, 2002; Tula Connell, "Workers Wronged: The NLRB Is Stacked against Labor," *In These Times*, May 26, 2002, 5–6. See also the union's Web site at http://www.2110uaw.org/gseu. For an updating of the situation at Columbia as of May 2004, see below, note 45.

2. A tragedy of the current left is the extent to which many academic leftists have turned their backs on the notion of agency. At the Columbia conference, one faculty participant repeatedly rent her garments, justifying her inactivity by saying that the "'00s are different from the sixties," and that today "there is no alternative." In saying this, she was unthinkingly echoing conservative British Prime Minister Margaret Thatcher's (1979–1990) "TINA" (There Is No Alternative) doctrine, which is well analyzed in Daniel Singer's *Whose Millennium? Theirs or Ours?* (New York: Monthly Review, 1999). Singer describes his book as "a gesture of revolt against Tina, a refusal of the prevailing religion of resignation. . . . We are not doomed to impotence and inaction by fate. . . . We are not prisoners of this system. Though sobered up by past defeats and burdened by the weight of our environment, we . . . can try to be masters of our fate and fight for a different future" (8–9).

3. A. M. Rosenthal, "Combat and Compassion at Columbia," *New York Times*, May 1, 1968.

4. Available at http://www.proskauer.com/practice_areas.

5. Jesse Lemisch, "A Movement Begins: The Washington Protests against IMF/ World Bank," *New Politics* 29 (2000): 9 (available at http://www.wpunj.edu/~newpol/issue29/lemisc29.htm).

6. Jack Newfield, "The Senate's Fighting Liberal," *The Nation*, March 25, 2002. Ads in subsequent issues show, over and over *ad nauseam*, photographs of famous liberals and leftists holding their copies of this issue.

7. *The Nation*, May 13, 2002, 28; June 3, 2002, 32; and other issues.

8. Available at http://www.berksconference.org. One older historian I spoke to also found the program unpromising, but found the actual conference better than her expectations had been.

9. For the call to the NUC conference, see Mitchell Goodman, ed., *The Movement towards a New America: The Beginnings of a Long Revolution* (New York: Knopf, 1970), 711. A history of NUC, with attention to both its rise and fall, would make an excellent dissertation topic. Records are available at the Tamiment Library, NYU, and at the State Historical Society of Wisconsin. Thanks to Andrew H. Lee of Tamiment for this archival information.

10. There are opportunities for important research around Lynd's firing from Yale in 1968. See presidential records of Kingman A. Brewster, record unit 11, boxes 138–40, Sterling Memorial Library, Yale University, New Haven, CT, for Files concerning Lynd, including alumni letters, history department chairman's review, statements by William Sloane Coffin, and speeches. Thanks to Yale's Public Services Archivist William R. Massa Jr. for calling these to my attention. C. Vann Woodward of Yale played a central role in Lynd's firing—as he did later in the nonhiring of Communist historian Herbert Aptheker to teach a one-semester undergraduate course at Yale. See James R. Green, "Past and Present in Southern History: An Interview with C. Vann Woodward," *Radical History Review* 36 (1986): 80–100; Jesse Lemisch, "If Howard Cosell Can Teach at Yale, Why Can't Herbert Aptheker?" *Newsletter of the Radical Historians Caucus* 22 (1976): 1–9; Staughton Lynd, "The Bulldog Whitewashed: A Critique of the Investigation of Herbert Aptheker's Nonappointment at Yale University," in *African American and Radical Historiography: Essays in Honor of Herbert Aptheker*, ed. Herbert Shapiro (Minneapolis, MN: MEP, 1998), 119–54. Woodward's papers are now available at the Sterling Memorial Library, Yale University, including material on the Aptheker controversy, the American Historical Association radical caucus, and much else. These materials cry out for a dissertation-seeking graduate student interested in tracing a major liberal's movement rightward in the sixties and after.

11. Jim O'Brien has a fine article about some of these themes in the *Radical History Review* 82 (2002): 65–90, entitled, "'Be Realistic, Demand the Impossible': Staughton Lynd, Jesse Lemisch, and a Committed History."

12. Staughton Lynd, "Intellectuals, the University, and the Movement," New England Free Press, 1968, reprinted in *Journal of American History* 76 (1989): 479–85. In this talk, Lynd also made another remark that might be reexamined, contending that it is "intellectual hubris . . . to hope . . . that upper-middle-class white professors can have much illumination to shed on black power." Both Lynd's talk and my response were originally published in the *NUC Newsletter*, but were then given wider circulation as a New England Free Press broadside/pamphlet (Boston, n.d. [1968?], unpaginated). NEFP, *ca.* 1968–1981, was an important left print shop and pamphlet publisher, and research should be done on it.

13. Jesse Lemisch, "Who Will Write a Left History of Art while We Are All Putting Our Balls on the Line?" *Journal of American History* 76 (1989): 485–86.

14. John McMillian, "Love Letters to the Future: REP, *Radical America*, and New Left History," *Radical History Review* 77 (2000): 49. McMillian is a graduate student in history at Columbia, currently teaching at Harvard.

15. For the best account of FSM, see the magnificent study by Robert Cohen and Reginald E. Zelnik, eds., *The Free Speech Movement: Reflections on Berkeley in the 1960's* (Berkeley: University of California Press, 2002).

16. For this and the following, see Alice and Staughton Lynd, eds., *Rank and File: Personal Histories by Working-Class Organizers* (Boston: Beacon, 1973), 42; Staughton Lynd, *Living Inside Our Hope: A Steadfast Radical's Thoughts on Rebuilding the Movement* (Ithaca, NY: Cornell University Press, 1997), 6–7, 14–15, 37, 46, 234. It should be added that attorney Lynd's creative role in developing the legal notion of a community right to industrial prop-

erty belies his own doctrine, for this fertile intellectual work goes far beyond mere "accompaniment." See Lynd, *The Fight against Shutdowns: Youngstown's Steel Mill Closings* (San Pedro, CA: Singlejack, 1982), 141, 163, 166.

17. See Jesse Lemisch, "Students for a Democratic Society, Heroically Portrayed, before the Inexplicable Fall: Consensus History in a Left Film," *Film and History* 31.1 (2001): 54–57.

18. I have enormous affection and respect for Terkel, but I disagree with important elements of his re-creation of the American past. Research cries out to be done on the Popular Front line that I believe he lays over his interview material. It would be interesting to scrutinize the kinds of questions he asks and does not ask, and to see what makes it through his editing and what does not. Possibly useful in this connection are the Chicago Historical Society's Studs Terkel/WFMT Oral History Archives.

19. For a recent strong critique of this tendency, see Dorothy E. Fennell, "Labor's Rose-Colored Glasses," *New Labor Forum* (Fall/Winter 2001), a review-essay of James R. Green's otherwise impressive, *Taking History to Heart: The Power of the Past in Building Social Movements* (Amherst: University of Massachusetts Press, 2000).

20. For a powerful defense of the idea of objective truth, and a critique of poststructuralist subjectivity, see Naomi Weisstein, "Power, Resistance and Science," *New Politics* 22 (1997): 150–51 (available at http://www.wpunj.edu/newpol/issue22/weisst22.htm): "[One scholar] mentions the 'tentativeness,' 'anxiety,' and 'paralysis' of postmodernist post-structuralist counter-Enlightenment feminism. *Of course*, there is paralysis: once knowledge is reduced to insurmountable personal subjectivity, there is no place to go; we are in a swamp of self-referential passivity. Sometimes I think that, when the fashion passes, we will find many bodies, drowned in their own wordy words, like the Druids in the bogs. Meanwhile, the patriarchy continues to prosper. . . . [I]n times of no movement, reality itself falls into question. In times of dynamism, change and movement, people abandon doubts about reality, properly seeing [such doubts] as part of the conservative past which they are rejecting. The fog lifts. The fact of movement gives us a clearer picture of what is really out there."

21. It's my understanding that some graduate student unions-in-the-making have yielded to universities' dread that TA's might "interfere" with curricular matters (which would bring Western Civilization and the entire Judeo-Christian Tradition, as it used to be called, to an immediate end). This yielding has taken the form of union commitments not to involve themselves with course content and other "academic issues" that are thought to be the sole prerogative of faculty, but rather to stick to bread-and-butter issues such as job descriptions, stipends, benefits, etc. This is a position that may come back to haunt these unions, a kind of tacit sweetheart deal that places very narrow limits on TAs' academic freedom, while creating a dangerous two-tier system distinguishing those who have it from those who do not. Forty years ago, as a TA at Yale (with its customary pollution of language, Yale called TA's "assistants-in-instruction"), I found myself teaching a course whose accompanying reader, coedited by Yale Eminence David Potter, carried the implication that approximately 50 percent of former slaves had happy memories of the institution. I resisted this, and offered my students supplementary primary materials. (For a brief accouny of this conflict, see David W. Wills, "Research and Training in American Religious History," p. 2 and note 1: www.amherst.edu/~aardoc/Yale-1.html.) I'm glad I was not constrained by a contract that prevented me from making an independent assessment of the curriculum, and acting on that assessment.

22. Except where otherwise noted, information about this organization comes from my experience or from the HAW Web site: http://www.historiansagainstwar.org

23. Available at http://www.hnn.us/articles/1170.html.

24. It was published in *The Nation*, January 6, 2003; *The New York Times*, February 10, 2003; and elsewhere; the full text and the list of 5261 signers may be found at http://www.cpdweb.org.

25. For accounts of the Radical Caucus's peak year at the AHA, 1969, see: Lemisch, *On Active Service in War and Peace: Politics and Ideology in the American Historical Profession* (Toronto: New Hogtown Press, 1975); Lemisch, "Radicals, Marxists and Gentlemen: A Memoir of Twenty Years Ago," *Radical Historians Newsletter*, no. 59, November 1989; Peter Novick, *That Noble Dream: The "Objectivity Question" and the American Historical Profession* (Cambridge: Cambridge University Press, 1988), chapter 13 ("The Collapse of Comity.")

26. The New York Police Department did its best to prevent this demonstration. See HAW's website for pictures of historians in the demonstration, including unsatisfactory ones of the author :-).

27. History News Network, April 5, 2003: http://www.hnn.us/articles/1369.html; see also HAW Web site.

28. History News Network, April 7, 2003: http://www.hnn.us/comments/10478.html; History News Network, April 6, 2003: http://www.hnn.us/comments/10525.html.

29. The session may be seen on videotape available from "Videotography," http://www.cmillervideo.com.

30. For a short account of HAW's May 31 New York City meeting, see History News Network, June 2, 2003: http://www.hnn.us/comments/13039.html].

31. I took a position critical of the latter.

32. I took the position that the peace movement's cry for multilateralism has been wrong, an effort to provide a kosher veneer to the construction of a U.S. empire (by bringing in other dominant economic powers), which should in fact be opposed in an unqualified way. For an updating on developing political disagreements within HAW, see below, p. 200, and note 41.

33. For HAW activities at the 2004 AHA and the 2004 OAH, see Jesse Lemisch, "Historians, Repression, and the Iraq War," *New Politics* 37 (in press).

34. Available at http://www.chmn.gmu.edu/rhr

35. Available at http://www.urpe.org

36. The following is based on e-mails and direct participation in meetings; the "Call for Founding Meeting," which includes the organization's draft statement of purpose, background, goals, and preliminary constituent groups, may be found at History News Network, July 18, 2003: http://www.hnn.us/comments/15341.html.

37. Another relevant problem involves posting on internet lists tasks to be done by some unknown and unnamed person. Not discussed here are the myriad other problems, both technical and interpersonal, involved in communication by Internet and conference call.

38. Of course, leadership can often be put on a rotating basis. But this device hardly solves all the difficult issues, especially differences in leadership skills. For an instructive account, from a different area, of problems arising from the assumption of equal skills and a group's failure to face the reality of leadership, see Naomi Weisstein, "Days of Celebration and Resistance: The Chicago Women's Liberation Rock Band, 1970–1973," in Rachel Blau DuPlessis and Ann Snitow, eds., *The Feminist Memoir Project: Voices from Women's Liberation* (New York: Crown Publishing, 1998). Weisstein's essay is also available at http://www.cwluherstory.com/cwlumemoir/Naomirock.html.

39. Just try to get through to an academic at home by telephone between 8 and 11 p.m. Sunday.

40. I am a signer of CPD's statement, "Anti-War, Social Justice and Human Rights Advocates Oppose Repression in Cuba," March 2003: http://www.cpdweb.org.

41. I disagree. By April of 2004 there was increasing disagreement in HAW, and I wrote the following:

"At the 2004 AHA and OAH meetings, many HAW members supported resolutions brought in by Yale's Graduate Employees and Students Organization (www.yaleunions.org/geso, www.leftalliance.org) against Yale's intimidation and coercion of union organizing efforts. But the GESO resolutions were not endorsed by HAW *organizationally*, on grounds that HAW is and should remain a 'single-issue' organization.

This is part of a larger debate within HAW: Are we just against the Iraq war, or do we seek new directions in American foreign policy? Do we oppose U.S. empire, and the wars to come? Are we anti-corporate, anti-imperial, anti-privatization, anti-IMF/WTO, against militarization, and for women's rights and social justice, both domestically and internationally? Do we seek to scrutinize the domestic roots of U.S. foreign policy?

. . . HAW is divided on issues of organizational democracy and leadership and on political questions, especially regarding calling for immediate U.S. withdrawal from Iraq vs. a 'Popular Front' strategy. [After Staughton Lynd and I had said that HAW should clearly state its advocacy of immediate withdrawal, one member of the HAW steering committee adopted classic left sectarian language on behalf of a liberal purpose, characterizing our position as the repetition of "the anti-occupation mantra," "absurd ideological fussing," and "ideological righteousness."] And while opposing Bush's policies and seeing them as in part departures from the past, we also have disagreements as historians about continuities and discontinuities in the history of American foreign policy. I do not look back on the era of Cold War 'containment' as some sort of golden age, nor would I uncritically accept past and present Democratic Party foreign policy. I would seek to persuade a broad constituency of the relevance of radical alternatives to American foreign policy. My answer to the questions asked in the preceding paragraph is, 'yes.' Since there is some ABB (AnybodybutBush) feeling in HAW, I want to be sure that HAW does not become a *de facto* supporter of likely Democratic presidential candidate John Kerry, whose position on the war is unacceptable, including sending more U.S. troops and seeking multilateral means to continue the war, and/or the use of the U.N. as a 'beard' to cover continued U.S. domination of Iraq. I favor immediate withdrawal from Iraq and the termination of plans for U.S. bases there, and I support greater organizational democracy in HAW."

Jesse Lemisch, "Historians, Repression, and the Iraq War," *New Politics* 37 (2004, in press).

42. The left, often driven by a kind of class bias, honors manual crafts but often refuses to see the work of intellectuals in this way as similarly involving labor, creativity and polished skills.

43. New York: Vintage Books, 1953. Translated by Peter Putnam. For the above and the following, see especially Joseph R. Strayer's introduction (pp. vii–xii), Lucien Febvre's "Note on the Manuscripts of the Present Book" (xiii–xviii), and Bloch's introduction (3–19). For additional biographical details, I have used Pratique de l'histoire et devoiements negationnistes, "Marc Bloch": www.phdn.org/histoire/bloch; and Hal Goldman, "Marc Bloch: Israelite de France," University of Vermont *History Review*, 6, December 1994: http://www.uvm.edu/~hag/histreview/vol6/goldman.html.

Strangely, the above-cited U.S. edition gives no French source; it is in fact a translation of Bloch's *Apologie pour l'Histoire ou Metier d'historien* (1949). My thanks to Maria Fernanda Justiniano, History, Universidad Nacional de Salta, Argentina, for information about Bloch.

44. For this and the following, see *Craft of History*, 3, 7, 8, 18.

45. We began with the Columbia TA/RA strike of 2002. As I am reading proof on this chapter in May 2004, GSEU is on strike again, seeking recognition and a counting of the ballots, and once again the inflated rat sits outside Columbia's main gate. For a brief account early in the strike, see Alan Brinkley, Jesse Lemisch, Staughton Lynd, and David Montgomery, "Liberalism and the Columbia Strike" (including my speech under that title delivered on the steps of Columbia's Low Library on April 21, 2004): History News Network, April 23, 2004: http://www.hnn.us/articles/4820.html

What had happened to bring the rat back? Columbia had appealed the 2002 graduate student vote on a union to the NLRB, thus colluding with the Bush administration, since the university had reason to think that Bush's NLRB would simply sit on the impounded ballots—which it did. As time passed, however, a development took place that suggested some liberalization of the Columbia administration: the appointment to the university's highest offices of two nationally known liberals, Lee Bollinger and Alan Brinkley.

Bollinger had established an illustrious liberal record as president of the University of Michigan before he became president of Columbia on June 1, 2002. At Michigan, he had supported affirmative action and had become the defendant in a major affirmative action case before the Supreme Court. And, as president at Michigan, he had bargained with the Graduate Employees' Organization and had said that graduate student unionization did not harm the educational process there.

Alan Brinkley, a historian of the twentieth century and Allan Nevins Professor of History at Columbia, is also a nationally known liberal. His students at Columbia had heard him saying in class that he would not oppose a graduate student union there (interview excerpted in History News Network, April 23, 2004; for the full interview, see Adyn Barkan, "Provost Alan Brinkley on the Strike," *Columbia Daily Spectator*, April 21, 2004). Bollinger appointed Brinkley provost effective July 1, 2003. In taking the job, perhaps Brinkley persuaded himself that he could get Columbia to change its anti-union policies. But in accepting this appointment, he had to have known that he would likely be called on to implement those policies.

More time passed, and the impounded ballots grew moldier. Bollinger and Brinkley did nothing to break the status quo, presumably hoping that they could simply outlast GSEU. In mid-April 2004, GSEU voted to strike for recognition beginning April 19. As of this writing, the strike continues, with a large picket line (with cries of "What's disgusting? Union busting;

What's appalling? Columbia's stalling"), rallies on the line and on the steps of Low Library (where Grayson Kirk's office had been occupied in 1968), marches through the campus and in one case through Low, with baton twirlers, whistles, drums (Columbia's crowded urban campus has fine acoustics), and support by other unions including the Transport Workers Union, Professional Staff Congress of CUNY, and John Sweeney, president of the AFL-CIO, who spoke on the line. Undergraduates rallying in support cried out, "2, 4, 6, 8; don't fuck with my TA!"

Many academics and intellectuals from outside Columbia have been supportive of the strike, with letters sometimes addressed directly to Brinkley and/or Bollinger. GESO people regularly came down from Yale, one with a sign reading, "Workers of the Ivy League, Unite." When I spoke on the steps of Low Library (calling Columbia's conduct "low-down, sleazy, hypocritical"), other speakers included Stanley Aronowitz, Distinguished Professor of Sociology in CUNY. I had organized a national support campaign, to which the historians who responded included Yale's David Montgomery, Rick Perlstein, and Staughton Lynd (who wrote, in part, "Were I in New York City I would be [picketing] at [Lemisch's] side"). Labor historians Nelson Lichtenstein and Joshua Freeman organized a letter to Bollinger urging Columbia to withdraw its NLRB appeal; the letter was signed by more than 130 faculty members at universities that have TA unions.

Liberals Bollinger and Brinkley have not distinguished themselves for liberal behavior before or during the strike. At one point, Bollinger said "there's nothing the university can do" [to expedite the appeal to NLRB], to which a student rightly pointed out that Columbia could drop its appeal. But Bollinger has not been interested in this sane alternative.

As the strike began, Brinkley gave an interview to the *Columbia Spectator*, which may be seen as poignant, hypocritical, or both. Brinkley stumbles, conveying confusion and surprise that a strike has occurred, and says "There wasn't a lot of time for planning . . . looking back maybe it would have been a good thing to try to talk to some graduate students . . . we don't have a plan for ending the strike . . . Well, the plans as of now are that we've taken our position, and we'll try to ride out the strike . . ." The student interviewer points out to him that, a year before, he had said that he would not oppose a graduate student union, and asks, "is your personal position at odds with that of the Administration?" Brinkley replies:

"Well, I can't answer that. I'm a great supporter of unionization. I think that the decline in unions is one of the great catastrophes of our recent economic life. I think there are many areas in economic life in which unions can play a constructive role, do play a constructive role. On this campus, we have lots of unions—we don't have unions for students. I don't know what else to say.

This seems another episode in that endlessly running soap opera, "The Crisis of Liberalism." Either these people aren't liberals, or liberalism means hypocrisy. During these hard Bushian times, many former radicals of my generation have blurred the lines between radicalism and liberalism, and forgotten that they are not the same. The situation at Columbia, with liberals playing so central a role, should serve as a strong reminder of the difference.

Meantime, at Columbia, the struggle continues: people know the difference between liberals and radicals. I dedicate this essay to the scholar-activists of GSEU, and look forward to a sequel.

Contributors

Kathleen M. Brown is an Associate Professor of History at the University of Pennsylvania where she teaches early American history and the history of women and gender. She is the author of *Good Wives, Nasty Wenches, and Anxious Patriarchs: Gender, Race, and Power in Colonial Virginia* (1996) and numerous articles. She is currently completing a book on the history of cleanliness in the United States to 1865 which explores the links among care of the body, housework, spirituality, and morality entitled *Foul Bodies and Infected Worlds: Cleanliness in Early America.*

Drucilla Cornell is Professor of Law, Women's Studies and Political Science at Rutgers University. Prior to beginning her academic life, she was a union organizer for a number of years, working for the U.A.W., the U.E., and the I.U.E. in California, New Jersey, and New York. Cornell was professor at the Benjamin N. Cardozo School of Law from 1989–1994 and spent the 1991–1992 academic year at the Institute for Advanced Study at Princeton. She has authored numerous books and articles on critical theory, feminism and postmodern theories of ethics, including *Beyond Accommodation, The Philosophy of the Limit, At the Heart of Freedom*, and most recently, *Defending Ideals*. She is also a produced playwright—productions of her plays *The Dream Cure* and *Background Interference* have been performed in New York and Los Angeles.

Jim Downs received his BA from the University of Pennsylvania. He is currently a doctoral candidate in history at Columbia University, where he is working on his dissertation, "Diagnosing Reconstruction: The History of the Medical Division of the Freedmen's Bureau." He has published articles in the *Southern Historian* and *Women and Performance: A Journal of Feminist Theory*.

209

Eileen Eagan is an Associate Professor of History and member of the Women's Studies Council at the University of Southern Maine. She received her BA from D'Youville College in 1968, an MA from the University of Wisconsin-Milwaukee, and PhD from Temple University. She is the author of *Class, Culture and the Classroom: The Student Peace Movement of the 1930s*. Her current scholarship and community work focus on redefining history (the history of Maine in particular) and public space to include, among others, women, workers, and non-Yankee immigrants. Issues of war and peace continue to have a central place in her teaching and activism.

Eric Foner, DeWitt Clinton Professor of History, specializes in the Civil War and Reconstruction, slavery, and nineteenth-century America. He received his BA from Columbia in 1963 and his PhD from Columbia in 1969. His publications include *Free Soil, Free Labor, Free Men: The Ideology of the Republican Party Before the Civil War* (1970), *Tom Paine and Revolutionary America* (1976), *Politics and Ideology in the Age of the Civil War* (1980), *Nothing But Freedom: Emancipation and Its Legacy* (1983), *Reconstruction: America's Unfinished Revolution, 1863–1877* (1988), *Freedom's Lawmakers: A Directory of Black Officeholders During Reconstruction* (1993), and *The Story of American Freedom* (1998). In 2000, he served as President of the American Historical Association. His latest book, *Who Owns History? Rethinking the Past in a Changing World*, was published in 2002 by Hill and Wang

Glenda Gilmore is the Peter V. and C. Vann Woodward Professor of History at Yale University. In 1970, after graduating from Wake Forest University with a major in psychology, she found herself in Beaufort, South Carolina, teaching U.S. history in the first years of public school integration there. After three years in the classroom, she pursued a career in business for fifteen years, working as a human resources manager and affirmative action officer. She returned to graduate school at UNC-Charlotte to learn something about Central America, ended up earning a master's degree, and then went on to earn the PhD from UNC-Chapel Hill in 1992. Her book, *Gender and Jim Crow: Women and the Politics of White Supremacy in North Carolina, 1896–1920*, came out in 1996. Since then she's co-edited, with Jane Dailey and Bryant Simon, *Jumpin' Jim Crow: Southern Politics from Civil War to Civil Rights*, and edited *Who Were the Progressives?*

Nancy A. Hewitt is Professor II of History and Women's & Gender Studies at Rutgers University. In the early 1970s when she had dropped out of college to pursue a career as an activist, this seemed an unlikely outcome. Her decision to pursue a PhD in History and study grassroots women's activism allowed her to combine her two passions, resulting in the publication of *Women's Activism and Social Change: Rochester, NY, 1822–1872* (1984) and *Southern Discomfort: Women's Activism in Tampa, Florida, 1880s–1920s* (2001). Hewitt has also organized teach-ins, brought activists and scholars together in workshops and seminars, and consulted on editorial projects and films documenting women's activism past and present.

Martin Klimke studied at the University of Göttingen, Amherst College and the University of Heidelberg, where he received his MA in history and English in 2002. He has taught at the college and high school level in the U.S. and Germany, and is currently a Research Fellow and PhD-candidate at the History Department at the University of Heidelberg. He is working in a joint research project with the History Department at Rutgers University sponsored by the Volkswagen Foundation entitled "The Other Within Us: Collective Identities, Intercultural Relations, and Political Protest in West Germany and the U.S. During the 1960s and 1970s."

Kitty Krupat is Associate Director of the Queens College-City University of New York Labor Resource Center and a doctoral candidate in American Studies at New York University. A life-long trade unionist, she has been active in the movement to organize graduate students and adjuncts and is an advocate for U.S. Labor against the War. Her research interests include labor and working-class history, intellectual history of the American left and the academic left. With Patrick McCreery, she is co-editor of *Out at Work: Building a Gay-Labor Alliance* (2001). Her essays have appeared in *Social Text, International Labor and Working-Class History, New Labor Forum* and in the anthologies *No Sweat: Fashion, Free Trade and the Rights of Garment Workers* (ed. Andrew Ross), and *The World The Sixties Made* (eds. Van Gosse and Richard Moser).

Jesse Lemisch, Professor of History Emeritus, John Jay College of Criminal Justice, CUNY. Best known for his work on the politics of merchant seamen in Revolutionary America and on "The American Revolution Seen from the Bottom Up," he has also published widely on left culture, history and politics. His books include: *Jack Tar vs. John Bull* (1997) and *On Active Service in War and Peace: Politics and Ideology in the American Historical Profession* (1975). In the 1960s, he was an SDS member, arrested in civil rights and antiwar protests, and fired for his politics from academic jobs. A founder of the New University Conference and the Radical Historians Caucus, he is currently on the steering committees of Historians Against the War and the Alliance of Radical Academic and Intellectual Organizations.

Jennifer Manion received a BA in history from the University of Pennsylvania in 1997. She is a doctoral candidate in history and a lecturer in the department of women and gender studies at Rutgers University. She is working on her dissertation, "Women's Crime and Penal Reform in Early Pennsylvania, 1776–1835." She received a dissertation fellowship from the McNeil Center for Early American Studies for the 2004–2005 academic year.

Vania Markarian was born in Uruguay in 1971. She got her BA from the Universidad de la República (Montevideo, Uruguay) in 1996. In 2003, she completed her PhD in Latin American history at Columbia University. Her main area of interest for some years now has been human rights activism on a global scale with particular reference to the experience of Latin American countries. She has taught at Queens College, City University of New York, and is currently a Post-Doctoral Fellow at the International Center for Advanced Studies at New York University. She has several publications on Latin American contemporary history.

John McMillian teaches history and literature at Harvard University. He is co-editor of *The Radical Reader: A Documentary Anthology of the American Radical Tradition* with Timothy Patrick McCarthy and *The New Left Revisited* with Paul Buhle. His articles and review essays have appeared in *American Quarterly, Radical History Review, Rethinking History,* and elsewhere.

Kimberly Phillips-Fein is a doctoral candidate at Columbia and teaches economy, history and culture at New York University. She is working on a dissertation called, "The Roots of Reaganism: Business Activism in the Liberal Age," which is on the role of business in the rise of the postwar right. A book based on the dissertation will be published by Norton in 2006. Phillips-Fein is also a journalist who has written for the *Baffler, The Nation, New Labor Forum,* the *Washington Post Book World, Newsday, In These Times,* and *Dissent,* among other publications. She is currently an active organizing committee member for GSEU-UAW.

David Rosner is Professor of History and Public Health at Columbia University and Director of the Center for the History of Public Health at Columbia's Mailman School of Public Health. He and Gerald Markowitz co-authored and edited numerous books and articles, including *Deceit and Denial: The Deadly Politics of Industrial Pollution.* Rosner is also author of *Deadly Dust: Silicosis* (2002), *The Politics of Occupational Disease in Twentieth Century America* (1991), *Children, Race, and Power: Kenneth and*

Mamie Clarks' Northside Center (1996), and *Dying for Work* (1987). In addition to numerous grants, he has been a Guggenheim Fellow, a National Endowment for the Humanities Fellow and a Josiah Macy Fellow. Presently, he is the recipient of a Robert Wood Johnson Investigator Award. He is also the author of *A Once Charitable Enterprise* (1982). Dr. Rosner is testifying on behalf of workers who are diseased by industrial pollutants and for the state of Rhode Island in a suit against the lead industry.

Anita Seth is a doctoral candidate in history at Yale University, where she has organized with the Graduate Employees and Students Organization (GESO) since 1999 and served for two years as its Chair. From 1996 to 1999 she worked with communities in the United States and Russia suffering the environmental and health consequences of the nuclear arms race. Her dissertation compares the economic and social effects of defense production in Los Angeles and Novosibirsk during the Cold War.

Tracey M. Weis has been on the faculty of the History Department of Millersville University since 1992. She grew up in Pittsburgh, PA, but came of age in the South, spending four years in Durham, NC at Duke University and another four years in the coalfields of central Appalachia as a community organizer. The Women's History program at the State University at Rutgers enabled her to refine her sense of the possibilities of collective scholarship directed to public and practical applications. Since 1997, her engagement in the American Social History Project's New Media Classroom Program has prompted her to incorporate digital resources and technologies in her teaching. From 2000–2003, she directed an NEH-funded curriculum and faculty development program on the Underground Railroad in Lancaster County, PA, a project that has brought her scholarly research on race relations in post-emancipation Virginia full circle.

Index